ANCIENT INDIAN TRADITION & MYTHOLOGY

Translated by

A BOARD OF SCHOLARS

Edited by

G.P. Bhatt

VOLUME 78

ANCIENT INDIAN TRADITION AND MYTHOLOGY

Mahāpurāṇas *Translated into English*
Gen. Ed. Dr. G.C. Tripathi
Founder Eds. Late J.L. Shastri and Late G.P. Bhatt

PUBLISHED VOLUMES

Vols. 1-4 ŚIVA PURĀṆA *Tr.* J.L. Shastri

Vols. 5-6 LIṄGA PURĀṆA *Tr.* J.L. Shastri

Vols. 7-11 BHĀGAVATA PURĀṆA *Tr.* G.V. Tagare

Vols. 12-14 GARUḌA PURĀṆA *Tr.* J.L. Shastri

Vols. 15-19 NĀRADA PURĀṆA *Tr.* G.V. Tagare

Vols. 20-21 KŪRMA PURĀṆA *Tr.* G.V. Tagare

Vols. 22-26 BRAHMĀṆḌA PURĀṆA *Tr.* G.V. Tagare

Vols. 27-30 AGNI PURĀṆA *Tr.* N. Gangadharan

Vols. 31-32 VARĀHA PURĀṆA *Tr.* S. Venkitasubramonia Iyer

Vols. 33-36 BRAHMA PURĀṆA *Tr.* J.L. Shastri

Vols. 37-38 VĀYU PURĀṆA *Tr.* G.V. Tagare

Vols. 39-48 PADMA PURĀṆA *Tr.* N.A. Deshpande

Vols. 49-71 SKANDA PURĀṆA *Ed.* G.P. Bhatt, *Tr. & Annot.* Shridhar Balooni & Pratosh Panda

Vols. 72-73 VĀMANA PURĀṆA *Tr. & Annot.* R.S. Shiva Ganesha Murthy

Vols. 74-76 GAṆEŚA PURĀṆA *Tr. & Annot.* Greg Bailey

Vols. 77-82 BRAHMAVAIVARTA PURĀṆA *Tr. & Annot.* G.P. Bhatt

PURĀṆAS UNDER PREPARATION

Viṣṇu Purāṇa • Harivaṃśa Purāṇa • Bhaviṣya Purāṇa • Matsya Purāṇa • Devī Bhāgavata Purāṇa • Kālika Purāṇa • Mārkaṇḍeya Purāṇa • Viṣṇudharmottara Purāṇa

Brahmavaivarta Purāṇa

Part- II

Prakṛti Khaṇḍa

(Book-I)

Translated and annotated by

G.P. Bhatt

MOTILAL BANARSIDASS PUBLISHERS
PRIVATE LIMITED • DELHI

First Edition: **Delhi, 2017**

ISBN: 978-81-208-4031-7 Part II (Book I)
ISBN: 978-81-208-4032-4 Part II (Book II)

MOTILAL BANARSIDASS
41 U.A. Bungalow Road, Jawahar Nagar, Delhi 110 007
8 Mahalaxmi Chamber, 22 Bhulabhai Desai Road, Mumbai 400 026
120 Royapettah High Road, Mylapore, Chennai 600 004
236, 9th Main III Block, Jayanagar, Bengaluru 560 011
8 Camac Street, Kolkata 700 017
Ashok Rajpath, Patna 800 004
Chowk, Varanasi 221 001

UNESCO COLLECTION OF REPRESENTATIVE WORKS—*Indian Series*
This book has been accepted in the Indian Translation Series of the UNESCO Collection of Representative Works, jointly sponsored by the United Nations Educational, Scientific and Cultural Organization (UNESCO) and the Government of India

MLBD Cataloging-in-Publication Data
Brahmavaivarta Purana (Part-II) (Book I)
Prakrti Khanda by G.P. Bhatt
Includes Notes
ISBN: 978-81-208-4031-7 Part II (Book I)
ISBN: 978-81-208-4032-4 Part II (Book II)
I. Hinduism II. Purana III. Brahmavaivarta
IV. Prakrti Khanda V. Bhatt, G.P.

Printed in India

by RP Jain at NAB Printing Unit,
A-44, Naraina Industrial Area, Phase I, New Delhi–110028
and published by JP Jain for Motilal Banarsidass Publishers (P) Ltd,
41 U.A. Bungalow Road, Jawahar Nagar, Delhi-110007

PUBLISHER'S NOTE

The purest gems lie hidden in the bottom of the ocean or in the depth of rocks. One has to dive into the ocean or delve into the rocks to find them out. Similarly, truth lies concealed in the language which with the passage of time has become obsolete. Man has to learn that language before he discovers that truth.

But he has neither the means nor the leisure to embark on that course. We have, therefore, planned to help him acquire knowledge by an easier course. We have started the series of Ancient Indian Tradition and Mythology in English Translation. Our goal is to universalize knowledge through the most popular international medium of expression. The publication of the Purāṇas in English Translation is a step towards that goal.

Acknowledgement

It is our pleasant duty to put on record our sincere thanks to Dr. R. N. Dandekar and the UNESCO authorities for their kind encouragement and valuable help in the publication of the volumes in this series.

NOTE OF THE GENERAL EDITOR

With a certain mingle of the feelings of joy and sorrow we are presenting herewith one of the most important Purāṇas in its English translation. While being happy to bring this work to light, we are deeply sorry to note that the translator of this work Dr. G.P. Bhatt, one of the best experts on Purāṇic lore who has been associated with this our grand endeavour of AITM for a long time, is unfortunately no more to see the fruit of his labour in print. During his life time he could finish the translation of only half of this Purāṇa, i.e. the first two khaṇḍas (Brahma & Prakṛti), whereas the other two still need to be translated.

The Purāṇakāra has created the title of his work from a technical term of the Advaita Vedānta. '*Vivarta*' is used to describe a phenomenon which we perceive and experience as *real* but which in its substance is totally different from it. According to Advaita Vedānta this whole creation is a '*vivarta*' of Brahman, which is to say that intrinsically every phenomenon and every object is essentially and substantially Brahman but it appears to us in various universal forms. Brahman is the ultimate and the only reality of everything that we perceive and experience.

Our Purāṇa thus seeks to stress the point that all objects of the world, all creatures and even the divine beings about which it speaks are ultimately manifestations of Brahman who or which is none else than Kṛṣṇa and his Śaktis, though they may not appear as such.

The word '*vivarta*' in this technical sense has been made popular especially by Śankarācārya in his exposition of the Brahmasūtras. It appears therefore likely that the author of the Purāṇa was well acquainted with this great philosopher and his works.

Our Purāṇa does not choose to elaborate any one particular subject or theme, nor has it any single plan of narration, in fact few Purāṇas have it.

Our Purāṇa can very well be described as a quadrology of four completely independent works, however with a marked Krishnaite bias permeated through the whole text. Whereas this first section (Brahmakhaṇḍa) mainly (though not exclusively) deals with the earlier manifestation of the creation from god Brahma-Kṛṣṇa, the other three are more coherent, dealing with god Ganeśa, five main Goddesses and exploits of Kṛṣṇa, along with Rādhā.

The most important section of this Purāṇa for which it is known and also held in high esteem by the Gauḍīya Vaiṣṇavas especially, is its fourth section in which the person of Rādhā is depicted in its full glory. There is no other Purāṇa among the major eighteen ones which depicts the character, personality and the sportive activities of Rādhā with Kṛṣṇa. Not even Bhāgavata Purāṇa mentions her name in its Xth Skandha which is solely devoted to the exploits of Kṛṣṇa. The only other text which describes the love sports of Rādhā and her female mates with Kṛṣṇa is *Garga Saṃhitā*. But it does not have the status of a Purāṇa.

Although stray references to Rādhā can be traced back to the 1st c. of the current era (first mention in the *Gathāsaptaśtī* of Hāla) yet it is in fact in this Purāṇa as well as in the *Gītagovinda* of Jayadeva (12th c.) that she receives her true personality in flesh and blood. But whereas the Rādhā of Gītagovinda is a shy, love-lorn maiden not married to Kṛṣṇa, the Rādhā of our Purāṇa is the first wife of Kṛṣṇa, also his eternal consort, well versed in love games.

Gītagovinda was composed by an Oriya poet, and the section on Kṛṣṇa of our Purāṇa seems to have been composed in Bengal because the concept of Rādhā as a married woman elder in age to Kṛṣṇa is still prevalent in that region. In any case, the provenance of the present reworked version of our

Purāṇa appears to be the Eastern part of India in all likelihood because not only a few sub-castes of Bengal find mention in its first Khaṇḍa, but also the holy river Virajā flowing through north Odisha is referred to in the very beginning of fourth section. The glorification of Mother Goddess in its third section, her various forms and exploits mentioned in BVP also point towards this direction, which is corroborated by a detailed description of the ceremony of the marriage between Kṛṣṇa and Rukmiṇī (IVth Khaṇḍa) which is not substantially different from the rites that take place today in central-eastern and Eastern India. This also point towards its relatively late origin, much later than the classical age. By the way, this also gives us some clue about the approximate date of the BVP which must be around 10th-12th c. or a little later.

I hope that the present translation of this Purāṇa finds the same warm welcome with the scholars, especially with those who are interested in the development of Kṛṣṇa cult, which they have accorded to the previous volumes of this series.

—Dr. G.C. Tripathi

ADDITIONAL NOTE

The present volume of the *Brahmavaivaivarta Purāṇa* deals mainly with the goddesses worshipped chiefly in Bengal, although not exclusively there. Whereas Manasā, Maṅglā and Tārā, etc. are typically the goddesses of the Bengal region, Rādhā and Lakṣmī have a pan-Indian character. However the person of Rādhā and her worship as described in this Khaṇḍa has a strong imprint of the Eastern part of India.

The title "Prakṛti" for this Khaṇḍa has been taken from the Sāṃkhya philosophy. As is well known, this technical term in Saṃkhya stands for that female Cosmic Force which gives rise to the whole creation, is conceived as feminine and the supreme mother, whereas the male "Puruṣa" stands for pure individual consciousness.

—Dr. G.C. Tripathi

CONTENTS

BRAHMAVAIVARTA PURĀṆA

Prakṛti Khaṇḍa

Book-I

ABBREVIATIONS

Common and self-evident abbreviations such as Ch(s)—Chapter(s), p—page, pp.—pages, v—verse, vv—verses, Ftn—Footnote, Hist. Ind. Philo.—History of Indian Philosophy are not included in this list.

ABORI	*Annals of the Bhandarkar Oriental Research Institute,* Poona
AGP	S.M. Ali's The Geography of *Purāṇas,* PPH, New Delhi, 1973
AIHT	*Ancient Indian Historical Tradition,* F.E. Pargiter, Motilal Banarsidass (MLBD), Delhi
AITM	*Ancient Indian Tradition and Mythology Series,* MLBD, Delhi
AP	*Agni Purāṇa,* Guru Mandal Edition (GM), Calcutta, 1957
Arch. S. Rep.	*Archaeological Survey Report*
AV	*Atharva Veda,* Svādhyāya Maṇḍal, Aundh
BdP	*Brahmāṇḍa Purāṇa,* MLBD, Delhi 1973
BG	*Bhagavadgītā*
BhP	*Bhāgavata Purāṇa,* Bhagavat Vidyapeeth, Ahmedabad
Br	*Brāhmaṇa* (preceded by name such as Śatapatha)
BsP	*Bhaviṣya Purāṇa,* Vishnu Shastri Bapat, Wai
BVP	*Brahma Vaivarta Purāṇa,* GM, 1955-57
CC	*Caturvarga Cintāmaṇi* by Hemādri

CVS	*Caraṇa Vyūha Sūtra* by Śaunaka, Commentary by Mahīdāsa
DB	*Devī Bhāgavata, GM,* 1960-57
De or GDAMI	*The Geographical Dictionary of Ancient and Mediaeval India,* N.L. De, Oriental Reprint, Delhi, 1971
DhS	*Dharma Sūtra* (preceded by the author's name such as Gautama)
ERE	*Encyclopaedia of Religion and Ethics* by Hastings
GP	*Garuḍa Purāṇa,* ed. R.S. Bhattacharya, Chowkhamba, Varanasi, 1964
GS	*Gṛhya Sūtra* (preceded by the name of the author such as Āpastamba)
HD	*History of Dharma Śāstra,* P.V. Kane, G.O.S.
IA	*The Indian Antiquary*
IHQ	*The Indian Historical Quarterly*
JP	*Purāṇa* (Journal of the Kashiraj Trust), Varanasi
KA	*Kauṭilya Arthaśāstra*
KP	*Kūrma Purāṇa,* Veṅkaṭeśvara Press Edn., Bombay; also Kashiraj Trust Edn., Varanasi, 1971
LP	*Liṅga Purāṇa,* GM, 1960; also MLBD, Delhi, 1981
Manu	*Manusmṛti*
Mbh	*Mahābhārata,* Gītā Press, Gorakhpur, VS 2014
MkP	*Mārkaṇḍeya Purāṇa*
MN	*Mahābhārata Nāmānukramaṇi,* Gita Press, Gorakhpur, VS 2016
MtP	*Matsya Purāṇa,* GM, 1954
MW	Monier Williams' *Sanskrit-English Dictionary,* MLBD, Delhi 1976

NP	*Nāradīya* or *Nārada Purāṇa*, Veṅkaṭeśvara Press, Bombay
PCK	*Bhāratavarṣīya Prācīna Caritrakośa*, Siddheshwar Shastri, Poona, 1968
PdP	*Padma Purāṇa*, GM, 1957-59
PE	*Purāṇic Encyclopaedia*, V. Mani, English version, MLBD, Delhi, 1975
PR or	*Puranic Records on Hindu Rites and Customs*,
PRHRC	R.C. Hazra, Calcutta, 1948
ṚV	*Ṛg-Veda*, Svādhyāya Maṇḍal, Aundh
Śat Br	*Śatapatha Brāhmaṇa*
SC or SMC	*Smṛti Candrikā* by Devanna Bhaṭṭa
SEP	*Studies in Epics and Purāṇas*, A.D. Psalkar, Bharatiya Vidya Bhavan (BVB), Bombay
SkP	*Skanda Purāṇa*
SP	*Śiva Purāṇa*
VāP	*Vāyu Purāṇa*
VR	*Vālmīki Rāmāyaṇa*
VdP	*Viṣṇudharmottara Purāṇa*
VmP	*Vāmana Purāṇa*
VP	*Viṣṇu Purāṇa*
VrP	*Varāha Purāṇa*

INTRODUCTION*

It is believed that the study of the Purāṇas is beneficial to the knowledge of the *vedas*. As the *Mahābhārata*[1] states, the *veda* should be supplemented with the Itihāsa and Purāṇa, for the *veda* is afraid of being hurt by a person who is not well-versed (in the mythological and traditional lore). The traditionalists take the word Purāṇa to mean the Purāṇic texts like *Matsya*, *Kūrma*, etc. and attach to them great authority and veneration. They hold that the Purāṇic texts are repositories of very ancient knowledge because they have been referred to in the *Bṛhadāraṇyaka Upaniṣad*.[2] Modern Scholars dispute this claim and say that not the extant Purāṇic texts but some parts of the *vedas* which preserve very old traditions, alluded to in other places of the *vedas*, are referred to in the *Bṛhadāraṇyaka Upaniṣad*, as the Purāṇa. They quote, in support of their thesis, Śaṅkarācārya's interpretation of the said passage of the *Bṛhadāraṇyaka Upaniṣad*: "*Mythology*, such as "The universe was in the beginning unmanifest' etc.".[3]

It is true that the extant Purāṇa texts are much posterior to the early Upaniṣads and, hence, could not have been referred to in the *Bṛhadāraṇyaka Upaniṣad*. But this position does not reduce the usefulness and authority of the Purāṇas. The Purāṇa is not a particular set of texts, it is a branch of ancient Indian learning, a class of ancient Indian literature. The nucleus of

---

*Courtesy : *Brahmavaivarta Purāna of Kṛṣṇa Dvaipāyana Vyāsa* (Original Sanskrit text with Introduction in Sanskrit and English, and alphabetical Index by Prof. Satkari Mukhopadhyaya) in 2 Parts, Ed. by Acharya Jagdish Lal Shastri, MLBD, 1984 (Reprint 2004).

this branch of class existed in the body of the *vedas*, which gradually developed into the *Purāṇasaṃhitā* and then into the present *Mahāpurāṇas, Upapurāṇas*, and later apocrypha. The authority of the Purāṇa, as mentioned in the *Mahābhārata*, is vested in this whole class. In this way, we can reconcile the interpretation of Śaṅkarācārya[4] with the classical five characteristics of the Purāṇas, e.g. primary creation (*sarga*), dissolution (*pratisarga*), genealogy (*vaṁśa*), ages of Manus (*manvantara*) and history of Royal dynasties and some illustrious personages (*vaṁśānucarita*).

There is no controversy about *Brahmavaivartapurāṇa*'s being a major Purāṇa (*Mahāpurāṇa*).

The *Brahmavaivartapurāṇa* figures as the tenth in the traditional lists of the Purāṇas.

The *Brahmavaivartapurāṇa* is divided into four parts called *khaṇḍas*, comprising 267 chapters. The *khaṇḍas* are : *Brahmakhaṇḍa* : 30 chapters, *Prakṛtikhaṇḍa* : 67 chapters, *Gaṇapatikhaṇḍa* : 46 chapters and *Śrikṛṣṇajanmakhaṇḍa* : 133 chapters.

The *Matsya*[5] and *Nāradapurāṇa*[6] describe the total number of verses of the *Brahmavaivartapurāṇa* as 18,000. The *Brahmavaivarta*[7] itself mentions the same number. But the actual counting of the verses of the Purāṇa, now available, gives a total of little over 20,500 verses.

The *Brahmavaivarta*[8] rejects the traditional five characteristics as covering the *Upapurāṇas* only and holds that ten topics are dealt with in a Mahāpurāṇa : they are : primary creation (*sṛṣti*), secondary creation (*visṛṣṭi*), stability of the creation (*sthiti*), protection (*pālana*), desire for work (*karmavāsanā*), information about different Manus (*Manu-vārtā*), description of the final destruction of the world (*pralaya-varṇanā*), showing the way to emancipation (*mokṣa-nirūpaṇa*), discourses on Hari (*Harikirtana*), and discourses on other gods (*devakirtana*).[9] The purpose of this substitution of list of topics in the *Bhāgavata* and *Brahmavaivarta* has been discussed by Dr. R.C. Hazra and his opinion on this point deserves serious consideration.[10]

A complete table of contents (*anukramaṇikā*) is included in the chapter 132 of the *Śrikṛṣṇajanmakhaṇḍa*.

It is well known that the *Brahmavaivarta* is a Vaiṣṇavite Purāṇa and the sole objective of the work is to glorify the life and achievements of Śrī Kṛṣṇa, an incarnation of Viṣṇu and his Śakti Rādhā. Many episodes and topics have been interwoven to embellish the main theme of the work. In this Purāṇa, Kṛṣṇa is not simply an incarnation, he is far superior to and even creator of Prakṛti. He is God above all gods.

Part I, i.e., *Brahmakhaṇḍa* deals with the creation of the universe including the gods and animate and inanimate beings by Brahman, the creator God, who is, according to this Purāṇa, none other than a manifestation of Kṛṣṇa and acts under the guidance of the latter.

Part II, i.e., *Prakṛtikhaṇḍa* deals with Prakṛti, the primordial matter. According to this Purāṇa, Prakṛti is not inert as she is conceived by the Sāṅkhya philosophy, but is intelligent; she is the primary goddess of creation.[11] In compliance with Kṛṣṇa's desire, she is manifested as the five goddesses,[12] viz. Durgā, Rādhā, Lakṣmī, Sarasvatī, and Sāvitrī.[13] Many stories about these deities have been narrated and rituals for their worship described in this part.

Part III, i.e., *Gaṇapatikhaṇḍa* narrates many legends about Gaṇeśa, the elephant-headed god, widely worshipped throughout India and even outside. Though named *Gaṇapatikhaṇḍa*, this part deals with the birth and life of both sons of Śiva, viz. Gaṇeśa and Skanda Kārttikeya. According to this Purāṇa, Gaṇeśa is also a manifestation of Kṛṣṇa. Hence, there is no mention of Gāṇapatya sects who worshipped Gaṇeśa as the Supreme Godhead. The variations in the images of this deity, found in literature and on icons find no mention in the Purāṇa.

Part IV, i.e., *Śrikṛṣṇajanmakhaṇḍa* is the most important of all books of this Purāṇa. It deals not only with the birth of Kṛṣṇa, as signified by the title, but also his whole life, especially his battles and love dalliances with the cowherdesses (*gopīs*), in particular, with Rādhā. Rādhā, who is not even mentioned in the major Vaiṣṇava Purāṇas like *Bhāgavata, Viṣṇu*, and

Harivaṃśa, has risen in this Purāṇa, to a great importance. It is interesting to note that she is depicted here as a married wife of Kṛṣṇa.[14]

Authority of the Text

Much can be discussed about the authority of extant *Brahmavaivartapurāṇa*. The authority of the Purāṇa is apparently established, because it is mentioned in older texts *Matsya, Nārada,* etc.[15] But there exists a great discrepancy between the *Brahmavaivarta* as mentioned in the *Matsya* and *Nārada* purāṇa and the text that is available now. The *Matsyapurāṇa* says that the story of the *Brahmavaivarta* has been narrated by Sāvarṇi to Nārada, it includes the episode of Brahmavarāha, and it comprises 18,000 verses. But, we do not find even the name of Sāvarṇi in the *Brahmavaivarta* now extant, nor the episode of Brahmavarāha can be traced to it. It can, therefore, be inferred that the original form of the Purāṇa has undergone a great change. It is also interesting to note that only 30 lines out of 1500, quoted from the *Brahmavaivarta* in medieval *smṛti-nibandhas*, like *Smṛticandrikā, Caturvargacintāmaṇi, Kālanirṇaya, Smṛtitattva, Varṣakriyākaumudi,* etc. can be traced to the extant text.[16] It may, therefore, be presumed that a considerable part of the older text, containing genealogies, geographical descriptions, etc. has been purged and replaced by later compositions which suit the purpose of Vaiṣṇava sects. This transformation has diminished the authority of the Purāṇa to a great extent.

Date of Composition

It is not easy to determine, with any amount of certainty, the date of composition of the *Brahmavaivartapurāṇa*, because it contains both ancient and medieval materials. It is then obvious that there would be difference of opinion among scholars about the date of this Purāṇa. Wilson's view[17] that the *Brahmavaivartapurāṇa* was composed after the Mohammadan conquest of Northern India, need not be taken seriously. On the basis of its mention in the *Matsya* and other old Purāṇas, we can accept its existence, in some form or other, much prior to the Mohammadan invasions to the North. Jogesh Chandra Roy holds that the Purāṇa was composed during the 8th century A.D. The upper limit of the date of composition may tentatively be fixed in the 8th century because Śaṅkarācārya who flourished in the same century, is mentioned in the *Śrikṛṣṇajanmakhaṇḍa.*[18] It is also probable that by the tenth century, it began to be changed.[19]

Jayadeva, the Sanskrit poet, who flourished in the 12th century, was acquainted with the *Brahmavaivartapurāṇa,* the text of which was almost settled by that time.[20] The opening verse of Jayadeva's *Gitagovinda* (*Meghairmeduramambaram,* etc.) definitely alludes to an episode narrated in the 15th Chapter of the *Śrikṛṣṇajanmakhaṇḍa.* Jayadeva also describes Kṛṣṇa in his two aspects, *aiśvarya* and *mādhurya,* in the same line with *Brahmavaivarta.* It cannot, of course, be ruled out that interpolations, particularly of the *smṛti* material, continued till the 16th century or even till a little later. It can be safely presumed that the additions and alterations were carried out in Bengal. A close examination of the idiom and diction proves the fact beyond any reasonable doubt. The mixed castes like *Haḍḍi, Bāgatita,* etc. as mentioned in the Purāṇa, are found in no other part of the country than Bengal.[21] Gopālabhaṭṭa, one of the early Gosvāmīs of the Chaitanya sect, who flourished in the 16th century, found the *Brahmavaivarta-purāṇa,* almost in its present form, because, a little over sixty verses quoted by him in his *Haribhaktivilāsa,* from *Brahmavaivarta,* can be traced to that text.

It has already been mentioned that the extant *Brahmavaivartapurāṇa* comprises both ancient and medieval materials. It is difficult to ascertain the time of composition of ancient portions. Dr. Hazra is quite justified in his statement: "it seems highly probable that before 700 A.D. there existed a *Brahmavaivarta* which is now lost."[22]

— **Prof. Satkari Mukhopadhyaya**

NOTES

1. इतिहासपुराणाभ्यां वेदं समुपबृंहयेत्।
   बिभेत्यल्पश्रुताद्वेदो मामयं प्रहरेदिति॥ MBh. 1.1.260
2. II.4.10; IV.1.2; IV.5.11.
3. "पुराणम् 'असद्वा इदमग्र आसीत्' इत्यादीनि।" on. II.4.10
4. *op. cit.*
5. रथन्तरस्य कल्पस्य वृत्तान्तमधिकृत्य च।
   सावर्णिना नारदाय कृष्णमाहात्म्यमुत्तमम्॥
   यत्र ब्रह्मवराहस्य चरितं वर्ण्यते मुहुः।
   तदष्टादशसाहस्रं ब्रह्मवैवर्तमुच्यते॥
   —*Matsyapurāṇa,* Ch 53.
6. व्यासश्चतुर्धा संव्यस्य ब्रह्मवैवर्तसंज्ञितम्।
   तदष्टादशसाहस्रं पुराणं परिकीर्तितम्॥
   —*Nāradapurāṇa,* Ch 101.
7. तदष्टादशसाहस्रं ब्रह्मवैवर्तमीप्सितम्।
   —*Brahmavaivarta Purāṇa,* IV.133.16.
8. IV. 133.7.
9. सृष्टिश्चापि विसृष्टिश्च स्थितिस्तेषां च पालनम्।
   कर्मणां वासना वार्ता मनूनां चाग्रमेण च॥
   वर्णनं प्रलयानां च मोक्षस्य च निरूपणम्।
   तत्कीर्तनं हरेरेव वेदानां च पृथक् पृथक्॥
   —*Brahmavaivarta Purāṇa,* IV.133.8-9.

10. Hazra, R.C. *The Purāṇas in The Cultural Heritage of India,* Vol. II, 2nd edn., Ramakrishna Mission Institute of Culture, Calcutta, 1962, pp. 251-52.

11. प्रथमे वर्तते प्रश्च कृतिः स्यात् सृष्टिवाचकः।
   सृष्टेराद्या च या देवी प्रकृतिः सा प्रकीर्तिता॥
   —*Brahmavaivartapurāṇa,* II.1.8.

12. स्वेच्छामयस्येच्छया च श्रीकृष्णस्य सिसृक्षया।
साऽऽविर्बभूव सहसा मूलप्रकृतिरीश्वरी॥
तदिच्छया पञ्चविधा सृष्टिकर्मणि भेदतः।
अथ भक्तानुरोधाद्वा भक्तानुग्रहविग्रहा॥

—*Ibid.*, II.1.12-13.

13. गणेशजननी दुर्गा राधा लक्ष्मीः सरस्वती।
सावित्री वै सृष्टिविधौ प्रकृतिः पञ्चधा स्मृता॥

—*Ibid.*, II.1.1.

14. IV. 15. 120-130.

15. *loc.cit.*

16. Hazra, R.C., *Studies in Puranic records on Hindu Rites and Customs*, 2nd ed., MLBD, 1975, pp.166-167; *The Purāṇas, loc.cit.*

17. Wilson, H.H., *Essays*, Vol. 1, p. 120.

18. कारागारे च संसारे दुर्वहं निगडं परम्।
अच्छेद्यं ज्ञानखड्गैश्च महद्भिः शङ्करादिभिः॥

—*Brahmavaivarta Purāṇa, IV.* 24.18.

19. Hazra, R.C., *Studies in the Purāṇic records on Hindu Rites and Customs*, 2nd edn., MLBD, Delhi, 1975, pp.166-167.

20. De, Sushil Kumar, *Early history of the Vaishnava Faith and Movement in Bengal*, 2nd edn., Firma K.L. Mukhopadhyay, Calcutta, 1961, pp.11-12.

21. I.10.105, 118.

22. *Studies in the Purāṇic records on Hindu Rites and Customs*, p.167.

BRAHMAVAIVARTA PURĀṆA

PRAKṚTI KHAṆḌA

CHAPTER ONE

The Nature of Prakṛti and Its Different Forms

Obeisance to (lords) Gaṇeśa, Veṅkaṭeśvara, (Goddess) Sarasvatī and Lakṣmī-Narasiṁha! The Prakṛti Khaṇḍa begins:

Nārada said:

1. In the process of creation, *prakṛti* (Nature) is known to be of five forms: Durgā, the mother of Gaṇeśa, Rādhā, Lakṣmī, Sarasvatī and Sāvitrī.

2. Why did the Nature, outstanding among the learned, manifest ? Who was she ? What is her feature ? Describe me as to how she had five forms ?

3. You are fit to explain me the legends relating to all of them, the modes of worshipping them and why, where and how her manifestations were made ?

Nārāyaṇa said:

4. O Child ! Who will be capable of describing the characteristics of Nature. Even then I shall describe you a little that I have heard from the mouth of (lord) Dharma.

5. (The syllable) *pra* expresses excellence and (the term) *kṛti* expresses creation. Hence the goddess who excels in creation is glorified as *prakṛti*.

6. The syllable *pra* is used in the scriptures when there is excellence of good quality, the middle (letter) *kṛ* for *rajas* and the letter *ti* is used to denote *tamas.*

7. One who is vested with the three qualities, endowed with all the powers and is the principal in creation is hence termed as *prakṛti.*

8. (The letter) *pra* occurs first. The term *kṛti* is an expression of creation. The goddess who is the first in (the process of) creation is glorified as *prakṛti.*

9. In the process of creation the Supreme Being split Himself into two by means of abstract meditation. The right half of the body was a male and the left half was known to be *prakṛti.*

10. She is stated to be of the form of Brahman. She is illusory, eternal and without a change. She is known to be like the soul or the power of burning existing in fire.

11. That is why an ascetic never holds any distinction between a woman and man. O Nārada ! A realised soul always beholds everything as an embodiment of Brahman.

12. The Suzerain Primordial Nature suddenly manifested by the will of Lord Kṛṣṇa, an embodiment of free-will, desirous of creation.

13. At His command She had five forms either on account difference in the process of creation or at the behest of the votaries. She was an embodiment of benevolence to the votaries.

14. (Goddess) Durgā, the mother of (Lord) Gaṇeśa, is a form of (Lord) Śiva and is dear to (Lord) Śiva. (Goddess) Nārāyaṇi, the illusion of (Lord) Viṣṇu, is of the form of the whole Brahman.

15. She is always adored by Brahmā and other gods, sages and Manus. That presiding deity of all the beings is of the form of Brahman and is eternal.

16. She confers fame, auspiciousness, virtue, prosperity, truth and merits. This conferrer of beatitude and rejoice is the destroyer of grief, misery and distress.

17. She is bent on offering protection to indigent in distress seeking her refuge. She is of the form of lustre. She is supreme. She is the presiding deity of the indigent.

18. She is of the form of all energy and she is always the energy of the lord. She is the governess of accomplishment. She is of the form of accomplishment. She is the conferrer of perfection. She is the governess that yields perfection.

19-20. (She is) intellect, sleep, hunger, thirst, shadow, lassitude, compassion, remembrance, caste, forbearance, peace, lustre, delusion, consciousness, satisfaction, nourishment, fortune and livelihood. She is the mother. She is of the form of all energy of the Supreme Soul (Lord) Kṛṣṇa.

21. Her virtues described in the scriptures are very few. Boundless are the virtues of that infinite one. You listen (to me) for the other one.

22. Padmā, who (is the consort) of the Supreme Being, is of the form of pure *sattva* (quality). She is of the form of all prosperity. She is the presiding deity of that.

23-24. She is charming, forbearing, very tranquil, endowed with good disposition and all auspiciousness. She is devoid of greed, stupor, lust, anger, haughtiness and pride. She is devoted to her husband. She is the first among all. She is chaste. She is dear to the lord like the life. She is an object of love. She is sweet-speaking.

25-26. She is the soul of all grains. She is of the nature of means of existence of all beings. She is (Goddess) Mahālakṣmī, in Vaikuṇṭha (abode of Lord Viṣṇu) bent on serving her lord. She is the celestial goddess of fortune in the heaven. She is the royal goddess of prosperity in the kings. She is the goddess of the houses for the mortals and householders.

27-30. She is the form of grace of all the beings and substances. She is charming. She is of the form of satisfaction for the meritorious. She is of the form of lustre for the kings. She is of the form of commerce for tradesmen. She is the cause of dissension among sinners. She is an embodiment of compassion. She is the mother of devotees. She extends her grace on her devotees. She is fickle-mindedness in the fickle-minded. She is bent on the protection of the wealth of her devotees. O Sage ! The entire beings in the world are dead without that goddess. The second form of the energy described in the scriptures, regarded by all, worshipped and saluted by all has been explained. Listen (to me) I shall explain the other one.

31. The goddess presiding over speech, intellect, knowledge and wisdom of the Supreme Soul is the goddess Sarasvatī of the form of all knowledge.

32. She confers good intellect, poesy, genius, wisdom, and remembrance on the virtuous. She is the bestower of settlement relating to the sense of different theories of conflicting nature.

33. She is of the form of comprehension of the expositions. She destroys all doubts. She is the investigator, composer of works and is of the form of energy.

34. She is of the form of the determining cause of all music and rhythm. She is of the form of wisdom relating to worldly things and speech for every being in this universe.

35. All the beings in this universe are dumb and almost dead without her. She holds the posture of hands giving exposition. She is tranquil. She holds the lute and a book (in her hands).

36. She is of the form of pure *sattva* (quality). She has good disposition. She is dear to (Lord) Hari. She has the complexion of snow, sandal (paste), jasmine, moon, lily and lotus.

37. She is muttering (the name) of Śrīkṛṣṇa, the Supreme Soul with the garland of gems. She is of the form of penance. She confers the fruits of penance. She is a doer of penance.

38. She is of the form of knowledge pertaining to accomplishment. She is always the conferrer of all perfections.

39. Listen to my (narration) a little (about the other form of nature) according to the scriptures. She is the mother of the four *vedas*, *vedāṅgas* (six auxiliary texts of the *vedas*) and *metrices.*

40. She is well-versed in the mystic formulae for the twilight worship and the *tantras* (religious treatises dealing with magical and mystical formulae for worship). She is of the form of the castes such as the twice-born etc. (the castes entitled for investiture of the sacred thread). That doer of penance is of the form of repetition (of sacred syllables).

41. She is of the nature of the effulgence of Brahmā. She is of the nature of all refinements. She is of the form of sanctity. She is Sāvitrī, Gāyatrī and the dear one of (Lord) Brahmā.

42. The sacred places desire to have her touch and sight for gaining purity. She has the complexion of a pure crystal. She is of the nature of pure *sattva* (quality).

43. She is of the form of Supreme Bliss. She is Supreme. She is eternal. She is of the form of the Supreme Brahman. She is the conferrer of beatitude.

44. She is the energy, an embodiment of the lustre of (Lord) Brahmā. She is its presiding deity. O Nārada ! The entire world gets purified by the dust of Her feet.

45. I have described you the fourth form of the goddess. I shall describe you the fifth one (now). She is the presiding deity of love and life. She is of the form of the five life-breaths.

46. She is dearer than the life. She is the first (among all). She is most beautiful. She is endowed with all prosperity. She is respectful and dignified.

47. She is the left half of the body (of the Lord). By her virtues she is resplendent. She is higher and lower. She is the mother of all. She is the earliest one. She is eternal.

48. She is of the form of Supreme Bliss. She is fortunate, respectable and adored. She is the presiding deity of the *rāsakrīḍā* (sportive dance) of (Lord) Kṛṣṇa, the Supreme Soul.

49. She has her place in the dancing circle. She is adorned with the dancing circle. She is the presiding deity of *rāsa* (dance) and a good appreciator. She resides in the dancing place.

50. That goddess is a dweller in the world of cows. She wears the dress of a cowherdess. She is of the form of supreme delight, mirth and forbearance.

51. She is devoid of attributes, without form and unstained. She has the natural state of the soul. She is desireless, without ego and an embodiment of conferring favour on the devotees.

52. She should be known by the wise by means of meditation as laid down in the scriptures. Her look has been perceived by the chiefs of gods and foremost sages in thousands (of kine).

53. She is clad in a dress pure like the fire. She is adorned with gem-studded ornaments. She is endowed with charm graced by the lustre of crores of moons. She is an embodiment of the devotees.

54-55. She serves the devotee of (Lord) Kṛṣṇa. She is the sole conferrer of all prosperities. She was the daughter of Vṛṣabhānu at the time of the manifestation (of Lord Viṣṇu) as the Boar. The Earth became sanctified by the touch of her lotus feet. She is not beheld by (Lord) Brahmā and others. She beholds everything in Bhārata.

56. She stays in the midst of exquisite gem-like women. She rests on the chest-region of (Lord) Kṛṣṇa. O Sage ! She is the dangling lightning in the fresh clouds of the rainy season.

57. In olden days (Lord) Brahmā had done penance for sixty thousand years in order to behold the nails of her lotus feet and for his own purification.

58. She could not be beheld even in the dream. Then what to speak about in one's immediate presence. He himself has beheld her by meditation repeatedly at the Vṛndāvana forest.

59-60. The fifth form of the goddess has been described. She is glorified as Rādhā. All the women in the universe are a part or digit or part of digit-part manifestation of Nature. The five forms of the goddess are glorified as full forms.

61-62. Listen to me ! I shall describe you the principal part manifestations. Ganges, the sanctifier of the world, had her origin from the lotus-feet of (Lord) Viṣṇu. She is volatile and eternal. She is of the form of glowing fuel for burning the sticks in the form of the sins of the sinners.

63. She is capable of conferring beatitude by sight, touch, bathing and drinking. She is of the form of good steps to reach the region of the world of cows.

64. She is the sanctity of sacred places. She is the highest and lowest among the rivers. She is of the form of row of pearls adorning the tuft of Lord Śiva resembling the Meru.

65. She enables the penance of the ascetics to get fulfilled at once. She resembles the hue of conch, lotus and milk. She is of the form of pure *sattva* quality.

66. She is stainless, without ego and chaste. She is dear to (Lord) Nārāyaṇa (Viṣṇu). Tulasī (Holy Basil) is of the form of principal part (of Nature). She is the beloved of (Lord) Viṣṇu.

67. She is an ornament of (Lord) Viṣṇu. She remains at the feet of (Lord) Viṣṇu. She is chaste. O Sage ! She bestows at once (the fruits of) penance, resolve and worship.

68. She is the foremost among flowers, pure and conferrer of merits always. She is capable of bestowing beatitude at once by sight and touch.

69. She is of the form of fire for burning the dry fuel of sins in the *kali* (*yuga*).[1] The earth gets purified by the touch of her lotus-feet.

70. The sacred places desire to have her touch and sight for their purification. All actions in the universe are fruitless without her.

71-72a. She is the conferrer of beatitude for those desirous of liberation. She is the bestower of all desires for those who desire (worldly objects, etc.). She is the wish-yielding tree in Bhārata in the form of a tree. She is the Supreme goddess for the protection and worship (of the people) of Bhārata.

72b-73. (Goddess) Manasā, daughter of Kaśyapa is also a principal part (manifestation of Nature). She is a favourite disciple of (Lord) Śaṅkara (Śiva). She is extremely wise. She is the sister of Ananta, the lord of serpents. She is adored by the serpents.

74. She governs the serpents. She is the mother of the serpents. She is beautiful. She has the serpent as her vehicle.

She is in the company of hosts of serpents. She is adorned by the serpents as ornaments.

75. She is saluted by the chief of the serpents. She is an accomplished practitioner of meditation. She has the serpents as her attire. She is a devotee of (Lord) Viṣṇu. She is a form of (Lord) Viṣṇu. She is bent on worshipping (Lord) Viṣṇu.

76. She is an emblem of penance. She is the bestower of the fruits of penance. She is an ascetic. She did penance for a divine three lakh years (meditating) (lord) Hari (Viṣṇu).

77. She is adorable among male and female ascetics in Bhārata. She is the presiding deity of all the mystic formulae. She is glowing with the lustre of Brahman.

78-79a. She is of the form of Brahman. She is supreme. She is bent on meditating Brahman. She is the wife of sage Jaratkāru. She is devoted to (Lords) Kṛṣṇa and Śambhu (Śiva). She is the mother of sage Astīka, the foremost among the ascetics.

79b-80. O Nārada ! (Goddess) Devasenā, another part-manifestation (of Nature) is the most respected mother. She is glorified as Ṣaṣṭhi. She is the protector of all children in the universe.

81. She is an ascetic. She is a devotee of (Lord) Viṣṇu. She is the beloved of (Lord) Kārtikeya. She is the sixth part-manifestation of the Nature. Hence she is glorified as Ṣaṣṭhī.

82. She is the conferrer of sons and grandsons. She is always the supporter of the world. She is beautiful, young and always graceful near her husband.

83. In the place of children she is of the form of a very old ascetic woman. (Goddess) Ṣaṣṭhī should always be worshipped in the twelve months.

84. She should be worshipped on the sixth day (after the birth) of the child in the confinement room. Worship done on the twenty-first day causes good.

85-86a. The worship as laid down is done always or optionally done. She is always the guardian in the form of the mother and as compassion. She appears in the dream of the child in the water, on the earth and in the sky.

86b-87. Another form of principal part-manifestation is goddess Maṅgalacaṇḍikā. She had Her origin from the face of Nature. She confers all auspiciousness always. At the time of creation she is of the form of auspiciousness. At the time of destruction she is of the form of wrath.

88. That is why she has been glorified by the learned as Maṅgalacaṇḍī. She is worshipped on every Tuesday everywhere.

89. When she is worshipped by women with devotion offering five kinds of services,[2] she confers sons, grandsons, wealth, prosperity, fame and auspiciousness.

90. She destroys grief, agony, sin, misery, unhappiness and poverty. When she is pleased, she yields all the desires for women.

91a. That great goddess is capable of destroying the universe if she is angry.

91b-92. Lotus-eyed Kālī is a part-manifestation (of Nature). She had her origin from the forehead of (goddess) Durgā at the time of the battle with (the demons) Śumbha and Niśumbha.[3] She is of the form of half-part of (goddess) Durgā. With her attendants she is equal to the lustre (of goddess Durgā).

93. Her beautiful divine frame has the radiance of a crore suns. She is the principal among all the energies. She is outstanding, strong and supreme.

94. That goddess is capable of conferring all perfections. She is a foremost accomplished ascetic. She is a devotee of (Lord) Kṛṣṇa. In her lustre, valour and virtues she is on par with (Lord) Kṛṣṇa. On account of her meditation of (Lord) Kṛṣṇa always, she is eternally having dark complexion.

95. She is capable of destroying the entire cosmic egg by her mere breath. Her battle with the *daityas* (demons) (progeny of Diti) was done sportively for the sake of the protection of the world.

96. If she is well-worshipped she is capable of giving virtue, wealth, object of desire and beatitude. She is always adored by (Lord) Brahmā and others, sages, Manus and men.

97. The earth is also a principal part-manifestation of Nature. She is the sustainer of all the beings. She yields all the grains.

98. She is the mine of gems. She has the gems in her womb. She is the substratum of all the oceans. She is always worshipped and saluted by people and their rulers.

99. She is the sustainer of all the beings. She is the conferrer of all prosperity. Bereft of her the entire world, the movables and immovables, are without a support.

100. O Foremost sage ! You know from me the different digits (manifestations) of Nature. I shall describe you who are all the consorts of which (gods).

101. Goddess Svāhā, the wife of Fire-god, is worshipped in the three worlds. The gods are not capable of partaking of the *havis* (cooked rice) offered to them without her.

102. Dakṣiṇā, the wife of sacrifice is worshipped everywhere. All the actions in the universe are fruitless without her.

103. Svadhā, the wife of the manes, is adored by the sages, Manus and men. The gift intended for the sake of the manes is fruitless without her.

104. Goddess Svasti, wife of Wind god, is worshipped all over the world. Receiving and giving away are fruitless without her.

105. Puṣṭi, the consort of (lord) Gaṇapati, is worshipped all over the world. Men and women get emaciated without her.

106. Tuṣṭi, the consort of Ananta, is always adored and saluted. All the people everywhere do not get pleased without her.

107. Sampatti, the wife of Īśāna, is worshipped by the gods and men. All men in the universe are indigent without her.

108. Dhṛti, the wife of Kapila, is adored by all everywhere. All the people will not be valorous in this world without her.

109. Kṣamā, the consort of Yama, is chaste. She has a good disposition and is worshipped by all. All the people are insane and wrathful without her.

110. Rati, the chaste wife of Kāma, is the presiding deity of sport. All the people are bereft of sport and amusement without her.

111. Mukti (liberation), the chaste consort of Satya (truth), is the favourite of the world and adored. The people will always be without kinsman bereft of her.

112. Dayā (compassion), the pious wife of Moha (stupefication), is dear to the world and is worshipped. All the people everywhere are harsh without her.

113. Pratiṣṭhā (Firmness etc.), the consort of Puṇya (merit), is of the form of merit and adored. O Sage ! Without her the entire world is almost dead even though living.

114. Kīrti (fame), the wife of Sukarma(good act), is fortunate, respectable and adored. The entire world is without fame just like the dead without her.

115. Kriyā (act), the wife of Udyoga (endeavour), is adored and associated with all. O Nārada ! The entire world bereft of her is as if extirpated.

116-118. Mithyā (falsehood), the wife of Adharma (unrighteousness), is worshipped by all rogues. Without her all the world created by (Lord) Brahmā is destroyed. She is invisible in the *satya* (*yuga*).[4] She is subtle in the *tretā* (*yuga*). She has half the body in the *dvāpara* (*yuga*), yet (remains) concealed on account of shame. She is shameless in *kaliyuga* because she is pervasive everywhere. She roams in every house along with her brother Kapaṭa (conceit).

119. Śānti (peace) and Lajjā (shame) are the two wives of Suśīla (good conduct)and are adored. O Nārada ! Without them the entire world is like an insane person.

120. Buddhi (intellect), Medhā (retentive power) and Smṛti (remembrance) are the three wives of *jñāna* (wisdom). Without them the entire world is ignorant like the dead.

121. The graceful *mūrti* (embodied form) is the wife of Dharma (piety). She is charming. The all-pervasive Supreme soul is supportless without her.

122. (Goddess) Lakṣmī who is omnipresent embodied as beauty is an embodiment of chastity. She is respected, fortunate and adored in the forms of Śrī and Mūrti.

123. The consort of Kālāgnirudra who is the sleep of accomplished ascetics, enwraps (the world) by means of her illusion in the nights.

124. *Sandhyā* (twilight), *rātri* (night) and *dināni* (days) are the three wives of *kāla* (time). Brahmā will not be able to create without their help.

125. Hunger and thirst are the two wives of avarice. They are blessed, respectable and adored. The world pervaded by these two gets agitated and anxious.

126. *Prabhā* (lustre) and *dāhikā* (the power of burning) are the two wives of *tejas* (splendour). Without whom Brahmā has no power to create.

127. *Mṛtyu* (death) and *jarā* (decrepitude)are the two daughters of *kāla* (time). They are the wives of high fever. Through their influence the world created by Brahmā comes to an end.

128. Lassitude and Satisfaction are the two daughters of Sleep. They are the wives of Happiness. The world is pervaded by them and they control the Fate, son of Brahmā.

129. The adorable Faith and Devotion are the two wives of Non-attachment. O Sage ! Being influenced by them the world is always liberated while living.

130-131. Aditi, the mother of gods, Surabhi, the mother of cows, Diti, the mother of *daityas* (demon), Kadrū, Vinatā and Danu associated with the process of creation are all digits of Nature. There are many other digits. Some of them you know from me.

132-142. Rohiṇī, the wife of Moon; Saṁjñā, the consort of Sun; Śatarūpā, the wife of Manu; Śacī, the spouse of Indra; Tārā, the wife of Bṛhaspati; Arundhati, the wife of Vasiṣṭha; Ahalyā, the wife of Gautama; Anasūyā, the wife of Atri; Devahūti, (the wife) of Kardama; Prasūti, the beloved of Dakṣa, Menakā, the mind-born daughter of the Pitṛs and the mother of Ambikā; Lopāmudrā, Hūti, the wife of Kubera;

Varuṇānī, the wife of Yama; Vindhyāvalī, (wife) of Bali; Kuntī, Damayantī, Yaśodā, Devakī, the chaste, Gāndhārī; Draupadī, the wife of Arjuna; Sāvitrī, the wife of Satyavān; Sādhvī, the wife of Vṛṣabhānu; Kalāvatī, the mother of Rādhā; Mandodarī, Kausalyā, Subhadrā, Kaikayī, Revatī, Satyabhāmā; Kālindī, Lakṣmaṇā, Mitravindā, Nāgnajitī (daughter of Nagnajit); Jāmbavatī, Lakṣmaṇā, Rukmiṇī, Sītā, glorified as Lakṣmī herself, Kalā, Yojanagandhā, the chaste mother of Vyāsa; Uṣā, the daughter of Bāṇa; Citralekhā, the companion (of Uṣā), Prabhāvatī, Bhānumatī, the chaste Māyāvatī, Reṇukā, the mother of Bhṛgu, Rohiṇī, the mother of Balarāma, and Durgā, the sister of Kṛṣṇa are all part manifestations. Thus there are many digital manifestations of the Nature in Bhārata. All the village goddesses are also digital manifestations of Nature.

143. The women all over the world had their origin from a part of the digital manifestation (of Nature). Insult of women is humiliation of Nature.

144. Honouring a brahmin lady having her husband and children amounts to adoration of Nature with dress, ornaments and sandal paste.

145. The worship of a brahmin girl aged eight years with dress, ornaments and sandal paste amounts to adoration of Nature.

146-148. All women–good, mediocre and bad– are born from the Nature. Those having the *sattva* quality are known to be good. They are of good conduct and chaste. The mediocre are those having the *rajas* quality. They are declared as enjoyable. They court pleasure and are always after their selfish goals. The bad one are those having the *tamas* quality. They had their origin from unknown family. They are hideous, unchaste, wicked, independent and quarrelsome.

149. Those who are unchaste on the earth are the hosts of *apsara* women in the heaven. They are stated to be harlots arising from the *tamas* part of Nature.

150. Thus I have described you everything about the five divisions of Nature. They are all worshipped on the earth in the sacred land of Bhārata.

151. Durgā, the destroyer of hardship and misfortune was first worshipped by (King) Suratha. The second one (was worshipped) by Rāmacandra desirous of killing Rāvaṇa.

152. Then the mother of the world worshipped in the three worlds was born at first from the wife of Dakṣa in order to kill the demon progenies of Diti and Danu.

153. Thereafter discarding her life on account of the insult of her husband at the sacrifice, she was born (as the daughter) of the wife of Himavān. She gained Paśupati (Śiva) as her husband.

154. Gaṇeśa is (Lord) Kṛṣṇa himself. Skanda had the origin from a digit of (Lord) Viṣṇu. O Nārada ! They were born as her sons.

155. (Goddess) Lakṣmī was first worshipped by King Maṅgala. Then (she was adored) in the three worlds by gods, sages and men.

156. Sāvitrī was also worshipped first with devotion. Then she was adored by the gods, sages and men in the three worlds.

157. Goddess Sarasvatī was first worshipped by (Lord) Brahmā. Then (she was worshipped) by the gods, sages and men in the three worlds.

158. Rādhā was first worshipped in the world of cows in the dance circle by (Lord) Kṛṣṇa, the Supreme Soul, on the full-moon day in Kārttika (November).

159. Then (she was worshipped) by cowherdesses, cowherds, girls and boys, hordes of cows, hosts of gods by the illusion of (Lord) Hari (Viṣṇu).

160. Then she was worshipped and saluted always with flowers incense etc., with devotion by Brahmā and other gods, sages and men.

161. The goddess was first worshipped on the earth by Suyajña as directed by (Lord) Śaṅkara (Śiva) in the holy land of Bhārata.

162. Then she was worshipped in the three worlds with flowers, incense etc., with devotion by sages and gods at the command of the Supreme god.

163. Then all the digital manifestations were worshipped in Bhārata. O Sage ! The village goddesses were worshipped in the villages and towns.

164. Thus I have described you all the auspicious legend and traits relating to Nature as in the scriptures. What more do you desire to listen ?

CHAPTER TWO

The Description of the Origin of the Gods and Goddesses

Nārada said:

1. O Lord ! I have heard all the legend relating to the goddesses briefly (described by you). You can describe me in detail for my perfect comprehension.

2. How did the first creation manifest in the process of creation ? Foremost amongst learned in the scriptures ! Tell me how it became five ?

3. Now I am desirous of knowing in detail the legends about what all manifested from her digits on account of the three qualities.

4. After narrating me about their origin, describe me their meditation, modes of worship, glorification, amulet, affluence, valour and auspiciousness.

Śrī Nārāyaṇa said:

5. Just as the soul, sky, time and direction are eternal, the herd of kine belonging to the universe and the world of cows are eternal.

6. It is an extensive part of the Vaikuṇṭha (abode of Lord Viṣṇu) and is eternal. Similarly the Nature is eternal. She is absorbed in Brahman and is perpetual.

7. Just as the power to burn rests always in fire, beauty in Moon and Lotus, radiance in Sun and they never remain separate, so also Nature (rests) in the Supreme Soul.

8-9. The goldsmith is not capable of making a pendant without gold. The potter cannot make a pot without mud. In the same way (Lord) Brahmā cannot do the creation without her. She is of the form of all the energies. One gets endowed with energy on account of her.

10. (The syllable) *śak* is an expression of opulence and (the syllable) it is an expression of valour. One who is characterised by these and is their sustainer is hence stated to be Śakti.

11. (The word) *bhaga* is an expression for abundance, intellect, prosperity and fame. Hence Śakti, Bhagavatī is always of the form of '*bhaga*'.

12. The Supreme Soul always endowed with her is hence called Bhagavān. He is (Lord) Kṛṣṇa, an embodiment of free-will. He is both with form and formless.

13-14. The ascetics contemplate always that embodiment of lustre without form. They describe him as Brahman, Supreme Soul, Master, imperceptible, all-perceiving, omniscient, cause of all things, all-yielding, present in all forms, formless and nourishing all.

15. *Vaiṣṇavas,* the devotees of Viṣṇu, the knowers of subtle things do not accept it. They say that the lustre (is impossible) without a possessor of that lustre.

16-23. The devotees of Viṣṇu meditate that Supreme Brahman in the midst of an orb of lustre. He possesses lustre. He is an embodiment of free will. He is of all forms. He is the cause of all causes. He is having an extremely beautiful form that is very attractive. He is young, tranquil, dear to all and most supreme. He is having the complexion of a fresh cloud. He has a beautiful dark complexion in the midst of a dancing circle. His eyes bear the lustre of autumnal lotus blooming in the noon. His rows of teeth are charming and spotless like the exquisite pearls. He has the tuft adorned by peacock plumes. He is adorned by a garland of *mālatī* flowers.

He has a beautiful nose. He is smiling. He always extends His grace on the devotees. He is gracious with the silken garment as pure as the glowing fire. He has two arms. He holds a flute. He is adorned with a gem-studded ornament. He is the sustainer of all. He is the Lord of all. He is endowed with all powers. He is the master. He is the conferrer of all prosperity. He is everything. He is independent. He is all auspiciousness. He is whole. He is an accomplished person. He bestows perfection. He is the cause of accomplishment. He is perpetual. He is the supreme person that dispels (the cycle of) birth and death, decrepitude, disease, grief and fear.

24. A minute (of the Lord) is served by the whole life of (Lord) Brahmā. That soul is the Supreme Brahman designated as (Lord) Kṛṣṇa.

25. (The term) *kṛṣi* is an expression for devotion to him and (the syllable) *naḥ* (denotes) the service to him. One that confers devotion and service is declared as Kṛṣṇa.

26. (The term) *kṛṣi* expresses 'all'. The letter *na* expresses 'seed'. Supreme Brahman, that is the seed of all things is named as Kṛṣṇa.

27-28. O Nārada ! Even after the fall of innumerable Brahmās and (a long) period had elapsed, the virtues of whom do not get destroyed and there is no one as much virtuous like him, that Kṛṣṇa desirous of creation was alone at the time of the beginning of creation. The lord who was about to create was directed by *kāla* (time), a part-manifestation (of the Lord).

29. An embodiment of free-will, the Lord, assumed two forms by his own desire. The left part was that of a female and the right part was a male.

30. The voluptuous, perpetual one, sustainer of desire, beheld her. She was very beautiful and had the complexion of charming *campaka* flower.

31. She had a pair of rumps resembling the disc of the full-moon. She was beautiful with her loins resembling charming plantain trunk.

32. She was attractive with her pair of breasts graceful like the *śrīphala* (*bel* fruit) in shape. She had a well-developed and delicate body with slender waist and captivating.

33. She was very beautiful, tranquil and smiling. Her eyes were like those of the crane. She was wearing a dress as pure as the fire. She was adorned with gem-studded ornaments.

34. She was always drinking with delight with her *cakoras* (birds), the eyes, the beautiful face of (Lord) Kṛṣṇa, that was humiliating crores of moons.

35. She was having the marks of musk with dot of sandal and vermillion below them at the centre of the forehead.

36. She had a curly fine head of hair adorned with the garland of *mālatī* (flowers). She had a necklace made of exquisite gems. She was desirous (of union) with her lord.

37. She was endowed with beauty humiliating the lustre of crores of moons. She was putting to shame the gait of the royal swan and the wag-tail.

38. The lord of dance indulged in excessive amorous sports with her in privacy in the dance circle in the midst of delightful dancing.

39. He made different kinds of love, as if love-incarnate. He enjoyed her happy union for a period equal to the longest years of Brahmā.

40. O Disciplined one ! At last he was exhausted. Then that ever-blissful Lord impregnated her at an auspicious moment at the conclusion of the copulation.

41-45. Sweat flowed from her exhausted body on account of the lustre of (Lord) Hari. Being exhausted on account of prolonged sexual enjoyment, she was breathing hard. The sweat due to exhaustion which was the support became the universal globe. That exhalation became the support of all. It became the exhalation of all the beings in the (different) worlds. From the left-side of the embodied wind god (sprang up) his dear one. She became his wife. Their sons were the five life-breaths of beings *prāṇa, apāna, samāna, udāna* and *vyāna*.[1] These became her sons, the five vital airs of the lower region (abdomen).

46. Varuṇa became the great presiding deity of the sweat (that flowed from her). Varuṇāni, his wife, manifested from his left side.

47. Then (*prakṛti*) that energy of Kṛṣṇa, sustained the embryo from Kṛṣṇa for hundred *manvantaras*[2] glowing with the lustre of Brahman.

48. She was the presiding deity of the life of Kṛṣṇa. She was dearer than the life of Kṛṣṇa.

47.1. A *manvantara* is equal to 4,320,000 years. She always had the company of Kṛṣṇa. She rested on the chest region of Kṛṣṇa.

49. After a period of hundred *manvantaras* had elapsed, the most beautiful woman delivered a golden egg that is the supreme support of the universe.

50. Beholding the egg, that goddess got distressed in her heart. She discarded that egg in the spherical water with rage.

51. Beholding her forsaking that (egg) Lord Kṛṣṇa lamented. The Lord of gods cursed the goddess appropriately that very moment.

52. O Wrathful and Cruel one ! Since you have abandoned the foetus, you be without progeny from now onwards.

53. Whichever celestial women have the part manifestations from you let them be without progeny and be perpetual maidens like you.

54. In the meanwhile a beautiful girl having white complexion sprang up suddenly from the tip of the tongue of the goddess.

55. She was having a yellow garment and holding a lute and book. She was adorned with gem-studded ornaments. She was the presiding deity of all the sciences.

56. Then in course of time she divided herself into two forms. The left half of the body (was) Kamalā and the right half (was) Rādhikā.

57. In the meantime (Lord) Kṛṣṇa divided himself into two forms, the right half having two arms and the left half four arms.

58. Lord Kṛṣṇa said to Vāṇī (Sarasvatī): You become his consort. As Rādhā would be jealous, it would not augur well for you.

59-60. Thus he gave away Lakṣmī to Nārāyaṇa with pleasure. The Lord of the universe then repaired to Vaikuṇṭha along with them since the two part manifestations of Rādhā had no progeny (on account of the curse). The attendants (of Nārāyaṇa) having four hands had their origin from the body of Nārāyaṇa.

61. They were equal to Hari in their lustre, age, form and virtue. Innumerable female attendants equal to her came up from the body of Kamalā.

62. O Sage ! An equal number of cowherds (came up) from the pores of the master of Goloka equal in age and valour.

63. Then the attendants of the master became all dear and equal to his life by their forms, good virtues, dress and valour.

64. Cowherd damsels sprang up from the hair pores of the body of Rādhā. They were all equal to Rādhā and no one else. (All of them) were speaking sweet.

65. They were all adorned with gem-studded ornaments. They were perpetually young. All of them never had any progeny on account of the curse of the male.

66. O Brahmin ! In the meanwhile that goddess Durgā, the veil of Viṣṇu, the perpetual one, suddenly manifested from the body of Kṛṣṇa.

67. That goddess was Nārāyaṇī, Īśānā and of the form of all energies. She was the presiding deity of the intellect of Kṛṣṇa, the Supreme Soul.

68. That Primordial Nature, the governess, was of the form of a seed of all the goddesses. She had the full form. She was of the nature of lustre. She was composed of the three qualities.

69. She had the complexion of heated gold. She had the lustre of a crore Suns. Her face was little smiling. She had thousand arms.

70. She was well-versed in all the sciences and was wielding different weapons. She had three eyes. She was wearing a dress as pure as fire. She was adorned with gem-studded ornaments.

71. All the women had their origin from a digital part of her part manifestations. The people of the entire universe were stupefied by her veil.

72. She is the bestower of all the wealth for the aspirants and householders. She is the conferrer of devotion to (Lord) Kṛṣṇa. She is (goddess) Vaiṣṇavī for the devotees of (Lord) Viṣṇu.

73. She is the giver of beatitude for those aspiring liberation and yielder of happiness for those seeking happiness. She is the celestial goddess of fortune in the heaven and the household goddess of fortune in the houses.

74-75. She is penance in the ascetics. She is of the form of prosperity in the kings. She is the power of burning in fire. She is of the form of lustre in the sun. She is of the form of beauty in the moon and lotus. She is of the form of all energies in the Supreme soul Lord Kṛṣṇa.

76. The soul possesses energy on account of her. The world has energy on account of her. Without her the whole world is almost dead even though living.

77. She is the perpetual seed of the tree of mundane existence. O Nārada ! She is of the forms of existence, intellect and fruit.

78. She is of the forms such as hunger, thirst, compassion, earnestness, sleep, lassitude, forbearance, firmness, tranquility, bashfulness, satisfaction, nourishment, doubt, radiance etc.

79. She eulogised the lord and stood in front of him. The Lord of Rādhā offered her a gem-studded throne.

80. O Sage ! In the meanwhile there manifested from the navel lotus (of Kṛṣṇa) the four faced one (Brahmā) together with his wife.[3]

81. He was holding a pitcher. He was endowed with prosperity. He was an ascetic and foremost among the wise.

The four-faced one glowing with the lustre of Brahman glorified him (Lord Kṛṣṇa).

82-83. The beautiful woman with graceful teeth wearing a dress as pure as fire and adorned with gem-studded ornaments eulogised the lord, the cause of everything and sat with delight on the beautiful gem-studded throne along with her master in front of (Lord) Kṛṣṇa.

84. In the meanwhile Kṛṣṇa divided himself into two, the left half of the body being Mahādeva (Śiva) and the right, the Lord of the cowherd women.

85. Hara (Śiva) was having the colour of pure crystal. He had the splendour of hundred crore Suns. He was bearing the trident and spear. He was clad with the tiger-skin.

86. He was having the matted hair resembling the colour of heated gold. His body was adorned with the ashes. He had a gentle. He was having the moon on his head.

87-88. He was nude. He had a blue throat. He was adorned with the serpents as the ornaments. He had a sanctified gem-studded garland in his right hand. He was muttering the Brahman-lustre with his five mouths.

88b-90. He was eulogising (Lord) Kṛṣṇa, the embodiment of truth, the Supreme soul, the master, the cause of all causes, the auspiciousness of all auspiciousness, and the supreme dispeller of birth, death, decrepitude, disease, grief and fear. He was death of death. Hence he was known as conqueror of death. He sat on the beautiful gem-studded throne in front of Hari.

CHAPTER THREE

The Creation of the Different Worlds

Śrī Nārāyaṇa said:

1. Then that egg remained in that water for a period equal to that of the longevity of Brahmā. Then at the appropriate time it suddenly divided into two.

2. Then there manifested a child possessing the lustre of a hundred crore Suns. Being afflicted with hunger that child was wailing for a while.

3. Discarded by the parents and without any resort (it remained) in the water. That lord of many universal eggs beheld upwards like an orphan.

4. He was more gross than the most gross. The lord was known as Mahāvirāṭ. Just like the infinitesimal particle is more (subtle) than the subtle, he was more gross than the gross.

5. He was the sixteenth part of the lustre of (Lord) Kṛṣṇa, the Supreme Being. That Mahāviṣṇu, the lord of the gods, was the sustainer of innumerable universes.

6. All the universes (are contained) in each one of the pores on his skin. (Lord) Kṛṣṇa is not capable of telling their numbers.

7. Just as the tiny dust in the universe can never (be counted) so also there is no count of Brahmā, Viṣṇu, Śiva and others.

8. In the same way there are Brahmā, Viṣṇu and Śiva in each universe. The Brahmāṇḍa (the primordial egg) is said to be extending from the nether world to the world of Brahmā.

9. Above that is the Vaikuṇṭha. That is outside the Brahmāṇḍa. It is of the nature of truth just like Nārāyaṇa (Viṣṇu) himself always.

10. Goloka is fifty crores *yojanas* [1] above that. It is eternally of the nature of truth similar to (Lord) Kṛṣṇa himself.

11. The earth has the seven continents, the seven oceans, forty nine minor continents and innumerable forests.

12. There are seven celestial worlds, including the Brahmaloka, above (the earth). There are the seven nether worlds below (the earth). This is the primordial egg.

13. Bhūrloka is above the earth. Bhuvarloka is above that. Svarloka is above that. The Mahaloka and Janaloka are beyond that.

14. Tapoloka and Satyaloka are above that. Then above is the Brahmaloka, made of heated gold.

15. Thus both outside and inside all these are artificial. O Nārada ! When the world is destroyed, all of them get destroyed.

16. All these are like the water bubble. The entire universe is transient. The Goloka and Vaikuṇṭha are eternal. They are real and always not artificial.

17. It (The Virāṭ) has a Brahmāṇḍa in each one of the pores of the skin. (Lord) Kṛṣṇa does not know their numbers. Then what about others ?

18-19a. There are Brahmā, Viṣṇu, Śiva and others in each Brahmāṇḍa. O Child ! The number of gods in all the worlds are thirty crores. (There are) regents and guardians of directions, stars and planets.

19b. There are four castes on the earth. There are snakes, movable and immovable beings in the nether world.

20. In course of time that Virāṭ looked up again and again. In spite of his great efforts he did not find any other world and everything was a void.

21. He began to reflect. Becoming hungry he cried again and again. He then gained wisdom and contemplated (Lord) Kṛṣṇa, the Supreme Being.

22-23 He then beheld there itself that perpetual Brahman lustre, black like the fresh rain-bearing cloud, having two arms, clad in yellow dress, smiling, holding the flute in the hand and an embodiment of conferring boons on the devotees. After beholding the father, the Lord, the child got pleased and smiled.

24-27. The Lord of boons became pleased and bestowed on him appropriate boons: O Child ! You become equal to me endowed with wisdom and devoid of hunger and thirst. You be residing without any desire and without fear in the Brahmāṇḍa until its dissolution and be the foremost among the conferrer of boons on all, devoid of disease, death, decrepitude, grief and other afflictions. After having stated thus he imparted three times the six-lettered great formula in his right ear. He first muttered the foremost *vedas* and then (the word) Kṛṣṇa consisting of two letters preceded by the Praṇava (syllable *om*) followed by the fourth case (ending), and ending with the flame of fire,[2] that was dear and capable of removing all obstacles.

28. After imparting the formula the lord prescribed the diet. O Son of Brahmā ! Listen to me. I shall describe you. You understand.

29. A *vaiṣṇava* should offer a sixteenth part as the *naivedya* (offering made to a deity) in every world for the fifteen faces of the material (Lord)Viṣṇu.

30. There is no purpose in making an offering to (Lord) Kṛṣṇa who is without attributes and who is the supreme soul that is whole.

31. Whatever thing is offered to any god, he consumes the entire offering. But it is restored by the look of (goddess) Lakṣmī.

32. After having imparted that formula and boon, the Lord told him again: What other favoụr is desired by you? Tell me. I shall bestow upon you.

33. After having the words of Kṛṣṇa, Mahāvirāṭ, the toothless replied appropriately.

Mahāvirāṭ said:

34. Let me have firm devotion at your lotus feet as long as I am alive, whether it would be for a while or a long period.

35. One who is endowed with devotion to you he is always a liberated one even while living. But one who is devoid of devotion to you is dead even though he may be living.

36. What is the use of repetition (of a formula), penance, sacrifice, worship, austerity, fasting and pilgrimage.

37. For a person devoid of devotion to (Lord) Kṛṣṇa, the life would be worthless. He never recognises the very soul on account of which he exists.

38. So long as the soul remains in the body, one is endowed with energy. After the soul had left the body the energies go away. They are not independent.

39. O Blessed one ! You are the soul of everything and are above Nature. You are an embodiment of free will. You are the first being. You are the perpetual Brahman lustre.

40. O Nārada ! After stating thus, the boy ceased (talking). (Lord) Kṛṣṇa spoke sweet words that were pleasing to the ears as reply.

Śrī Kṛṣṇa said:

41. Just like me you be firm and remain for a long time. You will not have a fall even after the fall of innumerable Brahmās.

42. You be the Virāṭ in each Brahmāṇḍa by means of part-manifestation. Brahmā will have his origin in your navel lotus as the Creator of the universe. Eleven Rudras (will manifest) from the forehead of Brahmā as a part-manifestation of Śiva for the purpose of continuing the process of creation.

44. One among them, namely, Kālāgnirudra, will be the destroyer of the universe. Viṣṇu, the protector, the materialist, would be born by means of a little part-manifestation.

45-46. By means of my favour you will always be endowed with devotion to me. By means of contemplation you will always be beholding me, the attractive one, certainly and the beautiful mother resting on my chest-region. He told: O Child ! I will go back to my world. You remain here. Then he disappeared.

47. After reaching the heaven, he directed Brahmā, the Creator, to create and Īśa (Śiva), the destroyer (to do his work at the appropriate time).

Śrī Kṛṣṇa said:

48. O Child ! Listen ! You go away in order to carry on creation of the tiny worlds of Brahmā from the pores of the skin of Virāṭ by manifesting from the navel lotus (of Virāṭ).

49. O Child Mahādeva ! You have your genesis from the forehead of Brahmā by part-manifestation. O Blessed one ! You engage yourself in contemplation for a long time.

50. After having stated thus, the son of Brahmā stopped talking. After making obeisance Brahmā and Śiva, the bestower of good, went away.

51. (Then they two penetrated) the spherical mass of water (and entered) the Brahmāṇḍa on the pores of the skin of Mahāvirāṭ. Virāṭ also then assumed a reduced form as a part-manifestation of the Virāṭ.

52. Janārdana, the Universal form, manifested as a dark-complexioned youth wearing yellow garment reclining on the bed of water with a gentle smile and pleasing face.

53. Brahmā, the lotus born, manifested from his navel lotus. After his birth, he wandered in the lotus stalk for a lakh *yuga* period.

54. The lotus born was not able to reach the end of the stalk of the navel lotus. Then Brahmā contemplated the lotus in the navel.

55-57. He returned to his place and then contemplated the lotus feet of (Lord) Kṛṣṇa. Then after contemplating with divine eyes he beheld that tiny form reclining on the bed of water encompassing the mass of Brahmāṇḍa on the pores of his skin and the Supreme Lord Śrīkṛṣṇa and the Goloka together with the cowherds and cowherdesses. He then eulogised that Lord, gained his favour and began his creation.

58. The mind-born sons of Brahma, Sanaka and others were born. The eleven Rudras holding the skull as a form of Śiva had (come).

59. The protector Lord Viṣṇu, the venerable one, had his genesis from the left side of that tiny form possessing four arms and as a resident of Śvetadvīpa.

60. Brahmā created the universe, heaven, mortals, nether world, the three worlds, the movables and immovables from the navel lotus of the tiny form.

61. Thus each one of the entire universe (had its origin) in the pores of the skin. In each universe there are tiny Virāṭ, Brahmā, Viṣṇu, Śiva and others.

62. O Child ! Thus I have described you the auspicious glorification of Lord Kṛṣṇa yielding happiness and beatitude and that which is the essence. What else would you like to hear ?

CHAPTER FOUR

The Worship of and Eulogy on Sarasvatī

Nārada said:

1. By your grace I have heard all rare matter equal to ambrosia. O Lord ! Describe me the severalty (of the forms of) *prakṛtis*.

2. Whose worship was done by whom ? How was it imparted to the mortals ? O Sage ! Which goddess was worshipped by whom ? Which goddess was eulogised by whom ?

3. Kindly explain me who had favoured whom the amulet, the eulogy, meditation, glory and auspicious legend (about them).

Nārāyaṇa said:

4. In the process of creation, Nature is stated to be five kinds—Durgā, the mother of Gaṇeśa, Rādhā, Lakṣmī, Sarasvatī and Sāvitrī.

5. They were adored. They became famous. Their glory was most wonderful. Their legends were equal to ambrosia. They were the cause of all auspiciousness.

6. I will describe you their auspicious legends about the part and digital manifestations of Nature. O Brahman ! Listen to me attentively.

7-8. Vāṇī, Vasundharā (earth), Gaṅgā, Ṣaṣṭhi, Maṅgalcaṇḍikā, Tulasī, Mānasī, Nidrā (sleep), Svadhā, Svāhā and Dakṣiṇā were equal to me in their lustre, form and virtue.

9. I shall describe you briefly their legends, meritorious and pleasing the ear and the fruits of action of the being.

10. The legends of Durgā and Rādhā are extensive. I shall describe them later. Listen to me (describing) briefly in order.

11. O Foremost sage ! The worship of Sarasvatī was first formulated by Śrī Kṛṣṇa by whose grace an ignorant person becomes wise.

12. When the goddess manifested from the mouth of the spouse of Kṛṣṇa, that passionate beautiful woman approached Kṛṣṇa with lust. That omniscient person understood her mental attitude and told her true and friendly words conducive to her happiness. Śrī Kṛṣṇa said :

13-15. O Pious woman ! Worship (Lord) Nārāyaṇa, a part of myself and having four arms. He is the conferrer of pleasures for those seeking them. He is the person that fulfils the desires. He has the beauty of crore god of love. Sportively he humiliates the god of love.

16. O Beautiful one ! If you want to stay here after making me your husband, Rādhā is more powerful than you. It will not be for your welfare.

17. If one is stronger than another person he will be able to protect a person. But if one is not a master how can he succeed (in controlling) others.

18. Although I am lord of all beings and the governor of all beings, I cannot rule Rādhā. She is equal to me in her lustre, form and virtue

19. She is the presiding deity of the life. Who is capable of discarding the life ? Is there anything more dear than the life for anyone, anywhere ?

20. O Good Woman ! You go to Vaikuṇṭha. It will be for your welfare. You make him (Viṣṇu) as your husband and enjoy happiness for a long time.

21. (Goddess) Lakṣmī is devoid of greed, stupefaction, lust, anger and harm. She is equal to you in lustre, form and virtue.

22. Be satisfied in her company. You will be spending your time happily there. As a husband he will honour equally both of you.

23-30. With great rejoice mortals, Manus, gods, foremost sages, aspirants for liberation, pious men, ascetics, accomplished persons, *nāgas*, *gandharvas* and *kinnaras* in the universe would worship you with devotion on the fifth day in the bright half of Māgha (February) in every *kalpa*[1] on account of my boon offering sixteen kinds of services.[2] Those who have subdued their senses and have controlled them (would invoke you) as laid down in Kāṇva branch of text with contemplation and eulogy, in the books and jars, make a small golden ball and adorn it with fragrance and sandal. They would then wear the amulet on the neck or right hand. The learned men would read the books at the time of worship, after completing the worship. After describing thus then the adored one worshipped the goddess. Then Brahmā, Viṣṇu, Maheśvara, Ananta, Dharma, the foremost sages Sanaka and others, the gods, Manus, kings, mortals and others worshipped her. Thus (goddess) Sarasvatī was perpetually worshipped by all the people.

Nārada said:

31-32. O Foremost among the learned in the scriptures ! Kindly describe me the mode of worship, eulogy, meditation, cherished amulet, the offering, flower, sandal and other things used in the worship. My curiosity to hear is growing now to know that which is pleasing the ear.

Nārāyaṇa said:

33. O Nārada ! Listen to me. I shall describe you the procedure laid down in the Kāṇva school containing the mode of worship of the universal mother (goddess) Sarasvatī.

34. On the fifth day in the bright fortnight of Māgha (February) or on the day of beginning the study (it is done). One has to practise self-control the preceding day. After

controlling the senses and becoming clean, one has to bathe, perform the daily duties and place the jar firmly with devotion.

35. After having bathed and performed the daily rites one should firmly place the jar, worship the six gods (listed below) making the offering.

36. After having worshipped the gods–Gaṇeśa, Sun, Fire, Viṣṇu, Śiva and Śivā (Pārvatī) with dedication, one has to worship the tutelary deity.

37. A wiseman should contemplate (the goddess) in the jar kept outside by the (mode of) meditation to be described. The person practising the vow should worship making the sixteen offerings after contemplation.

38. As known to me from the scriptures about the materials offered in the worship, I will now describe you a little as laid down in the scriptures.

39-44. Butter, curd, milk, fried corn, sweet balls made of sesamum, sugarcane, juice of sugarcane, purified white-coloured molasses, honey, *svastika* (a kind of cake), sugar, white coloured unbroken grains, balls of flour from dry white grains, white *modakas* (spherical cakes), cooked rice seasoned with ghee and *saindhava* (salt) together with side dishes, ball of flour of barley, wheat etc. seasoned with ghee, flour of *svastika*, cakes of ripe banana fruits, rice mixed with milk and sugar, sweet meat comparable to nectar, coconut and its juice, saffron, the root of ginger, ripe plantain fruit, fine *śrīphala* (bel fruit), jujube fruit, well-seasoned white ripe fruits of the season and region, fragrant white flower, fragrant white sandal, new white cloth, beautiful conch garlands of white flowers, ornaments set with pearls and diamonds (are the offerings to be made).

45. O Fortunate one ! Listen to me describing the commendable mode of contemplation (of the goddess) pleasing to ears and is the cause for the removal of doubts, as laid down in the scriptures.

46-48. I make obeisance to (Goddess) Sarasvatī having white complexion, smiling, charming, endowed with the beauty humiliating the lustre of crore moons, wearing white dress as pure as fire, adorned with excellent ornaments studded with exquisite gems, honoured well by hosts of gods, Brahmā, Viṣṇu, Śiva and others and saluted with devotion by foremost sages, Manus and mortals.

49. After contemplation and making all the offering reciting the basic formula, the wise one should eulogise (the goddess), wear the amulet and prostrate flat on the ground like a staff.

50. O Sage ! She should daily be worshipped thus by them for whom she is the tutelary deity. She should be worshipped by others on the day of commencing the studies or on the fifty day or at the end of the rainy season.

51-52. The Vedic eight-syllabled (formula) is (prescribed) as outstanding for all the rotaries. O Sage! Whichever formulae have been imparted they are the basic formula for the respective people. The formula would consist of the word Sarasvatī ending with (the declension of) fourth case followed by the term for the consort of Fire (*Svāhā*): *Śrīm hrīm* oblations to Sarasvatī. In the same way for the terms Lakṣmī and Māya. This formula is like a wish-yielding tree.

53. In olden days (Lord) Nārāyaṇa, the mine of compassion, imparted this (formula) to Vālmīka at a sacred place on the banks of the Ganges in Bhārata.

54. Bhṛgu imparted this to Śukra at Puṣkara in the dark fortnight. Mārīca imparted it with pleasures to Vākpati (Bṛhaspati) in the bright fortnight.

55. Brahmā imparted it with pleasure to Bhṛgu at Badarikāśrama. Jaratkāra instructed this to Āstīka in the vicinity of the Milky ocean. It was given to the wise Ṛṣyaśṛṅga by Vibhāṇḍaka at Meru.

56. O Sage ! (Lord) Śiva instructed this to sage Kaṇāda and Gautama. Sūrya gave it to Yājñavalkya and Kātyāyana.

57. Śeṣa imparted it to Pāṇini, the wise Bharadvāja and Śākaṭāyana at a sacred spot in the presence of Bali.

58. People get the benefit of the formula by the repetition of it four lakh times. One would become equal to Bṛhaspati if he gets accomplished in the formula.

59. O Foremost brahmin ! Listen to me (describing) the excellent and victorious amulet imparted by Brahmā in olden days to Bhṛgu at Gandhamādana.

Bhṛgu said:

60-61. O Brahmā ! The foremost among the knowers of Brahman ! The learned in the wisdom relating to Brahman! Omniscient ! Father of all beings ! Adored by all adorable ones ! O Lord! Impart me the amulet of (goddess) Sarasvatī, that could conquer the world, and to which has been added a collection of all rare formulae.

Brahmā said:

62. O Child ! Listen to me. I shall describe you the amulet that confers all desires, that is the essence of the scriptures, pleasing to the ears, prescribed and glorified in the scriptures.

63. It was imparted to me by (Lord) Kṛṣṇa, the Lord of dance, while dancing in the dance circle at Vṛndāvana (Basil grove) at Goloka.

64. It is equal to a wish-yielding tree. It has to be guarded with great care. It is endowed with a collection of unfamiliar, wonderful formulae.

65. O Brahman ! Bṛhaspati has become learned by wearing and mastering it. Lord Śukra is honoured among all *daityas* (demons) (similarly).

66. Sage Vālmīki has become a foremost poet and measured speaker, by wearing and mastering it. Svāyambhuva Manu also has been respected by all by wearing it.

67. Kaṇāda, Gautama, Kaṇva, Pāṇini, Śākaṭāyana, Dakṣa and Kātyāyana composed their respective works after wearing this.

68. Kṛṣṇa *dvaipāyana* himself sportively accomplished the division of the *vedas* and the composition of all the *purāṇas* by wearing this.

69. Śātātpa, Saṁvarta, Vasiṣṭha, Parāśara and Yājñavalkya composed the works after wearing and reciting this (amulet).

70. Ṛṣyaśṛṅga, Bharadvāja, Āstīka, Devala, Jaigīṣavya, and Jābālī were respected by all by wearing this.

71. O Foremost brahmin ! Prajāpati is the sage for this amulet. Bṛhaspati himself is the metre. The lord of the dance circle is the lord (of this amulet).

72. It is declared to have its application in having thorough knowledge about all philosophical principles and in gaining all the desired objects.

73. May *om hrīm* oblations to Sarasvatī ! Protect my head always. May *om śrīm* oblations to Vāgdevatā ! guard my forehead always.

74. May *om* oblations to Sarasvatī ! protect the ear always. May *om śrīm hrīm* oblations to Bhāratī ! guard the pair of eyes always.

75. May *om hrīm* oblations to Vāgvādinī ! protect my nose for ever. May *hrīm* oblations to Vidyādhiṣṭhātṛdevatā (presiding deity of knowledge)! guard the ears always.

76. May *om śrīm hrīm* oblations to Brāhmī (consort of Brahmā) guard the row of teeth always. May the single syllabled formula *aim* guard my throat for ever.

77. May *om śrīm hrīm* protect my neck. May *śrīm* guard my shoulders always. May *śrīm* oblations to Vidyādhiṣṭhātṛdevatā always protect my chest.

78. May *om hrīm* oblations to Vidyāsvarūpā always guard my navel. *om hrīm hrīm* oblations to Vāṇī ! May this always guard my back.

79. *Om* to *sarvavarṇātmikā* (Soul of all letters)! May this always protect my pair of feet. *Om* to the presiding deity of the desires. May this guard all my limbs always.

80. May *om* oblations to *sarvakaṇṭhavāsinī* (Resident in all the throats) protect in the east always. May *om hrīm* oblations to *jihvāpravāsinī* (Residents in the tongue) protect in the south-east.

81. *Om aim hrīm śrīm* oblations to Sarasvatī, the mother of the wise ! May this foremost formula guard me always in the south.

82. May the formula containing the three letters — *Om hrīm śrīm* guard me always in the south-west. Oblations to *kavijihvapravāsinī* (one who dwells in the tongue of poets). May this protect me in the west.

83. *Om* oblations to *sadambikā* (the pious mother)! May this guard me always in the north-west. *Om* oblations to *gadyapadyavāsinī* (resident in prose and poetry). May this protect me in the north.

84. *Om* oblations to *sarvaśāstravāsinī* (one who dwells in all the sciences)! May this protect always in the north-east. *Om* oblations to *sarvapūjitā* (worshipped by all). May it always protect the region above.

85. May *aim hrīm* oblations to *pustakavāsinī* (resident in the books)! Protect always the region below me. May *om* oblations to *granthabījarūpā* (of the form of syllables) guard me in all the directions.

86. O Brahmin ! Thus I have described you the embodiment of all collections of formulae. This amulet, known as the conqueror of the universe, is of the form of Brahmā.

87. In the past I have heard this from the mouth of Dharma on the Gandhamādana mountain. I have described you on account of my love for you. It should not be divulged to anyone.

88. After having worshipped the preceptor as laid down, offering him dress ornaments and sandal, and prostrating him like a staff on the ground, a wise man should wear this amulet.

89. One becomes accomplished in the amulet by the repetition of this five lakh times. If one gets accomplished in the amulet, he would become equal to Bṛhaspati.

90. One would become a great orator, great poet and a conqueror of the three worlds. On account of the glory of the amulet such a person would become capable of conquering all things.

91. O Sage ! I have described you this amulet, hymn, mode of worship, contemplation and worship (of goddess Sarasvatī) as described in the school of Kaṇva.

CHAPTER FIVE

Eulogy on Goddess Vāṇī made by Yājñavalkya

Nārāyaṇa said:

1. Listen to me for the eulogy on goddess of speech, that yields all the desires, sung by the great sage Yājñavalkya in olden days.

2. Once that sage had lost his knowledge on account of the curse of the preceptor. Being oppressed with grief he then came to the sacred spot dedicated to Sun God.

3. By his meditation at Koṇārka (on the eastern seashore of India), he had the vision of Sun god. He extolled the sun and wept again and again with grief.

4. The Sun god imparted him the *vedas* and their auxiliary texts. He also said : For the sake of regaining the memory, extoll the goddess of speech.

5. After having instructed him thus, the lord of the indigent disappeared. After having bathed, the sage glorified (the goddess) with his head bent on account of devotion.

Yājñavalkya said:

6. O Mother of the world ! Be gracious to me divested of my lustre, deprived of my memory on account of the curse of the preceptor, devoid of knowledge and grief-stricken.

7-9. O Presiding deity of knowledge! Confer on me wisdom, memory, knowledge, fame, poesy, the power to teach my pupils, ability to compose works, firmly devoted good disciples, intelligence in good assembly and good ability in inquiry. Just as the god produces the sprout by means of the magic power of creation, revive all that I have lost on account of providence.

10. Obeisance to Vāṇī that form of Brahman, outstanding, lustrous, perpetual and the presiding deity of all knowledge.

11. Obeisance to that (goddess) Sarasvatī without whom the living world is always dead and who is the presiding deity of wisdom.

12. Obeisance to that Vāṇī without whom the entire world is dumb and like insane and who is the presiding deity of speech.

13. Obeisance to that indestructible one, possessing the complexion of snow, sandal, jasmine, moon, lily and lotus and who is the presiding deity of the letters.

14. You reside in *visarga*,[1] dot and syllable. You are thus glorified by the pious. Obeisance to that Bhāratī (speech).

15. Obeisance to that goddess, an embodiment of time, without whom an enumerator cannot make the counts here.

16. Obeisance to that goddess embodying exposition, the presiding deity of exposition, and of the form of doubt and the doctrine.

17. Obeisance to that goddess representing the powers of remembrance, wisdom, intellect, genius and imagination.

18. When Sanatkumāra asked Brahmā for wisdom, he stood like the inert thing not being able to make the doctrine.

19. Then there arrived the venerable Lord Kṛṣṇa. He directed Brahmā to recite the excellent hymn on Vāṇī (Sarasvatī).

20. Obeying the directive of the Supreme Being, Brahmā glorified Her. Then by Her grace he made the outstanding doctrine.

21. When the Earth asked Ananta for wisdom he also remained like a dumb person not being able to make any doctrine.

22. Then being afraid he eulogised you at the command of Kaśyapa. Then he composed the blemishless doctrine that dispels the doubt.

23. Vyāsa requested Vālmīki for the Purāṇasūtra. He remained speechless and remembered you alone, the Mother of the world.

24. Then that foremost sage made the doctrine on account of your favour. He gained spotless wisdom that is the cause of dispelling doubts.

25-26a. That Vyāsa, the digital manifestation of Kṛṣṇa, after having heard the Purāṇasūtra served and contemplated you for hundred years at Puṣkara. Then after having gained a boon from you, he became a foremost poet. Then he divided the *vedas* and composed the *purāṇas.*

26b-29. (Goddess) Śivā (consort of Śivā) asked (Lord) Śiva true knowledge (about the creation of the world etc.) at the Mahendra mountain. Then the Lord meditated you for a moment and imparted her wisdom. Mahendra asked Bṛhaspati about the science of words (grammar). He contemplated you for a divine count of thousand years at Puṣkara. Then he obtained a boon from you after thousand divine years. Then he imparted Mahendra the science of words and its sense. The disciples who have been taught and the foremost sages who have learnt them, O Goddess of Gods! they carry on their task after contemplating you.

30. You are eulogised and worshipped by excellent sages, Manus, mortals, outstanding demons, gods, Brahmā, Viṣṇu, Śiva and others.

31. Those gods having thousand mouths (Lord Viṣṇu), five mouths (Lord Śiva) and four mouths (Lord Brahmā) have become dumb-founded to praise. How can myself, a mortal, eulogise you with a single face ?

32. After having stated thus, Yājñavalkya bent down his head with devotion and saluted. Without food he wept again and again.

33. Then the goddess assuming the form of lustre, although not perceived by him, blessed him to become a foremost poet and went back to Vaikuṇṭha.

34. Whoever reads with dedication this hymn on Vāṇī composed by Yājñavalkya, he would become an outstanding poet and a great orator equal to Bṛhaspati.

35. The most stupid and dull-headed one reading this for one year would become learned, wise and a good poet.

CHAPTER SIX

Legend of Sarasvatī

Nārāyaṇa said:

1. Sarasvatī who was at Vaikuṇṭha with Nārāyaṇa became a river in Bhārata by digit manifestation on account of the curse of Ganges after a quarrel with her.

2. O Sage ! She is a conferrer of merits and producer of merits. She is an embodiment of sacred places. She is to be served by the pious. She is the support of the virtuous.

3. She is of the form of penance for ascetics. She is an embodiment of penance. She is of the nature of glowing fire for burning the fuel of sins committed.

4. Those who had spent their lives on the earth in the wisdom, the water of Sarasvatī, they would have their firm place in Vaikuṇṭha for a long time in the company of (Lord) Hari.

5. The sinners in Bhārata after bathing (in the river) would get free from their sins by her grace and would stay in the world of Viṣṇu for a long time.

6-7. One who bathes in her water on the fourteenth day, or on a full moon day or on an *akṣaya*[1] day, or at the end of a day or at the time of the eclipse or at the time of *vyatīpāta*[2] or on some other auspicious day as a consequence or with contempt or with faith he gets oneness of the form of Hari in Vaikuṇṭha.

8. Even the most stupid who repeats the formula of Sarasvatī for a month would become a foremost poet without any doubt.

9. One who bathes daily in the Sarasvatī water and has the tonsure, that man never again has (the agony of) staying in the womb.

10. I have thus described a little of the glory of the virtues of Bhāratī. It confers happiness and beatitude. It is the essence. What else do you desire to hear ?

11. O Śaunaka ! After hearing the words of Nārāyaṇa, the foremost sage Nārada, immediately asked again that which dispels the doubt.

Nārada said:

12. How goddess Sarasvatī became the merit yielding river in Bhārata by digital manifestation on account of the curse of Gaṅgā after a quarrel with her ?

13. My curiosity increases after hearing the essence of the scriptures. There is no satiation after hearing the stories, as sweet as nectar. Who indeed, will be satisfied in (the gain of) the virtuous ?

14. How did the calm, virtuous, sanctifying, generous Gaṅgā curse the adorable Sarasvatī ?

15. Describe me the cause of the dispute between those two radiant ones. It is delightful to hear and difficult to be found in the *purāṇas.*

Nārāyaṇa said:

16. O Nārada ! Listen to me. I shall describe you this ancient legend by the mere remembrance of which one gets free from all sins.

17. (Lord) Hari also had three wives Lakṣmī, Sarasvatī and Gaṅgā. They always remained in the presence of (Lord) Hari enjoying equal affection.

18. Once Gaṅgā looked at the face of (Lord) Viṣṇu. Again and again she cast amorous glances with a smile and love.

19. The Lord also smiled at her looking at her face with pleasure for a while. Beholding that Lakṣmī condoned her but not Sarasvatī.

20-21. The smiling virtuous Lakṣmī consoled her. But the enraged Sarasvatī did not get pacified. With her face and eyes turned red, body shaking with anger and the lips always quivering she spoke to Gaṅgā and her husband.

Sarasvatī said:

22. A virtuous husband would have the same attitude towards all his wives. It is the general trait of the outstanding pious men. But it is the contrary in the case of the wicked.

23. O Gadādhara ! I have now known that you love Gaṅgā more and equally Kamalā (Lakṣmī) O Lord! You do not love me.

24. Your affection for Gaṅgā along with Lakṣmī has been accepted. Hence Lakṣmī (the spouse of Hari) has not taken it amiss.

25. What is the use of this unfortunate self living here now ? Fruitless is the life of a person deprived of the love of her husband.

26. Those men who speak about you as lord of all beings and an embodiment of piety are fools. They do not know the *vedas* and your mind.

27. After hearing the words of Sarasvatī and beholding her enraged he mentally reflected and left the assembly.

28. After Nārāyaṇa had left, that presiding deity of passion spoke fearlessly with rage unpleasant words to Gaṅgā.

29-30. O Shameless one ! Are you proud that your husband loves you ? Or do you desire to show that your husband loves you more? I shall crush your pride in the presence of Hari. O Beloved of your husband ! What will your husband do me?

31. After having stated thus, as she was about to seize the hair of Gaṅgā, Padmā (Lakṣmī) standing between them prevented her.

32-33. The enraged Vāṇī cursed Padmā : You will certainly become a tree or a river since you stand in the assembly like a tree or a river without saying anything though you are capable of saying something after beholding the contrary.

34. After hearing the curse, the goddess did not give a (counter) curse. Nor did she get angry. She stood there grief-stricken holding Vāṇī by the hand.

35. Beholding her (Sarasvatī) much excited, the lotus-eyed Gaṅgā with face tremulous with anger told goddess Lakṣmī.

Gaṅgā said:

36. O Lakṣmī ! Release that haughty one. What will she do me? This goddess, the presiding deity of speech has a vile tongue. She is quarrelsome.

37. Let that wicked one make a debate with me as much as she is capable and has the power.

38. Let the world know our strength. Let them know the glory and greatness of both of us.

39. After having stated thus the goddess gave Vāṇī a curse: She who angrily cursed you let her become a river.

40. Let her go down to the (world of) mortals where there are sinners. No doubt she would get a part of the sins in the *kali*(*yuga*).

41. After having heard these words, Sarasvatī cursed her. You alone will reach the earth. You will get the sins of the sinners.

42. In the meanwhile the god with four arms and accompanied by four courtiers having four arms arrived there.

43. He held Sarasvatī by her hand and placed her on the chest. The omniscient imparted all the old wisdom.

44. After having heard their quarrel and curse the Lord (explained) the secret and spoke appropriate words to those grief-stricken.

The Lord said:

45. O auspicious Lakṣmī ! As a digit manifestation you go to the house of Dharmadhvaja. You will become his daughter, not born of the womb.

46-47. You will become a tree on account of fate there itself. You will then become the wife of the demon Śaṅkhacūḍa, a part-manifestation of myself. Then doubtless you will become my wife by name. Tulasī, purifying the three worlds, in Bhārata.

48. O lady with beautiful face ! By your digital manifestation you become a river go quickly to Bhārata with the name Padmāvatī on account of the curse of Bhāratī (Sarasvatī).

49. O Gaṅgā ! You will later become by means of part-manifestation as purifier of the universe for burning the sins of men in Bhārata on account of the curse of Sarasvatī.

50. On account of the penance of Bhagīratha and being led by him with great difficulty, you will become the holy Bhāgīrathī by name on the earth.

51. At my command you become the wife of Samudra (ocean), a part-manifestation of myself. O Mistress of the gods ! You later become the wife of King Śantanu, a part-manifestation of myself.

52. O Sarasvatī ! On account of the curse of Gaṅgā, you go to Bhārata by means of digital manifestation. O Unerring one ! Enjoy the fruits of the quarrel along with co-wives.

53. You go to the abode of Brahmā and become his consort. Let Gaṅgā go to the place of Śiva. May Padmā alone remain her.

54. She is tranquil, devoid of wrath, a devotee of mine and is a form of myself. She is most pious. She is endowed with prosperity. She has good conduct. She is virtuous.

55. The women in the universe who are her part digital manifestations are virtuous, chaste, tranquil and have good conduct.

56. Three wives, three brothers-in-law, three servants and kinsmen are certainly contrary to vedic precepts and are not conducive to welfare.

57. For which householders the mistress in the house has the masculine traits and the husband is under the control of the wife, their birth is fruitless. They entertain inauspiciousness at every step.

58. Whose wife is ugly, unchaste and quarrelsome, such a person has to go to the forest. A great forest is better for him than the house.

59. It is always easy for such people to get people, places and cities which they cannot get even in the house.

60. It is better to stay in fire. One can be happy in the presence of cruel animals. But it is certainly leading to grief of people to be in the presence of wicked wives.

61. O Lady with beautiful face ! The flame of disease, and the flame of poison are better for men. The flame of the face of wicked women is above death.

62. For men who have been conquered by women, their lives are certainly fruitless. Whatever work is done during the day, one would not get its fruit.

63. Being censured here, everywhere and elsewhere he would go to hell. One who is devoid of fame and glory, such a person even if living is indeed dead.

64. It is not conducive to one's welfare to have too many co-wives in the same place. One having a single wife is happy. But one having many wives is never (happy).

65. O Gaṅgā ! You go to the abode of Śiva. Sarasvatī ! You go to the place of Brahmā. May the good-natured (Lakṣmī) resident of the lotus ! remain here at my abode.

66. The husband of a submissive, good-natured, chaste woman enjoys heavenly bliss here and beatitude due to virtues in the other world.

67. One whose wife is chaste, he is liberated, pure and happy. The husband of an unchaste woman is dead even if living, impure and happy.

68. O Nārada ! After having stated thus, the lord of the world stopped talking. The goddesses embraced one another and wailed aloud.

69. All of them spoke to the lord in turn trembling, eyes filled with tears and with grief and fear after thinking well.

Sarasvatī said:

70. O Lord ! Tell me the expiation for purifying this wicked birth of mine. Which women discarded by their husbands could live ?

71. I will certainly discard my body in Bhārata by means of meditation. One is sure to fall after attaining high position.

Gaṅgā said:

72. O Lord of the world ! For what fault of mine I have been discarded by you. I will discard my body. You reap the fruits of killing a faultless one.

73. In the mundane existence whichever person forsakes his innocent wife suffers torments of hell for a *kalpa* period even if he be the master of all the beings.

Lakṣmī said:

74. O Lord ! You are an embodiment of goodness. How can you be angry ? Show mercy on us. It is praiseworthy for a good husband to have forbearance.

75. If I go to Bhārata by means of digital manifestation on account of the curse of Sarasvatī, tell me how long I have to stay there and when I shall behold your feet.

76. The sinners would transfer their sins to me by bathing and immersion (in the water). How shall I get rid of them and reach your place ?

77. O Acyuta (Imperishable)! Tell me how shall I attain your lotus feet after becoming Tulasī, the chaste daughter of Dharmadhvaja by means of digital manifestation.

78. I shall become the presiding deity of a tree. O Mine of compassion! Tell me when you will liberate me.

79. If Gaṅgā goes to Bhārata on account of the curse of Sarasvatī, when will she attain you after becoming free from the curse and the sin.

80. If Vāṇī goes to Bhārata on account of the curse of Gaṅgā, when will she attain your place after becoming free from the curse.

81. O Lord ! You direct Vāṇī to go to Brahmā's abode and Gaṅgā to the abode of Śiva. You forgive their words.

82. After having stated thus Kamalā (Lakṣmī) held the feet of her lord and bowed down. Having encircled his feet with her lovely hair she repeatedly wept.

83. The compassionate Padmanābha (Viṣṇu) embraced that lustrous woman and spoke with a gentle smile and pleasant countenance.

Nārāyaṇa said:

84. O Goddess ! I shall comply with your request. But I shall honour my own statement also. Listen to me for its course of action.

85. Let Bhāratī (Sarasvatī) go to Bhārata as a river by digit manifestation. Let her remain in the abode of Brahmā as half part-manifestation.

86. That Gaṅgā would reach Bhārata being led by Bhagīratha. May she remain in my abode in order to purify the three worlds ?

87. She would attain there itself the head of Candramauli (having the moon on the head) (Śiva) that is difficult to get. Then that one already holy by nature would become more sanctified.

88. The Lotus-born ! You go to Bhārata as a digit part-manifestation as Padmāvatī, in the form of a river and as Tulasī, in the form of a tree.

89. After a lapse of five thousand years of *kali*(*yuga*), there will be liberation of you all rivers. (You all) would come to my abode again.

90. O Padmā ! Misfortune is the cause of prosperity of all living beings. In the mundane existence, who have glory without adversity ?

91. You will be relieved of the sins accruing to you on account of the contact with the sinners, by the bathing and dipping of the pious (in your water) adoring the formula of mine.

92. O Beautiful one ! All the countless sacred water on the earth would be sanctified by the touch and sight of my devotees.

93. My devotees who are the votaries of the formula of mine roam in Bhārata, in order to sanctify Bhārata and the earth.

94. The place where my devotees remain and wash their feet, would certainly become a great sanctified pilgrim spot.

95. Murderer of a woman, killer of a brahmin and cow, an ungrateful person, a person violating the bed of his preceptor would become pure and liberated while living by the touch and sight of my devotees.

96. One who does not practise *ekādaśi* (fasting on the eleventh day)and twilight worship, an atheist and one who rides a bull, would become sanctified by the touch and sight of my devotee.

97. One who subsists on the sword and ink, a washerman, one who officiates as a priest for the *śūdra* and one who rides a bull would become sanctified by the touch and sight of my devotee.

98. A traitor, a murderer of a friend, a false witness and an usurper of a deposit would become sanctified by the touch and sight of my devotees.

99. A debtor, a usurer, a bastard, the husband of a harlot, the son of a harlot would get purified by the touch and sight of my devotee.

100. A cook of the *śūdras*, a *devala* (a brahmin subsisting on offerings made to an idol), a village priest and an uninitiated person become cleansed by the touch and sight of my devotee.

101. The destroyer of the holy fig tree, the censurer of my devotees and a person partaking food without offering (to the god) would become purified by the touch of my devotee.

102-103. O Nārada ! A great sinner who does not maintain his parents, wife, brother, son, daughter, the family of the preceptor, sister, a kinsman devoid of descendants, mother-in-law and father-in-law would become sanctified by the touch and sight of my devotee.

104-105. The great sinners such as one who steals the material intended for the gods, one who robs the property of a brahmin, the seller of lac, iron and mercury, the seller of his daughter and those cremating the dead bodies of *śūdras*, would become purified by the touch and sight of my devotee.

Lakṣmī said:

106-110. O Lord Graceful to the devotees! Describe me the characteristics of your devotees – by whose touch and sight, the vile persons, people devoid of devotion to (Lord) Hari, egoistic persons, men bent on self-praise, the rogues, cheats, censurors of pious men get purified at once – who would purify all the sacred waters by their bathing and dipping (in them), whose dust of the feet, and the water used for washing their feet would purify the earth, and whom the gods wish to behold and touch in Bhārata. The contact with the *vaiṣṇavas* are highly beneficial for all. The holy places in the form of holy water and (images of) gods made of earth and stone would purify after a long time. But devotees of Viṣṇu (would purify) in a moment.

Sauti said:

111. O Foremost sage ! After listening to the words of Mahālakṣmī, the consort of Lakṣmī began explaining the hidden truth with a smile.

Śrī Nārāyaṇa said:

112-113. O Lakṣmī ! The characteristics of the devotees, that is the secret of the scriptures and *purāṇas*, the embodiment of merit, the destroyer of sin, yielding happiness, giver of enjoyment and liberation, of the form of essence, should be guarded and not divulged to the wicked. Listen to me. I shall describe you who are holy and equal to life.

114. That foremost person is spoken as holy in the *vedas* and auxiliary texts, in whose ear the outstanding formula of Viṣṇu enters from the mouth of a preceptor.

115. Hundreds of his ancestors get sanctified by his mere birth and either they are in the heaven or in the hell, they would be liberated that very moment.

116. Whoever had taken birth elsewhere or as animals, they would become liberated while alive, get sanctified and attain the place of Hari in course of time.

117-118. One who is devoted to me, engaged in worshipping me, endowed with my virtues, glorifying my virtue and always having his heart on me would get horripilation with rejoice with voice choked, eyes filled with tears and forgetfulness of the self as soon as listening to (the eulogy of) my virtues.

119. They do not aspire for happiness, liberation, the four-fold (benefits) such as *sālokya* (oneness of place with the lord) etc., and the positions of Brahmā or the gods. They desire only to serve me.

120. Such a person does not desire for the positions of Indra, Manu and gods, which are unobtainable and pleasures such as heaven and kingdom even in his dream.

121. The primordial eggs, Brahmā and other gods would perish. My devotee endowed with good devotion to me will not perish.

122. After gaining the most difficult birth, (my) devotees wander in Bhārata, consecrate the earth and attain my sanctified abode.

123. O Padmā ! Thus I have described you everything. Do that which is appropriate. They all did as instructed by him. Lord Hari remained in his comfortable position.

CHAPTER SEVEN

The Advent of Kaliyuga and the Manifestation of Viṣṇu as Kalki

Nārāyaṇa said:

1. That Sarasvatī being cursed by Gaṅgā came to Bhārata by digit manifestation while she herself stayed in the abode of Hari.

2. After going to Bhārata, Bhāratī (Sarasvatī) (was designated) as Brāhmī, the consort of Brahmā. As she was the presiding deity of speech, she was glorified as Vāṇī.

3. She is seen only as a stream encircling the entire universe. As Lord Hari is resting in the water she is known as Sarasvatī as belonging to him.

4. That river Sarasvatī as a sacred water is very holy (sanctifier). She is of the form of glowing fire for burning the fuel, the sins of the sinners.

5. The auspicious Bhāgīrathi was later brought to the earth by Bhagīratha. O Nārada ! She descended to the earth by digital manifestation on account of the curse of Vāṇī.

6. At the appropriate time Lord Śiva held her on his head there itself at the request of the earth unable to bear her force.

7. Padmā (Lakṣmī) became the river Padmāvatī in Bhārata by means of her digital manifestation on account of the curse of Bhāratī, while she stayed at the place of Hari (in her full form).

8. By means of her another digital manifestation she got her birth in Bhārata as Lakṣmī, the daughter of Dharmadhvaja and well-known as Tulasī.

9. She became a tree, the sanctifier of the universe, by means of her digit manifestation on account of the curse of Sarasvatī in the past and that of Hari later.

10. After having remained in Bhārata for five thousand years of *kaliyuga*, they all came back to the abode of Hari, discarding their forms as rivers.

11. All sacred places other than Kāśī and Vṛndāvana (Basil grove near Mathurā) go to Vaikuṇṭha (abode of Viṣṇu) together with them at the command of Hari (Viṣṇu).

12. Śālagrāma and Jagannātha, the forms of Hari, left Bhārata after the end of ten thousand years of *kali* and attained the place of Hari.

13. The *vaiṣṇavas* (devotees of Viṣṇu), *purāṇas*, conches, the rites for ancestors and the duties laid down in the scriptures, also went away along with him.

14. The worship of (Lord)Hari, the name Hari, the glorification of his fame and virtues, the auxiliary texts of the Vedas and the sciences also went away along with him.

15. Goodness, truth, piety, scriptures, the village goddesses, austerity, ascetic practice and fasting also went away with him.

16. All people would be bent on left-hand tantric practices and endowed with falsehood and fraud. Thereafter the worship will be devoid of basil (leaves).

17. All people will discard practising the *ekādaśī* (fasting on the eleventh day) and will be devoid of piety. Then they will turn away from the narratives of Hari.

18. Thereafter all people will become rogues, cruel, hypocritic, egoistic, thieves and harmful.

19. There will not be distinction of men and women. The marriages will be decided after debate. There will not be ownership of properties and materials thereafter.

20. All people will be submissive to the women. There will be prostitutes in every house. They will beat their husbands often threatening and abusing them.

21. The wife will be the mistress of the house. The husband will be worse than a slave. The daughter-in-law, mother-in-law and father-in-law will be treated as equal to maids and servants.

22. The kinsmen by marital relationship would wield authority in the house. But one would not converse with those related by knowledge (combined study, etc.).

23. Just as the people are acquainted so also men and kinsmen. The husbands would not be able to do anything without the command of the wives.

24. The determination of the *brāhmaṇas, kṣatriyas, vaiśyas* and *śūdras* based on duties appropriate with their castes, twilight (worship) and the sacred thread would certainly be devoid of their true significance.

25. All the four castes would follow the practices of barbarians. People would study the sciences of the barbarians discarding (the study of) their own sciences. In the *kali* (*yuga*), the *brāhmaṇas, kṣatriyas* and *vaiśyas* would be the servants of the *śūdras.*

26. They would become cooks, washermen and bearers of bulls. People will discard truth. The earth will be devoid of grains.

27. The trees will not bear fruits. The women will not have progeny. The cows will not yield milk. Milk will be devoid of butter.

28. Couples will be devoid of mutual love. The householders will not have happiness. The kings will not be possessing valour. The subjects will be possessed with tax.

29. The male and female rivers will not have water. The caves, etc., will be elongated. The four castes would be devoid of piety and merits.

30. Thereafter there will not even be a single meritorious person among a lakh. Men, women and children will be contemptible and ugly.

31. Thereafter they will use unchaste words and tread reproachable path. Some villages and towns will be deserted by people and hence frightening.

32. Some places will be having a few cottages and men. Villages and towns will be covered with jungles.

33-34. All the inhabitants will be afflicted by tax. Grains will not grow in tank-beds and river-beds. The fields will not have grains and the wealthy will lose their riches. Rich people will be powerful and haughty.

35. Noble people will be mean in disposition in the *kaliyuga.* Wicked will speak untruthful words. Rogues will speak truth.

36. Sinners will be meritorious. Not virtuous (will be regarded as) virtuous. Dispassionate will be lustful. Chaste women will be unchaste.

37. Ascetics will be sinners. The devotees of Viṣṇu will not be *vaiṣṇavas.* Compassionate people will be harmful. Thieves will be murderers.

38. Wicked people in the robes of religious mendicants will censure and ridicule others. They will be experts in serving the spirits and make people rejoice.

39. The ignorant and deceitful persons will be honoured. Men and women will be dwarfs and sick everywhere.

40. In the *kaliyuga* people will be short lived and become decrepit even as they are young. They will be grey-haired at the age of sixteen and very old at twenty.

41. A girl aged eight will become a young woman and pregnant. A woman delivering at the end of a year would become old at sixteen years.

42. Some among thousand would be barren in *kaliyuga.* All people belonging to all the four castes will sell away their daughters.

43. Men will be bent on earning by the prostitution of mothers, wives, daughters-in-law, daughters and sisters.

44-46a. In the *kaliyuga* people will sell away the name Hari (for their maintenance). After having made gifts for the sake of fame, they themselves will violate after second thoughts. They will usurp the wealth intended for gods, *brāhmaṇas*, the preceptor's family and that given away by the self or by others.

46b-50. In the *kaliyuga* some will approach their daughters. Some will have intercourse with their mother-in-law. Some will have sexual relationship with daughter-in-law. Some others will have with all. Some will copulate with the mothers of fellow wife. Others will copulate with the wives of brothers. In every house people will have sexual relation with those prohibited (in the codes). People will discard their wives and amuse with all. There is no determination regarding wives or husbands, people, materials, and villages especially in the *kaliyuga*. All will speak false and be covetous to gain wealth by robbery.

51-55. All will be mutually harmful and murderers. The descendants of the *brāhmaṇas, kṣatriyas* and *vaiśyas* will be sinners. They will be engaged in trading in lac, iron, mercury and salt. The descendants of the *brāhmaṇas* will ride the bullocks, cremate the dead bodies of *śūdras,* eat food from a *śūdra,* and have sexual relationship with *śūdra* women. They will abandon practising the five *parvans* (lunar periods). They will eat on New moon nights. They will not be wearing the sacred thread. They will not practise twilight worship and cleanliness. A harlot, usurer, woman without sons or husband, procuress and woman in menstrual period will become cooks in the kitchen.

56. There is no determination about food or womb, the (four-fold) institutions of life and people. All will be barbarians in the *kaliyuga.*

57-61. Thus when *kali* begins, the world becomes full of barbarians, the trees grow a cubit high and the men grow thumb high, Kalki will be born as the son of a Brāhmaṇa Viṣṇuvyaśas, being a digital part manifestation of (Lord)

Nārāyaṇa and most powerful. Holding a sword and riding a long mare, he will make the earth rid of barbarians in three nights. After making the earth rid of the barbarians he will vanish. Then the earth without a ruler will be seized by the *dasyus* (outcastes). Then being inundated by very thick showers of rain for six nights, the earth will be devoid of people, trees and houses.

62. O Sage ! Then the twelve Ādityas (Suns) will rise. By their radiant light, the earth will become dry.

63. When the unassailable Kali had gone and the *kṛtayuga* begins, piety will be completely endowed with austerity and truth.

64. The *brāhmaṇas* will be ascetics, pious and knowers of the *vedas.* In every house woman will be chaste and pious.

65. The kings and all *kṣatriyas* will be faithful to the *brāhmaṇas* and adhere to their own duty. They will always be valorous, pious and bent on doing meritorious deeds.

66. The *vaiśyas* will be bent on carrying on business, devoted to the *brāhmaṇas* and pious. The *śūdras* also will be meritorious, pious and serving the *brāhmaṇas.*

67. The descendants of the *brāhmaṇas, kṣatriyas* and *vaiśyas* will be bent on doing rites devoted to (Lord) Viṣṇu. All will be drawn towards the formula of Viṣṇu. The *vaiṣṇavas* will be devotees of Viṣṇu.

68. All will possess knowledge of the scriptures, codes of law and *purāṇas.* Knowing *dharma* (religious law) they will copulate (with their wives) at the appropriate menstrual period. In the *kṛtayuga* having piety in its complete form, there was not even a little bit of unrighteousness.

69. Virtue will have three feet in the *tretāyuga* and two feet in the *dvāpara* (*yuga*). When *kali* begins it has one foot and thereafter everything will be lost.

70. O Brahmin ! The days are seven. The lunar days are sixteen. Since the months are twelve, the seasons are six.

71. The fortnights are two and the *ayanas* (half years) are two. There are four *praharas* (parts) in a day and four parts in a night. A month consists of thirty days.

72. A year is of five kinds. You understand the reckoning of time. We get the four fold *yugas* by the revolution of years.

73. When a human year is completed, it is a day and night for the celestials. Three hundred and sixty mortal years is known to be one, divine year according to those proficient in reckoning time.

74. Seventy one *yugas* constitute one *manvantara.* Indra's life is said to be equal to (a span of) a *manvantara.*

75. Brahmā's one day and night gets completed after the twenty-eighth Indra has gone. After the lapse of one hundred and eight years, Brahmā's period comes to an end.

76-77. This is known as the *prākṛta* (relating to nature) dissolution. The earth becomes invisible. The universe gets inundated. Brahmā, Viṣṇu, Śiva and others, the sages and all the beings get merged in (Lord) Kṛṣṇa, the Supreme Being. The primordial nature gets merged in him. Hence it is called *prākṛtika* dissolution.

78. For this dissolution of the nature and the fall of Brahmā, it is only a *nimeṣa* (winking of eye) for Lord Kṛṣṇa, the Supreme Being.

79. When the entire universe gets destroyed, the Goloka, Vaikuṇṭha and Lord Kṛṣṇa with his courtiers alone remain.

80. The dissolution in which the universe gets inundated lasts only for a moment (winking of the eye). After this moment is over, the creation is resumed in order.

81. In this way, how many creations were there and how many destructions were there. Nobody knows the count as to how many times it has come and gone.

82. O Nārada ! Who knows the count of the creations, digits, universes and Brahmās in the universal egg.

83. There is only one Supreme Being for all these universes. Śrī Kṛṣṇa is the Supreme Soul of all these. He is above nature.

84. Brahmā and others are his parts. The Mahāvirāṭ (gross principle) and Kṣudravirāṭ (subtle principle) are his parts. The nature is also known to be his part.

85. That Kṛṣṇa had two forms one having two arms, and (the other) having four arms. He has four arms in Vaikuṇṭha and two arms in Goloka.

86. From Brahmā to the gross all things are of the character of nature. Whatever has been created out of nature is perishable.

87-92. You know that one as the root of creation the truth, eternal and ancient, an embodiment of free-will, unstained Supreme Brahman without attributes, limitless and formless, an embodiment of favour towards devotees, extremely charming, resembling the colour of the fresh cloud, having two arms, holding the flute in his hand, wearing the dress of a cowherd, a lad, omniscient, worthy of being served by all, the Supreme soul and Lord. Brahmā, the lotus-born, creates and possesses wisdom (on account of him). Śiva, the conquerer of Death, is the destroyer and knower of all principles (because of him). By comprehending whom and by devotion to whom, the Lord of beings (Viṣṇu) is as great as he and is endowed with great prosperity, always omniscient himself, omnipresent, protector of all the beings and the conferrer of all prosperity. Lord Viṣṇu is master of all beings and the lord of the world by comprehending him (Kṛṣṇa).

93. By knowing him, by austerities, devotion and service towards him, the great illusory Nature has all the powers and is a mistress.

94. Sāvitri, the Mother of the *vedas* is the presiding deity of the *vedas* and adored by the *brāhmaṇas* by comprehending him and serving him.

95. Sarasvatī has become the presiding deity of all knowledge and adorable by the learned by comprehending him, by penance and service rendered to him.

96. Mahālakṣmī the ancient one, the conferrer of all prosperity, has become the presiding deity of wealth by serving him and doing penance.

97-98. (Goddess) Durgā, the destroyer of misfortune, has been adored all over the universe, has become the presiding deity of all the villages, has been the conferrer of all prosperity, has been the mistress of all, omniscient, glorified and adored by all and has attained the paramount lord as her spouse, by virtue of serving him and devoted penance towards him.

99-100. Rādhikā, one originated from the left part (of the body) of Kṛṣṇa– the presiding deity of love towards Kṛṣṇa, has become dearer to him than the life by her affection and service rendered to Kṛṣṇa. She attained an exquisite beauty, prosperity, respectful honour, a position on the chest-region of Kṛṣṇa and the position of a spouse by serving him.

101. In olden days she practised penance on the Śataśṛṅga (having hundred peaks) mountain for a period of one thousand divine *yugas* without taking food and getting emaciated.

102. Beholding her emaciated, breathless and resembling the digit of the moon, Lord Kṛṣṇa placed her on the chest-region and wailed on account of compassion.

103. He conferred on her a boon that is the essence and most difficult to be obtained. You stay in my chest-region. May you have devotion towards me.

104. You will excel me in prosperity, honour, affection and respect. You will be the foremost among all women in your affection.

105. O Dear one ! Being excellent and grand, you will always be glorified and adored by me. I will be attainable by you and subject to your affection.

106. After having stated thus, the universal lord, revived her and made her his sole spouse without any co-wives.

107. O Sage ! Whichever goddesses have worshipped him by serving him, they have reaped their benefits according to their austerity.

108. After having performed penance for thousand divine years on the Himālaya and contemplating his feet, (goddess) Durgā has become (a goddess) adored by all.

109. After having performed penance for a lakh divine years on the Gandhamādana mountain, (goddess) Sarasvatī has become (a goddess) worshipped by all.

110. After having performed penance for a hundred divine *yugas* at Puṣkara, (goddess) Lakṣmī by serving him, has become the conferrer of all prosperity.

111. After having performed a penance and contemplating his feet foı sixty thousand divine years on Malaya mountain, (goddess) Sāvitrī has become adored by the *dvijas* (the first three *varṇas* eligible for the investiture of the sacred thread).

112. In days of yore (Lord) Śaṅkara did penance for hundred *manvantaras* (periods of Manu). Lord Brahmā devotedly (worshipped) him for hundred *manvantaras.*

113. After having performed penance for hundred *manvantaras,* (Lord) Viṣṇu has become the protector. (Lord) Dharma after having performed penance for hundred *manvantaras* became adored.

114. O Nārada ! (Lord) Śeṣa did penance for a *manvantara.* (Lords) Sun, Venus, Moon and Jupiter (did penance) for a *manvantara.*

115. After having done devotional austerities, for hundred divine *yugas,* Wind-god has become the life force, adorable by all and sustainer of all.

116. Thus all the gods were worshipped on account of their devotion to (Lord) Kṛṣṇa. The sages, men, kings and *brāhmaṇas* were adored.

117. Thus I have described you all the things as in the *purāṇas* and *āgamas* I have heard from the preceptor's mouth. What again do you wish to hear ?

CHAPTER EIGHT

The Origin of the Earth and Eulogy on Her

Nārada said:

1. You have described that the *prākṛtika* (relating to Nature) dissolution takes place at the fall of Brahmā caused by Hari in a trice.

2. It was mentioned (by you) that at the time of the *prākṛta* dissolution the earth (became) invisible, the entire universe was inundated and all merged in (Lord) Hari.

3. Where did the Earth disappear and remain then ? How did she manifest again at the time of the process of creation?

4. How did she become blessed, honoured, substratum of all and glorious ? Explain me in detail her blessed origin.

Śrī Nārāyaṇa said:

5. The scriptures state that at the time of the primary creation all had their origin from (Lord) Kṛṣṇa. The manifestation and disappearance (is a feature) in all the dissolutions.

6. Listen to me for the most auspicious (account of the) birth of the Earth. It is the destroyer of obstacles and sins and it causes the growth of merits.

7. Ah ! Some people state that the blessed Earth was made out of the fat of (the demons) Madhu and Kaiṭabha.[1] That is false. Listen to me.

8. In olden days they fought with (Lord) Viṣṇu and were pleased with his valour. They then asked : Kill us at a place where the earth is surrounded by water.

9. It is hence clear that the earth existed during their lifetime. The fat was there only after their death.

10. You listen to me for the view that she is well-known as Medinī. Since she was emaciated by being flooded with water and was developed through their (demons') fat (she was known as Medinī).

11. I shall describe you (the legend of) her origin that is fruitful, agreeable to all and sanctioned by the scriptures. It was heard by me in days of yore from the mouth of Dharma at Puṣkara.

12-13. The impurity of the body of Mahāvirāṭ remaining in the water for a long time, came out and in course of time spread all over his body. Then it entered all the pores of the skin. O Sage ! After a long time, the earth had its origin from that.

14. Remaining firm in each pore of the skin, she repeatedly manifested and disappeared and was thus unsteady.

15. At the time of creation she manifested and remained above outside the water. At the time of dissolution she disappeared and remained inside the water.

16-20. The earth is endowed with mountains and jungles, seven oceans and seven continents in each universe. It had Himādri (Himālaya), Meru (mount), planets, moon and sun. It was extolled by (gods such as) Brahmā, Viṣṇu, Śiva and others, the celestials and mortals. It was endowed with holy places and the sacred Bhārata. It had the golden soil and all mountains. There were seven nether worlds below that. The Brahmaloka (world of Brahmā) was above that. The world of Dhruva was also there. The entire universe was also there. Thus the entire universe was created on the earth. The Goloka and Vaikuṇṭha were above outside the universe.

22. The artificial and natural universe was perishable. O *brāhmaṇa* ! After the fall of Brahmā in the *prākṛta* dissolution (dissolution of Nature), the Mahāvirāṭ (great principle) was created by Lord Kṛṣṇa, the Supreme Soul, in the primary creation. He remained at the time of the dissolution along with the regents of the regions of the quarters.

23. That presiding deity of the Earth was adored by the celestials, Manus, sages, *brahmins, gandharvas* and others in the Varāha (*kalpa*).

24. According to the scriptures she was the spouse of Viṣṇu in his Boar form. Maṅgala (Mars) is known to be her son. Suyaśas was the son of Maṅgala.

Nārada said:

25-26. O Lord ! In which of her forms the Earth was adored by the celestials in the Varāha (*kalpa*)? How was she associated by all with the form of Boar (of Viṣṇu) and as the sustainer of all beings ? Describe me the mode of her worship, the process of her rescue from the nether world and the auspicious legend of the birth of Maṅgala.

Nārāyaṇa said:

27. In the past, Varāha (Boar form of Viṣṇu) was extolled by (Lord) Brahmā in the Varāha (*kalpa*). After having killed (the demon) Hiraṇyakṣa,[2] he rescued the earth from the nether world.

28. He placed her on the water just as a lotus leaf on the water. (Lord) Brahmā created the entire charming universe there itself.

29-34. Beholding that lustful goddess, the lustful Lord Hari assumed the form of a boar resplendant like crores of Sun. After having arranged for a lovely bedding, he assumed a handsome form and sported with her day and night for several divine years in secrecy. That beautiful lady fell into a swoon on account of the pleasant union. The union of gallant woman with a gallant person yields pleasure. (Lord) Viṣṇu did not wake up day and night on account of contact with her limbs. At the end of one year the passionate one gained consciousness and left the lustful woman. He once again assumed sportively his original boar form. After contemplating the pious Earth, he worshipped her with devotion. After having worshipped her with incense, lamps, offerings, vermilions, unguents, dresses, flowers and oblations, (Lord) Hari spoke to her.

The great Boar said:

35-37. O Auspicious one ! You be the support for all. You be worshipped by all the ascetics, Manus, celestials, accomplished persons and mortals. At the time of letting out water through a channel, consecration of a house, consecration of a well and tank and auspicious agricultural operations, celestials and others will worship you with reverence. Those who do not (worship) you would go to hell.

The Earth said:

38-41. O Lord ! At the command of your Boar form I shall sportively support the entire universe consisting of mobile and immobile things. O Lord ! Listen to me. I will not be able to bear the painful burden of pearl, oyster, offering made to (Lord) Hari, the liṅga form of (Lord) Śiva, stone, conch, lamp, gem, ruby, diamond, sacred thread, flower, book, holy basil petal, rosary of beads, garland of flowers, camphor, gold, *gorocana* (yellow pigment got from a cow), sandal and the water used for anointing the *śālagrāma* (stone symbol representing Lord Viṣṇu).

The Lord said:

42. O Beautiful one ! The ignorant people who dedicate these things to you, they will be caught in the cob-web of time for a divine hundred years.

43. O Nārada ! After having spoken thus, the Lord ceased talking. The lustrous planet Mars came into being from that impregnation.

44-45. They all worshipped Earth at the command of (Lord) Hari. They made offerings as laid down by Garga and extolled with eulogies. They made the offerings, etc., with the basic formula. She was extolled and worshipped in the three worlds (thereafter).

Nārada said:

46. I am curious to listen. Describe me the mode of contemplation, extollation, basic formula lying hidden in the *purāṇas.*

Nārāyaṇa said:

47. Goddess Earth was at first worshipped by the Boar (form of Viṣṇu). Then (she was worshipped) by (Lord) Brahmā and Pṛthu in the past.

48. Then (she was worshipped) by all the ascetics, Manus, Nārada and others. O Nārada ! Listen to me. I shall describe you the mode of contemplation, extollation and (basic) formula.

49. *Oṁ hrīm śrīm vām* oblations to Vasudhā (Earth, conferrer of riches). She was worshipped by (Lord) Viṣṇu with this formula in the past :

50-51. I adore (the goddess) resembling the hue of white *campaka* (flower), radiant like hundred moons, besmeared with sandal all over the body, adorned with all ornaments, source of the gems, filled with gems, endowed with the ocean, clad in a garment spotless as fire, smiling and adored.

52. That goddess would be worshipped by all with this (mode of) contemplation. O Excellent brahmin ! Listen to me the eulogy (on her) as described in the school of Kaṇva.

Viṣṇu said:

53-54. You are the consort of Yajñavarāha. The conferrer of victory ! Give us victory. O Victorious one ! Invincible one! Support of victory ! Victorious one ! Conferrer of victory ! O Support of all ! The germ of all ! One endowed with all powers ! O Goddess ! Conferrer of all desires ! The eternal one ! You bestow on me all the desired things.

55. The abode of everything ! One abound with all grain! Bestower of all grains ! Remover of all grains ! Abode of all grains at the appropriate time ! O Earth !

56. O Auspicious one ! Support of auspicious things ! Auspiciousness incarnate ! Conferrer of auspiciousness ! Import of auspiciousness ! Being a part of auspiciousness ! Bestow on me supreme auspiciousness.

57. O Earth ! Support of all kings ! One intent on protecting all kings ! One of the form of pride of the kings! O conferrer of prosperity ! Grant me land.

58. One who reads this meritorious hymn after worshipping her well, would be the glorious ruler of the earth for crores of births.

59. No doubt one would get the merits of gifting land by reading (this). There is no doubt that one would become free from the sin of stealing a gift.

60. One would certainly become free from the sin of digging the earth for water. One would certainly be free from the sin of setting foot in another's well.

61-62. One would become free from the sin of performing ancestral rite in another's land, discharging the semen and placing the lamp and other things (on the earth). O Sage ! A wiseman would certainly acquire the merits of (the performance of) hundred horse sacrifices by reading this hymn.

CHAPTER NINE

Merits and Demerits of Making Gifts on Earth

Nārada said:

1. Making a gift of land is meritorious and by usurping which accrues sin.

2. I would like to listen to you describe me the sin that would accrue by the performance of ancestral rite on another's land or encroaching in another's well or digging well in another's well or discharging semen (on the earth) or placing a lamp and other things (on the earth).

3. O Foremost among the learned in the *vedas* ! Describe me these and other sins accruing from deeds on earth as well as the remedial measures for the same.

Nārāyaṇa said:

4. One who makes a gift of land of 12 inches length (the space between the extended thumb and little finger) in Bhārata to a brahmin purified by (the performance of) twilight worship, would reach the abode of (Lord) Viṣṇu.

5. One who gives away land abound with all grains, etc., to a brahmin, would dwell in the place of (Lord) Viṣṇu for a period equal to the (quantum of) dust (on the piece of land).

6. One who would make a gift or receive a gift of a village or land or grains, would both be relieved of all their sins and would reside in Vaikuṇṭha.

7. A pious person who would approve of a gift of land, would go to Vaikuṇṭha with friends and kinsmen of his class.

8. Whoever robs a brahmin, the gift made by himself or someone else for his maintenance, would remain in the cobweb of time as long as the moon and sun stay.

9. The sons, grandsons etc., of such a person would be deprived of land, prosperity and happiness. He would be indigent and attain the *raurava* (hell) in the end.

10. Whoever snatches away the land (intended) for grazing of cattle and makes a gift of grains would remain in the *kumbhīpāka* (hell) for a hundred divine years.

11. Whoever snatches the cowpen or tank or grazing land and makes a gift of grains would remain in the *āsipatra* (hell having plants with spear-edged leans) for a period of the fourteen Indras.

12. Whoever bathes in another's well without offering five balls (of oblation) would reach the hell. The fruits of bathing would never accrue to him.

13. A lustful person who discharges semen secretly on earth would remain in the *raurava* (hell) as many years as the sticky particle.

14. A person making a pleasure trough or digging a well (in another's land) would go to (the hell known as) *kṛmidaṁśa* (bitten by insects) for a period of four *yugas* (43,20,000 mortal years).

15-16. If an ignorant person digs a well at another's destroyed well and dedicates a destroyed tank, all the benefits would accrue to the other person only. He would attain (the hell) *taptasūrmi* (heated iron or metallic image) and remain there suffering heat for a period of the fourteen Indras.

17. Whoever digs out clay from another's pond and throws it away, would remain in the world of Brahmā for a period of years equal to the dust particles.

18. An ignorant person who does not offer balls of oblation to the manes of the enjoyer of property and performs the ancestral rite would certainly reach the hell.

19. Whoever places a lamp on the earth would be blind for seven births. Whoever places the conch on the ground would become a leper in the next birth.

20. Whoever places the pearl, ruby, diamond, gold and gem on the earth, would be indigent for seven births.

21. Whoever places the *śivaliṅga* or the adorable stone on the earth, would remain (in a hell) *kṛmibhakṣa* (bitten by insects) for hundred *manvantaras* (periods of Manu).

22.Whoever places the (vedic) hymn, sacred formula, water (used for anointing) the(*śālagrama*) stone, flower and leaves of holy basil on the earth would remain in the hell for a *yuga* period.

23. Whoever places on the earth, the rosary of beads, garland of flowers, camphor, and *rocanā* (yellow pigment got from a cow)would certainly go to hell.

24. O Sage ! Whoever places on the earth sandal stick, *rudrākṣa* (berry of a holy tree) and bottom of the *kuśa* (grass) would dwell in the hell for a period of Manu.

25. Whoever places a book and sacred thread on the earth, he would not be born as a brahmin in his next birth.

26. One would certainly get a sin equal to that of killing a brahmin. The sacred thread having a knot is to be worshipped by all the class of people.

27. After performing a sacrifice whoever does not sprinkle the earth with milk, he would reach the *taptasūrmi* hell (heated molten metal) and suffer heat in all the births.

28. Whoever digs the earth at the time of earthquake or an eclipse would become a great sinner in the next birth and would certainly become disabled.

29. The earth is called as *bhūmi* because it is the *bhavana* (abode) of all (beings). It is known as Vasudhā or Vasundharā because it yields excellent riches (*vasuratna*).

30. Because she had her origin from the thigh of (Lord) Hari, she is known as *urvī*. Because she supports all (the beings) she is known as *dharā, dharitrī* and *dharaṇī*.

31. She is (known as) *ijyā* because she supports the sacrifice. She is *kṣoṇī* because she is emaciated at the time of the deluge. She is said to be *kṣiti* because she gets destroyed at the time of the great deluge.

32. She is *kāśyapī* because she had come into being from Kaśyapa. She is steady because of her (firm) position. She is *viśvambharā* because she supports the universe. She is endless because of her endless form.

33. She is *pṛthvī* because she was the daughter of Pṛthuka. O Sage ! She is *mahī* since she is extensive.

CHAPTER TEN

The Narration about Gaṅgā

Nārada said:

1. O Foremost among the learned in the *vedas* ! I have heard the attractive legend about the Earth. You tell me now the legend about the Ganges.

2. The goddess that is supreme and of the form of (Lord) Viṣṇu having remained in the place of (Lord) Viṣṇu had come to Bhārata on account of the curse of Bhāratī (Sarasvatī).

3. I would like to listen to the auspicious and meritorious legend that destroys sins as to how and where and being requested by whom and sent by whom (she came) in the past.

Nārāyaṇa said:

4. The prosperous great king Sagara was a descendant of the solar race. He had two beautiful wives Vaidarbhī and Śaibyā.

5. He was truth-incarnate. He liked truth. He spoke truth. He had a fancy for truth. He knew how to make inquiry in virtue of truth. He is the foremost and born in the *satyayuga* (*kṛtayuga*).

6. One of them gave birth to a beautiful son. Born to Śaibyā, he was known as Asmañjas. He was the perpetuator of the family.

7. The other one desirous of progeny propitiated (Lord) Śaṅkara (Śiva). On account of the boon of (Lord) Śiva she became pregnant.

8. After hundred years had gone she delivered a mass of flesh. Beholding that she contemplated (Lord) Śiva and wept aloud repeatedly.

9. (Lord) Śiva assumed the form of a brahmin and came to her. He divided that mass of flesh into sixty thousand pieces.

10. They all became very powerful and valorous sons, their physical frames humiliating the radiance of the midday sun of the summer season.

11. They were all reduced to the state of ashes on account of the wrathful look of sage Kapila. On hearing that the king wept and died on account of grief.

12. Asamañjas performed penance for the sake of bringing the Ganges (from the heaven). After having performed penance for lakh number of years he died after lapse of time.

13. Dilīpa was his son. He also did penance for lakh number of years for bringing the Ganges and died in course of time.

14. Aṁśumat was his son. He also died in course of time after doing penance for a lakh years in order to bring the Ganges.

15. Bhagīratha was his son. He was a great devotee of (Lord) Viṣṇu, a *vaiṣṇava* possessing good qualities, devoid of decrepitude and death.

16-20. He performed penance for lakh years in order to bring the Ganges. He then beheld (Lord) Kṛṣṇa with a pleasant countenance having the lustre of crore suns, having two arms, holding the flute in his hand, youthful, dressed as a cowherd, Supreme soul, lord, an embodiment of favouring the devotees, embodiment of free will, Supreme Brahman, the wholesome one, the master adored by (Lords) Brahmā, Viṣṇu, Śiva and others, having the company of hosts of ascetics, unstained–a witness devoid of quality, higher than Nature, gently smiling, one that favours the devotees, wearing a dress as pure as fire, adorned with gem-studded ornaments. Beholding him the king extolled him bowing down again and again.

21. On account of the sportive gesture (of the lord) he obtained the favour of redeeming his ancestors. That Ganges came there by the (mere) remembrance of the Supreme Being.

22. After saluting him she stood in front of him with folded palms. Beholding her beautiful form the lord spoke to her, who was making a divine extollation with horripilation.

Śrī Kṛṣṇa said:

23. O Celestial goddess ! You resort quickly to Bhārata on account of the curse of Bhāratī (Sarasvatī).

24-26. By my command you purify all the sons of Sagara. Being purified by the wind touching you they would attain my abode assuming celestial forms riding the celestial cars. They would be my attendants always without diseases shedding the enjoyment of their actions pertaining to different births. Manifold major and minor sins accrue to men in Bhārata.

27. It has been heard from the scriptures that (the sins) get destroyed by the wind touching the Ganges. Touching the goddess is ten times meritorious than beholding her.

28. It has been heard in the scriptures that sins of men accrued in crores of births get destroyed by immersion (in the Ganges)on an ordinary day.

29-30. Whatever sins had been committed wilfully such as the killing of brahmins etc., accrued by men in the course of several births, they all get destroyed by immersion (in Ganges). The *vedas* cannot adequately describe the merit of bathing on an auspicious day.

31. O Goddess ! Some describe it as your benefit as in the scriptures. Even all the gods such as Brahmā, Viṣṇu and Śiva do not know it.

32. O Beautiful one ! Listen to me. (I shall describe you) the resolve for bathing on an ordinary day. Having a dip is ten times more meritorious than that.

33. On the day of the entry of the Sun into a different constellation, it is thirty times more meritorious than that. It is the same on the New moon day. It is two-fold on the winter solstice.

34. It is ten-fold more meritorious for men than that in summer solstice. (Bathing) in *cāturmāsya* (four months commencing with the middle of June) and on full moon day (yields) infinite merits.

35. It has the same benefit on the *akṣaya* (day).[1] It has not been mentioned in the *vedas*. It yields immeasurable meritorious results by bathing and making gifts.

36. Bathing on an ordinary day yields hundred times more merits than contemplation. O Governess of Gods ! It is in the same way in the Manu periods and *yugas* etc.

37. (It is meritorious) to bathe on the seventh day of white fortnight in Māgha (February-March) *bhīṣmāṣṭamī* (eighth day sacred for Bhīṣma), *aśokāṣṭami* (eighth day in the first half of Caitra)and *navamī* (ninth day) for Lord Hari.

38. It is two-fold meritorious on Nandā (the first, sixth, and eleventh days of a fortnight). It is difficult to get. (Bathing) on the tenth day (of Jyeṣṭha) that removes ten sins is highly meritorious.

39. It has the same benefit in *vāruṇī* (the asterism *satabhiṣak*) as in Nandā four-fold much meritorious. It has four-fold benefits on the Mahāvāruṇī day.

40. Bathing at the time of lunar and solar eclipses has immense benefits than bathing on an ordinary day. It has ten-fold benefits.

41. It is hundred times meritorious at the partial rise of the Sun or the rise of half moon. In general all have to make a resolve. But it is the contrary in the case of the devotees of (Lord) Viṣṇu.

42. The devotees of (Lord) Viṣṇu are not attached to fruits. They are liberated even when they are alive. They are always bent on pleasing me and are devoted to me in all their actions.

43. All the *vedas* declare him a *vaiṣṇava*, liberated while alive, in whose ear the supreme formula of Viṣṇu enters from the mouth of the preceptor.

44-47. Immediately after the formula has been received one elevates along with himself hundreds of paternal ancestors and hundreds of descendants, hundreds of maternal ancestors, mother, mother's mother, sister, brother, sister's son, maternal uncle, mother-in-law, father-in-law, preceptor's wife, and son, preceptor imparting knowledge, friend that accompanies, attendant, pupil, maid-servant and people in the vicinity of one's own hermitage. One becomes liberated while alive soon after receiving the formula.

48. A sacred place on the earth in Bhārata gets sanctified soon after his touch. The earth gets sanctified at once by the dust under his feet.

49-52. The place where his feet were washed with water becomes certainly a sacred place. The food and water not dedicated to (Lord) Viṣṇu are faeces and urine and the *vaiṣṇavas* do not partake them. They always partake only that which has been offered (to Lord) Viṣṇu.

53-54. The *sudarśana* disc of (Lord) Viṣṇu protects them always. Those men who get horripilation, with their throats choking and eyes filled with tears on hearing my virtues etc., are the foremost *vaiṣṇavas*.

55. From Brahmā to a clump of grass, all the movable and immovable things had their origin from me. I am the lord of all the beings. Those who know me thus are the foremost *vaiṣṇavas*.

56. There are innumerable crores of universal eggs as well as Brahmā, Viṣṇu, Śiva and others. All these get absorbed in me at the time of deluge. Those who know thus are the foremost *vaiṣṇavas*.

57-58. I am a form of lustre, supreme, an embodiment of favouring the devotees, an embodiment of free-will, without any quality, without any desire and above Nature. All the things originated from Nature had their origin from me and get dissolved in me. O Goddess ! Those men who know thus are the foremost *vaiṣṇavas.*

59. After having spoken thus, the lord of the celestials stopped talking in front of those two. One that takes to three paths—the sky, atmosphere and earth, (the Ganges) spoke to him with her head bent on account of devotion.

Gaṅga said:

60-63. O Lord ! If I go to Bhārata on account of the past curse of Bhāratī (Sarasvatī), your command and penance done (by Bhagīratha) now, tell me what kinds of sins the sinners would give me and how these will perish. How long I may have to stay in Bhārata ? O Lord of all beings! When shall I attain the supreme place near (Lord) Viṣṇu ? You, the omniscient one, know all the rest I desire (to get). You are the inner soul, omniscient. O Lord ! You describe me the means.

Śrī Kṛṣṇa said:

64-66. O Gaṅga ! The goddess of celestials! I know what all you desire. This salt ocean of the form of Rudra will be your husband. The ocean (will be) a part of myself. You are a form of Lakṣmī. Union of the gallant with the gallant will be meritorious on earth. Your glory lies in the union of all the rivers in Bhārata with the salt ocean.

67. O Goddess of the celestials ! You will have your stay in Bhārata on account of the curse of Bhāratī (Sarasvatī) for five thousand years of Kali from now onwards.

68. You will have amorous union with the ocean daily in secret. O Goddess ! You are the connoisseur. You have been united with the foremost connoisseur.

69-70. All the people in Bhārata will please you with the eulogy made by Bhagīratha and will worship you with devotion. After having contemplated you as laid down by Kauthuma, one who worships you, glorifies you and bows down to you daily, will get the benefit of (doing) the Aśvamedha (horse sacrifice).

71. Whoever utters O Gaṅgā !, O Gaṅgā !, even at a distance of hundred *yojanas* [2] from you, he will become free from all sins and attain the world of Viṣṇu.

72. Whatever sin would accrue to you by the bathing of thousand sinners, that would get destroyed soon after beholding my devotee.

73. Whatever sin would accrue to you by the contact with the corpses of thousand sinners, that sin would get destroyed by the bathing of those who recite my formula.

74. O Gaṅgā ! Wherever there is glorification of my name, you get established there itself becoming free from sins.

75. O Auspicious one ! Where there is glorification of my name along with the excellent rivers Sarasvatī and others, that would become a holy place at once.

76. By contact with the dust of such places a sinner becomes purified. He would certainly reside in Vaikuṇṭha as many years as the count of dust.

77. After recollecting my name with devotion and knowledge, those persons who discard their lives in you, they would attain the place of (Lord) Hari.

78. They will become foremost among the attendants of (Lord) Hari for ever. Those men would witness innumerable dissolutions of Nature.

79. On account of the manifold merits of a dead person, that corpse shall be placed in you, and that person, would go to Vaikuṇṭha (and stay) as long as the bones remain in you.

80. After making him a part of my body and making him enjoy the fruits of his action, I will give him assimilation to me and make him my attendant.

81. If an ignorant person discards his life after touching your water, I will give him assimilation to me and make him my attendant.

82. Otherwise, whoever discards his life elsewhere after remembering your name, I would give him residence in my place for a period of innumerable deluges.

83. Otherwise, whoever discards his life in a place devoid of Gaṅgā, after remembering your name, I would give him residence in my place for a period of Brahmā's life.

84. There is no speciality dying in a sacred place or not for those votaries of my formula and those partaking offering made to me.

85. He is capable of making the three worlds sanctified sportively. He would go to the Goloka mounted on a chariot made of excellent gems.

86. O Auspicious one ! Whoever are associated with me as my devotees those pious persons go to inaccessible Goloka on a gem-studded chariot.

87. Whoever had died anywhere consciously or unconsciously, they would be sanctified and liberated while living merely in the vicinity of (my) devotees.

88. After having spoken to her thus Śrī Hari, spoke to Bhagīratha: You eulogise this Ganges and worship her now.

89. Bhagīratha extolled and worshipped her with devotion, contemplation as laid down by Kauthuma and extollation again and again.

90. Bhagīratha saluted Śrī Kṛṣṇa, the Supreme lord and the Ganges. Lord Hari then disappeared.

Nārada said:

91. O Foremost among the learned in the *vedas* ! Describe me with what eulogy, contemplation and procedure for worship, the king worshipped.

Śrī Nārāyaṇa said:

92-93. After bathing, doing daily duties, wearing washed clothes, washing one's feet, and sipping (three drops of water), a purified person should worship well (Lords) Gaṇeśa, Sun god, Fire god, Viṣṇu, Śiva and Śivā (consort of Śiva) with devotion and restraint. Such a person is qualified to worship.

94-95. One should worship (Lord) Gaṅeśa for the destruction of obstacles, Sun-god for becoming free from sin, Fire-god for his purification and (Lord) Viṣṇu for beatitude, Śiva for knowledge and (Goddess) Śivā for the growth of intellect. A wise person would obtain (the desired) by worshipping these. They would get the contrary if they violate.

96. O Nārada ! Listen to me for (the mode of) contemplation as laid down by Kauthuma that destroys all sins and by which (the above mentioned gods) have to be contemplated.

97-107. One should worship the Ganges, having the complexion of the white *campaka*, destroying the sins, originated from the image of Kṛṣṇa, equal to Kṛṣṇa, the foremost chaste Lady, wearing a dress as pure as fire, adorned with gem-studded ornaments, having a body humiliating the lustre of hundreds of autumnal full moons, having a gently smiling face, having an eternal and firm maidenhood, the beloved of (Lord) Nārāyaṇa, tranquil one, endowed with all prosperity, having a fine head of hair adorned by the jasmine garland, graceful with the vermilion on the forehead, together with dots of sandal, with variegated designs of the musk on the neck, with excellent lips graceful like the ripe bimba fruit, having charming rows of teeth humiliating rows of pearls, having a beautiful face and eyes with attractive side glances, having a pair of breasts hard and well-formed like the *śrīphala* (bilva), having a large and enduring waist adorned by loins resembling the plantain, having a pair of lotus feet humiliating the grace of land lotus, endowed with gem-studded ornaments, unointed with saffron and besmeared with lac-dye, ruddy with the drops of honey oozing-out from the coral flower adorning the head of Indra, always endowed with the respectful offer of water given by celestials, accomplished souls, and foremost ascetics and others and adored by the multitude of heads of ascetics resembling rows of bees, yielding beatitude for the aspirants, conferring heaven and enjoyment for the seekers, outstanding, distinguished, bestower of favour, eager to favour the devotees. I worship that chaste woman conferring the place of Viṣṇu and who had her origin from the feet of Viṣṇu.

108. O Brahmin ! After having contemplated the auspicious Ganges thus one should worship her making the sixteen kinds of services.

109-110. Seat, (water for) washing the feet, (respectful) water offering, (water for) bathing, unguent, incense, lamp, offering (of eatables), betels, cold water, dress, ornament, garland, perfumes, (water for) sipping and charming bed are the sixteen offerings to be offered.

111. After making the offering with devotion one should bow down after having extolled her with folded palms. After having worshipped thus one would get the fruits of Aśvamedha (horse sacrifice).

112. O Nārada ! Listen to me. I shall describe you the eulogy uttered by Kauthuma and the conversation between Viṣṇu and Brahmā that destroys sins and yields merits.

Śrī Brahmā said:

113. O Lord of the celestials ! Lord Viṣṇu ! Consort of Lakṣmī! Obeisance to you, O Lord. I am desirous of hearing the hymn on the feet of Lord Viṣṇu, that destroys sins and is the cause of merit.

Śrī Nārāyaṇa said:

114. My obeisance to Ganges who had her origin from the water issuing forth from the bodies of Kṛṣṇa and Rādhā excited after hearing the music of (Lord) Śiva.

115. I bow down that Ganges who had her origin before the creation in Goloka in the dancing circle in the presence of (Lord) Śaṅkara.

116. I salute that Ganges who had her origin at the time of full moon in Kārttika (November-December) in the auspicious celebrations of Rādhā surrounded by cowherds and cowherdesses.

117. I bow down that Ganges crore *yojanas* wide and lakh times surrounding the Goloka.

118. I salute that Ganges sixty lakhs *yojanas*[3] wide and four times long surrounding the Vaikuṇṭha (world of Viṣṇu).

119. I bow down that Ganges extending to twenty lakhs *yojanas* and four times that in length surrounding the Brahmaloka (world of Brahmā).

120. My obeisance to that Ganges thirty lakh *yojanas* wide and five times that in length surrounding the Śivaloka (world of Śiva).

121. I salute that Ganges six *yojanas* wide and ten times that in length, and which is (known as) Mandākinī in Indraloka (world of Indra).

122. I bow down that Ganges a lakh *yojanas* wide and seven times that in length surrounding the world of Dhruva.

123. My obeisance to that Ganges a lakh *yojanas* wide and six times that in length surrounding the Candraloka (world of moon).

124. I salute that Ganges sixty thousand *yojanas* wide and ten times that in length surrounding the Sūryaloka (world of Sun).

125. I bow down that Ganges a lakh *yojanas* wide and six times that in length encircling the Satyaloka (uppermost world above earth).

126. My obeisance to that Ganges ten lakhs *yojanas* wide and five times that in length surrounding the Tapoloka (lower to Satyaloka).

127. I salute that Ganges thousand *yojanas* wide and seven times that in length encircling the Janaloka (lower to Tapoloka).

128. I bow down that Ganges thousand *yojanas* wide and seven times that in length surrounding the Kailāsa (residence of Śiva and Kubera on the Himālayas).

129. My obeisance to that Ganges known as Bhagavatī in Pātāla (nether world) ten *yojanas* wide and ten times that in length.

130. I salute that Ganges known as Alakanandā on the earth only a *krośa* (1/4 of a *yojana*) wide and no where lesser than that.

131. I bow down that Ganges of the colour of milk in *satyayuga*, resembling the colour of the moon in *tretāyuga* and having the colour of sandal in *dvāparayuga.*

132. My obeisance to that Ganges having the colour of water in *kaliyuga* and nowhere else on the earth and always of the colour of milk in heaven.

133. I salute that Ganges whose glory has been described well in the *purāṇas* and scriptures and who is bestower of merits and remover of sins.

134. O Brahmā ! the touch of a particle of her water destroys the sins such as the killing of brahmins and the like accrued by the sinners in crores of births.

135. O Brahmin ! I have described you thus the twenty-one verse in the form of a hymn which is the supreme destroyer of sins and the germ of merits.

136. Whoever reads this with devotion after worshipping the celestial goddess he would no doubt get always the fruits of Aśvamedha (horse sacrifice).

137. One without progeny gets a son. A person without a wife would get a dear one. A sick person becomes free from illness. A person caught in the bondage gets released.

138-139. A person whose glory is not well-known becomes famous. An ignorant person would become learned. Whoever reads this auspicious hymn on the Ganges after getting up in the morning, his bad dream would become auspicious and he would gain the merit of bathing in the Ganges.

Nārāyaṇa said:

140. After having eulogised the Ganges with this hymn, Bhagīratha went with her to the place where the sons of Sagara were lost.

141. They all quickly attained Vaikuṇṭha by the wind that had touched the Ganges. She is remembered to be Bhāgīrathī because she was brought by Bhagīratha.

142. Thus I have described you fully the outstanding episode relating to Ganges, that is meritorious and bestower of beatitude. What else do you desire to hear ?

Nārada said:

143. What happened when Kṛṣṇa and Rādhā were excited by the music of (Lord) Śiva and water issued forth from their bodies ?

144. Who were the people present there then and what efforts were made by them ? O Lord ! You are competent to describe me in detail all these.

Nārāyaṇa said:

145. At the time of the great festival of Rādhā on the full moon in Kārttika (November-December), after worshipping Rādhā, Kṛṣṇa stayed in the dance-circle.

146. Brahmā and others, all the sages Sanaka and others spoke after having worshipped with reverence Rādhā, who had been worshipped by Kṛṣṇa.

147. In the meanwhile, Sarasvatī sang the charming glory of Kṛṣṇa with protracted notes on the lute.

148. Becoming pleased Brahmā gave her a necklace studded with valuable gems, and a crest-jewel very difficult to procure in the universe.

149. Kṛṣṇa (gave her) the excellent Kaustubha (a gem got from the ocean when it was churned), surpassing all the gems. Raḍhikā (presented her)an excellent necklace studded with invaluable gems.

150. Lord Nārāyaṇa (gave her) an attractive garland of flowers. (Goddess) Lakṣmī (presented her) an ear-ring in the shape of a fish-studded with invaluable gems.

151. Goddess Durgā, the Primordial Nature, the illusion of (Lord) Viṣṇu, Nārāyaṇī, Īśānī (gave her) devotion to Viṣṇu very difficult to be got.

152. Dharma (gave her) pious thoughts and wide fame in mundane existence. Fire-god (presented her) clothes as pure as fire and Wind-god gem-studded anklets.

153. In the meanwhile Lord Śiva sang the glory of Kṛṣṇa together with the rapturous *rāsa* dance at the repeated instance of Brahmā.

154. All the celestials fainted like painted pictures. After a moment they regained their consciousness and beheld the dance circle.

155. The entire place was inundated without Rādhā and Hari. All the cowherds, cowherdesses, celestials and brahmins wept aloud.

156. By means of contemplation Brahmā had understood all the desired things that along with Rādhā Kṛṣṇa has attained liquid state.

157. Then Brahmā and all the other gods extolled the Supreme lord : O God ! Favour us with what we desired and show us your form.

158. In the meanwhile there arose a voice (in the sky) from a formless one. All heard that explicit, sweet and auspicious voice.

159. I am universal soul and this form of energy is an embodiment of favouring devotees. O Gods ! what (use of) myself and this (Rādhā) possessing a body ?

160. The Manus, mortals, all ascetics and *vaiṣṇavas* would become purified with my formula and would come to my place in order to behold me.

161. If you gods are very keen to behold my form, let Śiva act as per my directive.

162-166. O Brahmā ! You are the creator. O Preceptor of the world ! You command (Lord Śiva) in order to compose a special text together with the auxiliary text that is attractive containing the modes of worship consisting of rare collection of formulae conferring the desired fruits, eulogies, amulets and contemplation. After composing my formula, amulet and eulogy, you maintain its secrecy.[4] One among thousand or hundred men would be a votary of my formula. Those who do not turn away would come to my place after getting purified by the formula. Otherwise all will become residents of Goloka.

All the creation of the Brahmāṇḍa by Brahmā would become fruitless.

167-168. There are five kinds of people in every creation of Brahmā: Some are residents of the earth, some of heaven, some others of the nether world and others of Brahmaloka. Some others are *vaiṣṇavas* and some others residents of my world.

169. Let Mahādeva make a firm resolve in the assembly of gods immediately in order to do this. Then you will behold the form.

170. After having spoken thus in the sky, the eternal one stopped talking. Beholding that Jagannātha (the Lord of the world) spoke to (Lord) Śiva with delight.

171. The Lord of knowledge and foremost among the learned after listening to the words of Brahmā, held the Ganges water on the hand and took a resolve.

172. I shall make the essence of *vedas,* an excellent *śāstra* containing the illusions of Viṣṇu and formula etc., honouring the command of Kṛṣṇa.

173. Whoever utters a lie after touching the Ganges water, he will be caught in the cob-web of mundane existence for a period of the life of Brahmā.

174. When Śaṅkara had spoken thus, Śrī Kṛṣṇa manifested with his dear Rādhā at Goloka amidst the assembly of gods.

175. Beholding him they were delighted. After extolling the foremost being they made the festivities again with great rejoice.

176. In course of time Lord Śambhu (Śiva) made the lamp of *śāstra.* Thus I have described you all matters to be kept secret and very difficult (to know).

177. That Ganges in her liquid state originated in the Goloka from the bodies of Rādhā and Kṛṣṇa is the conferrer of enjoyment and emancipation.

178. She was established at different places by the Supreme soul Kṛṣṇa. One who is of the form of Kṛṣṇa is supreme and is adored in all the worlds.

CHAPTER ELEVEN

The Legend of Gaṅgā

Nārada said:

1. You are fit to describe me as to where that fortunate one, the celestial goddess had gone five thousand years after the advent of *kali.*

Nārāyaṇa said:

2. At the wish of Lord she resorted to Bhārata on account of the curse of Bhāratī and she went back to Vaikuṇṭha once again at the end of the curse.

3. O Nārada ! Bhāratī left Bhārata and reached the place of (Lord) Hari. At the end of the curse of Gaṅgā, Padmāvatī also (returned to him).

4. Gaṅgā, Sarasvatī and Lakṣmī these three are dear to (Lord) Hari. O Brahmin ! Together with Tulasī they are declared as four in the scriptures.

Nārāda said:

5. Why did the goddess originating from the lotus feet of (Lord) Viṣṇu and contained in the pitcher of (Lord) Brahmā, reach the head of (Lord) Śiva ? O Foremost among ascetics ! How has Gaṅges become dear to Nārāyaṇa ? You are competent to describe me these.

Śrī Nārāyaṇa said:

6. The Gaṅges was in the liquid state in the Goloka. Originating from the body of Rādhā and Kṛṣṇa, she is a part and a form of them.

7-14. (Gaṅgā) presiding over the liquid form had a beautiful form on earth. She had a maiden form adorned with gem-studded ornaments. She had a smiling and charming face resembling the lotus in the autumnal midday. She had the complexion of heated gold and resembled the autumnal moon in her lustre. She had a glossy radiance and was extremely glossy. She was of the form of pure piety. She had large and hard hips with a pair of exquisite buttocks. She had a pair of large, raised, hard and round breasts. She had a pair of very attractive eyes. She had curved side-glances. She had curving braids of hair adorned with a wreath of jasmine. She had a graceful mark of vermilion together with dots of sandal paste. The pair of cheeks were charming with the designs of musk. The lower lip was beautiful resembling the *bandhūka* flower. The row of teeth was radiant like the seeds of ripe pomegranade. Her clothes as pure as fire adorn her waist.

15-17a. That lustful one stood by the side of Kṛṣṇa with bashfulness drinking with delight the face of the Lord with her unwinking eyes resembling the leaves of the lotus. She had her face blossoming on account of excitement. She was desirous of having fresh union with him. She fainted after getting horripilation (on beholding) the form of the Lord.

17b-26. In the meanwhile Rādhikā, present there in the company of thirty crores of cowherdesses, radiant like crore moons, having the face like the red lotus on account of wrath, with eyes like the red lotus, having the complexion of white *campaka* (flower), having the gait of an elephant in rut, adorned with various ornaments studded with invaluable gems, having an invaluable necklace as pure as fire and studded with rubies, wearing a pair of yellow dress and the loin cloth, placing her lotus feet together with respectful water offered by Kṛṣṇa, red, tender and humiliating the lustre of land lotus, climbing down from an aerial chariot studded with foremost gems, served by the female companions by the waving of white *chouries*, having a mark of musk (on the forehead) together with crescent-shaped sandal mark, having the beautiful vermilion resembling the lustre of a glowing lamp in the middle of the forehead below the parted hair that was radiant, as she herself was trembling, her curved beautiful braids of hair endowed with a garland of flowers such as the *pārijāta* shaking with her lips together with charming nose quivering with wrath went there and seated by the side of Kṛṣṇa on a gem-studded royal throne. The assembly of Lord was full with the hosts of female companions.

27. On beholding her, Kṛṣṇa stood up with respect. Acyuta hurriedly spoke to her sweet words with a smile.

28-29. The frightened cowherds saluted her with their bent heads. They all extolled her with devotion. Gaṅgā extolled the Supreme Lord after getting up and spoke to him. She enquired about his welfare with fright and extreme modesty.

30. With humility, fright and parched throat, lips and palates she sought refuge at the lotus feet of Śrī Kṛṣṇa.

31. Kṛṣṇa stationed in her lotus heart extended protection to that frightened one. She regained her normal countenance on account of the favour of the universal god.

32-39. Gaṅgā beheld Rādhā seated on the royal throne above, glossy, pleasing to look at, glowing with the lustre of brahman, first among innumerable Brahmās, first among the creation, eternal one, always youthful like a twelve year old girl, incomparable in her form and virtue among the hosts of women, a half of the body of Kṛṣṇa, equal to Kṛṣṇa in radiance, age and splendour, worshipped as Mahālakṣmī by the consort of Mahālakṣmī, covering the council of the Lord with her lustre, radiant, partaking the betel offered by the companion very difficult to be had by others, the unborn mother of all beings, the fortunate one, worthy of respect possessing self-respect, the goddess presiding over the life of Kṛṣṇa and Ramā dearer than life. Beholding the goddess of the dance-circle, the goddess of the celestials did not get satisfaction. She drank her (beauty) with unwinking eyes.

40. O Sage ! In the meanwhile calm, modest and smiling Rādhā spoke to the Universal God.

Rādhikā said:

41-42. O Dear Lord ! Who is this smiling good lady by your side always looking at your lotus face, with lust and red eyes, fainting after getting horripilation at your (beautiful) form, looking at you again and again covering her face with a cloth.

43. You also always used to be looking at me with passion and smile. When I am alive at Goloka how is this bad conduct on your part ?

44. Repeatedly you indulge in such immodest acts. On account of love towards you I forgive you as women are affectionate.

45. O lustful one ! You go away from this Goloka with that dear one. O Lord of celestials ! Otherwise it will not be for your welfare.

46. I had noticed you earlier in the sandal forest with Virajā. I had forgiven you then at the request of the companions.

47. You had disappeared in the past on (hearing) the sound of my arrival. Virajā had discarded her body and become a river.

48. She is still existing as a form of your good fame a crore *yojanas* wide and four times that in her length.

49. After I had gone home, you went near her and wailed aloud : O Virajā ! O Virajā, remembering her.

50. Then that accomplished one rose from the water by means of her ascetic power and manifested in an embodied form with ornaments.

51. Then you embraced her and impregnated her. Then the seven oceans came into being from her.

52. Then you were noticed in the *Campaka* forest in the company of cowherdess Śobhā. On (hearing) the sound of my arrival you disappeared.

53. Śobhā discarded her body and entered the orb of the moon. Then her body became shining splendour.

54-57. (Then her body) was divided by you with tormented heart and given to the gems, gold, excellent learned one, lotus faces of women, princes, excellent dress, silver, sandal paste, water, tender sprouts, flowers, fruits, ripe grains, mansions of kings and gods and refined men.

58. You were (once) noticed in the Vṛndāvana (bushes of holy basil) in the company of the cowherdess Prabhā. You had at once disappeared on (hearing) the sound of my arrival.

59. Prabhā discarded her body and entered the orb of the sun. Then her body became hot lustre.

60-63. You divided her body and gave it away with affection and lamentation to the eyes out of bashfulness and being afraid of her, to fire, kings, assembly of men, gods, service minded men, serpents, brahmins, sages, ascetics and prosperous and famous women. After having given to all those in the past, you started crying.

64-65. (Once) you were noticed in the dancing circle in the company of the cowherdess Śānti in the spring on a couch of flowers with sandal paste besmeared (on your body). (Then you were seen) in a gem-studded mansion endowed with gem-studded lamps adorned with gem-studded ornaments with that cowherdess adorned with gem-studded ornaments.

66. Fragrant betel was offered by you to her who had eaten. She also offered you betel. O Lord ! You also ate it.

67. On (hearing) the sound of my arrival you immediately disappeared. Śānti discarded her body out of fear and merged in you, O Lord !

68-70. Then her body became an exceedingly virtuous one. O Lord ! You divided her body and with affection and wailing you distributed them in the past to the things of the world, to Viṣṇu, the embodiment of goodness, to Lakṣmī, the embodiment of pure goodness, to the *vaiṣṇavas*, votaries of your formula, to ascetics, to *dharma* and to most pious ones.

71-75. Once you were noticed with the cowherdess Kṣamā. You were well-dressed, wearing a garland and besmeared with fragrant sandal with that lady adorned with gems and besmeared with charming sandal paste. You happily fainted on the sandal and flower bed. You fell asleep at once on account of happiness due to fresh union. You both were awakened by me. You recollect. Your yellow garment, charming flute, garland of flowers, Kaustubha (gem adorning the chest) and gem-studded ear pendants were seized from you. They were then returned to you on account of love and at the behest of the companions. O Lord ! You had a dark complexion on account of shame. That still exists.

76-78. Kṣamā discarded her body on account of fame and reached the earth. Then her body became most virtuous. You divided that affectionately and wailing and distributed to Viṣṇu, *vaiṣṇavas*, virtuous ones, *dharma*, weak people, ascetics, gods and learned.

79. I have told you everything. What else you desire to hear from me? O Lord ! I know that your virtue is very extensive and outstanding.

80. After having stated thus, Rādhā, possessing eyes like the red lotus, began to speak to the chaste Gaṅgā, bashful and having bent head.

81. Gaṅgā, the accomplished one, knew the secret by means of her ascetic power disappeared from the council and entered her own water.

82. Having known by means of ascetic power, that she (Gaṅgā) was omnipresent, Rādhā, the accomplished one began to drink her as if it was mouthful.

83. Gaṅgā, the accomplished ascetic woman, came to know of this by means of her ascetic power and resorted the lotus feet of Śrī Kṛṣṇa as the supreme refuge.

84. Rādhā beheld the Goloka, Vaikuṇṭha and Brahmaloka and other worlds. But she did not find Gaṅgā anywhere.

85. There was no water, where the lotuses dried up on the earth. The earth was abound with the dead bodies of watery creatures.

86-101. Brahmā, Viṣṇu, Śiva, Ananta, Dharma, Indra, Indu (moon), Divākara (sun), Manus, mortals, all gods, accomplished souls and ascetics came to Goloka with parched throats, lips and palates. All of them bowed down to Govinda, the lord of all and above Nature, the excellent one, adorable one, bestower of boons, most excellent one, cause of favour, lord of favour, foremost among all, the lord, desireless, formless, unstained, without any support, without quality, without desire, without a barricade, unstained, an embodiment of self-will, and embodiment of favouring his devotees, form of truthfulness, lord of truth, form of witness, eternal one, supreme one, lord of other, Supreme Soul and lord, and all of them extolled him after saluting with bent heads on account of devotion. They had choking throats, eyes filled with tears and horripilation on their bodies. They all extolled the lord, propitious one, supreme one, Lord Hari, the supreme brahman that is effulgent, cause of all causes, seated on a royal throne studded with invaluable gems, being served by the cowherds by waving the white *chowries*, watching with delight and smile the dance and song of the cowherdesses, surrounded by hundreds of cowherds in lovely dress, besmeared with sandal paste all over the body, adorned with gem-studded ornament, dark like fresh cloud, a young boy, wearing yellow dress, having a form as a cowherd like a boy of twelve years, having a body endowed with splendour humiliating the lustre of a crore moons, being encircled by his lustre as charming as his self, having an attractive body sporting the beauty of a crore gods of love, being looked at always by smiling cowherdesses, adorned with ornaments made up of invaluable gems and drinking with delight the lotus face of the lord with their eyes, remaining in the chest region of Rādhā, dearer than his life, partaking the fragrant betel given by her (Rādhā). The gods beheld that full one in the dancing-circle everywhere. The sages, mortals, accomplished souls, ascetics and others were all delighted and surprised.

102. After having discussed among themselves, they all requested Brahmā to convey Jagannātha their opinion and desire.

103-104a. Brahmā, after having heard those words came to the foremost Kṛṣṇa, seated on the right side of Viṣṇu and the left side of Vāmadeva, as endowed with supreme bliss and as an embodiment of supreme bliss.

104b-108. Brahmā beheld all things in the dancing-circle as forms of Kṛṣṇa, each one wearing similar dress and seated on similar seats, possessing two arms, with a flute in the hand, adorned with garland of wild flowers, having the diadem adorned by the peacock plumes and shining with the *kaustubha* (a jewel on the chest). Each one was attractive, beautiful and had a tranquil form. Each one was equal in the virtue, ornament, beauty, lustre, age radiance, dress, fame, form and beauty. They were all perfect and vested with divine attributes.

109. It was impossible to distinguish the worshipped and the worshipper. At one moment it was an embodiment of lustre. At another moment it was a collection of beauty.

110. At one moment it was one Kṛṣṇa in the company of Rādhā. At one moment it was seated on different seats and at another moment it was (seated) together with her.

111. Brahmā was not able to contemplate Kṛṣṇa assuming the form of Rādhā and Rādhā, the form of Kṛṣṇa, and unable to distinguish the female form and the male form.

112. Then Brahmā extolled with devotion Śrī Kṛṣṇa stationed in his heart after contemplating in the mind and repeated salutation.

113-114. Then he opened his eyes and again looked at his command. He then behold only one Kṛṣṇa stationed in the chest region of Rādhā, encircled by his courtiers and abound with the assembly of cowherdesses. After beholding him they (the gods) saluted and extolled him again.

115. After having known their intention the lord of the gods, the soul of all beings, the lord of all sacrifices, the lord of all beings and the cause of all beings spoke to them.

The Lord said:

116. O Brahmā ! O Viṣṇu ! O Mahādeva ! You all come. Are you fine ? May you all have prosperity.

117. O Fortunate ones ! You have all come here on account of the bringing of Gaṅgā. Gaṅgā has sought refuge at my lotus feet with fright.

118. Beholding her in my presence, Rādhā desires to drink her up. Making this one in bondage to come out you make her fearless.

119. After hearing the words of Śrī Kṛṣṇa, Brahmā smilingly extolled that Rādhā, the adorable by all and worshipped by Śrī Kṛṣṇa.

120. After having extolled her with his four faces with devotion, the four faced (Brahmā), the creator of the four *vedas*, spoke.

121. Gaṅgā had her origin from your body in the dancing-circle of the Lord. Being excited by the music of Śaṅkara, she has attained a liquid state.

122. Being a part of Kṛṣṇa and yourself, she is dear like your daughter. Let her worship you by receiving your sacred formula.

123. The four-armed one (Viṣṇu) will be her husband in Vaikuṇṭha and the salt-ocean (will be her husband) after she had reached the earth.

124. Rādhā, who is in Goloka, is omnipresent and hence the soul. O Goddess of the gods ! You are her soul and she is always your daughter.

125. After listening to the words of Brahmā, she accepted her with a smile. Then Gaṅgā came out from the tip of the toe-nail.

126. After having risen up from water, that presiding deity, sat in the midst of all with security and peace.

127. Brahmā put a little of that water in his pitcher. Candraśekhara (Śiva) put a little on the crescent moon on his head.

128-129. Lotus-born (Brahmā) imparted to Gaṅgā, the sacred syllable, hymn, amulet, mode of worship of contemplation of Rādhā and all the procedure that has been described in the Sāmaveda. The chaste Gaṅgā worshipped her alone and attained Vaikuṇṭha.

130. O Sage ! Lakṣmī, Sarasvatī, Gaṅgā and Tulasī, the sanctifier of the universe, all these are the consorts of Nārāyaṇa only.

131. Then Kṛṣṇa told Brahmā with a smile, all the legends of the time incomprehensible for the ignorant.

Śrī Kṛṣṇa said:

132-138. O Brahmā ! O Viṣṇu ! O Maheśvara ! Accept Gaṅgā. Listen to the narration of the past time. You all, the other gods, sages, Manus, accomplished persons, ascetics and all those who have come here, all of them live in the Goloka devoid of the cycle of time. At the time of the dissolution of Nature, the entire Universe gets inundated. Brahmā and others in the universe are merged in me now. O Brahmā! Behold the entire universe except Vaikuṇṭha are submerged in water. You go and make the creation. You then create the Brahmaloka and other (worlds) together with the Brahmāṇḍa. Then Gaṅgā would go there. In the same manner after having made the creation of Brahma (*loka*) and other (worlds) in the universe, I do creation. You go forth at once with the gods. Brahmā would have his fall merely by the winking of my eye. How many of Brahman have already gone and would be coming into being ?

139. O Ascetic ! After having described thus, the consort of Rādhikā went to the harem. The gods went away and made the creation once again only with effort.

140-141. Gaṅgā remained in Goloka, Vaikuṇṭha, Śivaloka, Brahmaloka and other places. Wherever she was present earlier that Gaṅgā went to those places by the command of the Supreme soul. As she had come out from the lotus feet of Viṣṇu, she is known as *viṣṇupadī* (originated from the feet of Viṣṇu).

142. Thus I have described you everything about the excellent episode of Gaṅgā, that confers happiness and beatitude and is the essence. What else you desire to hear?

CHAPTER TWELVE

The Legend of Gaṅgā (Continued)

Nārada said:

1. (You have stated) that Lakṣmī, Sarasvatī, Gaṅgā and Tulasī, the sanctifier of the world, these four are the consorts of Nārāyaṇa.

2. I have heard that Gaṅgā had gone to Vaikuṇṭha. O Keśava ! Describe me as to how she had become his consort (consort of Viṣṇu).

Nārāyaṇa said:

3. Gaṅgā went to Vaikuṇṭha and then went Brahmā. After going there he bowed down to lord of the universe along with her.

Brahmā said:

4. The goddess who in the liquid state had her origin from the body of Rādhā and Kṛṣṇa, this is the presiding goddess of unrivalled beauty of that (goddess) on earth.

5. She is endowed with a fresh maiden form, possessing good conduct. She is beautiful and excellent. She is of the form of pure goodness devoid of anger and pride.

6-7. She would not choose any one else other than that person from whose body she had her origin. There also the most radiant, excellent and proud Rādhā was intent on drinking her up. Being frightened she (Gaṅgā) consciously entered the lotus feet of the Supreme soul Kṛṣṇa.

8-9. Beholding that the entire Goloka was dry, I then came to Goloka where Krṣna, the inner soul of all the beings, sought our opinion in order to know the entire episode. He then made explicit Gaṅgā from the tip of the toe.

10. O Lord ! After having imparted her the formula of Rādhikā, I filled up the Goloka, saluted the lord of Rādhā and I have come here with her.

11. You accept this celestial goddess by *gāndharva*[1] form of marriage. You are the chief of the gods. You are a connoisseur. With the feeling of appreciation (you accept) this woman of taste.

12. You are a gem among the males and gods. This chaste woman is a gem among women. The union of the gallant woman with a gallant man will be meritorious.

13. Whoever on account of pride does not accept a girl that has approached, there is no doubt that Mahālakṣmī would desert him with wrath and go away.

14. Whoever is a wise man, he also does not slight Nature. All men are from Nature. The women are the digits of Nature.

15. You are the only glorious first person, void of attributes and above the Nature. Half of your body (as Kṛṣṇa) has two arms. You have four arms in the other half (as Viṣṇu).

16. The outstanding Rādhikā had her origin from the left side of Kṛṣṇa's body in the past. Just as Kamalā (Lakṣmī) had her origin from the left side, in the same way she had her origin from the right side.

17. Hence she has chosen you because she had her origin from your body. Just as the Supreme Being and Nature, the male and female have the same body.

18. After having spoken thus, Brahmā offered her and left. Hari himself married her by means of *gandharva* form of marriage.

19. After making couch suited for amorous sports adorned with flowers and sandal paste, Viṣṇu, the consort of Ramā sported there with Gaṅgā with delight.

20. She had gone to *gā*, the earth. She had come back to her place from (the place of Viṣṇu). As Gaṅgā had emerged from the feet of Viṣṇu she is known as *viṣṇupadī* (originated from the feet of Viṣṇu).

21. That goddess, the connoisseur, fainted soon after the fresh union, on account of the pleasant union with the lord of connoisseur of art.

22. Beholding that, Sarasvatī was sad as she was devoid of jealousy towards co-wife. Sarasvatī always had jealousy towards her but Gaṅgā did not reciprocate (jealousy) towards Sarasvatī.

23. The consort of Ramā had thus three wives together with Gaṅgā. O Sage ! It later became four including Tulasī.

CHAPTER THIRTEEN

The Legend Relating to Tulasī

Nārada said:

1-6. Where did Tulasī originate ? Who was she in her previous birth? How did she, the pious one, become the dear of Nārāyaṇa ? In whose family she had her birth ? Whose daughter was that ascetic ? By what austerities she attained a position higher than Nature, namely the incorruptible, desireless, witness of all beings, Nārāyaṇa, the Supreme Brahman, Supreme soul, lord, adorable by all, lord of all beings, omniscient, cause of all beings, support of all, forms of all and protector of all beings ? How had such a goddess attained the state of a tree? How did that ascetic lady get seized by a demon? My curious mind is inquisitive and impels me (to aṣk) again and again. O dispeller of all doubts you are fit to clear my doubt.

Nārāyaṇa said:

7. The Dakṣa Sāvarṇi Manu was a pure meritorious *vaiṣṇava.* He was famous and glorious and had his origin from Viṣṇu as a part-manifestation.

8. His son Dharma Sāvarṇi was a pious and pure *vaiṣṇava.* His son Viṣṇu Sāvarṇi was a *vaiṣṇava* who had controlled his senses.

9. His son Deva Sāvarṇi was bent on doing austerities towards Viṣṇu. His son Raja Sāvarṇi was devoted to Mahāviṣṇu.

10. Vṛṣadhvaja was his son devoted to Śiva, who had the bull in his banner. Lord Śiva stayed in his hermitage for three divine *yugas.*

11. Śiva had more affection towards the king than his own son. He (Vṛṣadhvaja) did not adore Nārāyaṇa or Lakṣmī or Sarasvatī.

12. He deserted the worship of all the gods. That proud king discarded the worship of Mahālakṣmī in the month of Bhādra (September-October).

13. He discarded the worship of Sarasvatī in the month of Māgha (February-March). He despised the sacrifice and the worship of Viṣṇu and did not practise them.

14. On account of Śiva no god cursed that king Sun-god cursed that king to become deprived of prosperity.

15. Śaṅkara (Śiva) himself held a spear and challenged him. Sun-god sought the refuge of Brahmā along with his father.

16. Holding the trident in hand Śiva went to the Brahmaloka with wrath. Being led by Sun-god, Brahmā went to Vaikuṇṭha with fear.

17. Śiva approached the Sun-god there also holding the spear. Brahmā, Kaśyapa and Sun-god had parched palates on account of fear.

18. Being afraid they sought the refuge of Nārāyaṇa, the lord of all beings. After going there they all saluted with their heads and extolled him again and again.

19. All of them informed Hari the cause of their fear.

20. O Sage ! On account of compassion Nārāyaṇa offered them protection (and said): O Frightened ones ! You be firm. What fear for you when I am here ?

21. Whoever remembers me when beset with misfortune and is having fear, I will go there hurriedly and protect them holding the disc in the hand.

22. I am the lord protecting the world and I am always the doer. I am the creator in the form of Brahmā and destroyer in the form of Śiva.

23. I am Śiva. I am you. I am Sun-god. I possess all the three attributes. After assuming various forms I will indulge in creation and such other activities.

24. You go away. You will be safe. Where (you may have) fear? Now onwards you will not have fear from Śaṅkara (Śiva) on account of my favour.

25. That lord gets pleased quickly. He is always the refuge for pious men. He is governed by the devotees. He is the lord of the devotees, soul of the devotees and fond of the devotees.

26. The *sudarśana* (disc) and Śiva are dearer to me than my life. O Brahmā ! There is no one possessing lustre superior to them in the Brahmāṇḍa.

27. Mahādeva (Śiva) is capable of creating a crore of Suns sportively and a crore of Brahmās in the same manner. What is impossible to be accomplished by Śūlin (Śiva) (the trident bearer)?

28. There is nothing which is outside the sphere of his knowledge for him who is contemplating me day and night. He recites my name and my attributes with his five faces.

29. I myself am contemplating that auspicious one day and night. Whoever is devoted to me in whichever way, I am devoted to that person in the same manner.

30. The lord is an embodiment of auspiciousness. He is the presiding deity of good. Wise people know him as Śiva, as auspiciousness proceeds from him.

31. In the meanwhile Śaṅkara (Śiva) himself came there with the spear in the hand and riding a bull and possessing eyes like the lotus.

32-36. O Nārada ! After getting down quickly from the bull, he saluted with his head bent on account of devotion (Viṣṇu), the consort of Lakṣmī, tranquil and most superior, seated on the gem-studded throne, adorned with gem-studded ornaments, wearing a crown and ear pendant, holding the disc and wearing the garland of wild flowers, having a dark complexion like the fresh cloud, beautiful, having four arms, being served with waving *chouries* by (gods) having four arms, besmeared with sandal paste on the entire body, adorned with yellow garment, one who had partaken the betel offered by Lakṣmī, smilingly listening with delight the dance-music of the Vidyādhara women, the master, the Supreme soul and an embodiment of favouring the devotees.

37. Mahādeva (Śiva) saluted him as well as Brahmā. Sun-god also saluted Candraśekhara (Śiva) (Lord with the crescent on the head) with devotion with fear.

38. Kaśyapa also extolled him with great devotion and saluted him. After glorifying the lord of all beings, Śiva sat on a comfortable seat.

39-41. Then in the assembly of gods, the propitious lord (Nārāyaṇa) spoke charming words as sweet as nectar to Candraśekhara (Lord Śiva) (having the crescent moon on the head) seated on a comfortable seat, relaxed, served by the attendants of Viṣṇu with white *chouries*, devoid of wrath and gracious on account of contact with good ones, smiling with pleasure and glorifying with his five faces, Lord Nārāyaṇa, the supreme one.

The Lord said:

42. It is extremely ridiculous to ask about the welfare of a person who is auspiciousness-incarnate. Still, I am asking you about worldly matters and those prescribed by the *vedas.*

43. It is improper now to enquire about prosperity and asceticism from one who confers the fruits of ascetic practices and who bestows all prosperities.

44. Why should I vainly enquire the omniscient one, the presiding deity of knowledge, about knowledge. It is vain to ask Lord Śiva (Hara), the conqueror of death and devoid of calamities, about calamities.

45. I am putting an important question to you who had come to my place. Why have you come here in a hurry? Thus spoke Viṣṇu, the consort of Ramā.

Śrī Mahādeva said:

46. Sun-god has cursed (King) Vṛṣadhvaja, my devotee and dearer to me than my life. That is the reason for my arrival (here) and wrath.

47. On account of grief due to affection for the son, I am intent on killing Sun. He has sought the refuge from Brahmā. That Sun and Brahmā have sought your refuge.

48. Whoever seeks your refuge by means of contemplation or expression, they are free from calamities and doubt. They conquer decrepitude and death.

49. O Sir ! How shall I describe the benefits of seeking direct refuge? Remembrance of Hari (Viṣṇu) bestows fearlessness (protection) and all prosperities always.

50. O Lord of the universe ! Describe me what is the future of my devotee deprived of prosperity and ignorant on account of the curse of the Sun.

The Lord said:

51. A period of twenty one *yugas* has elapsed on account of destiny during half a *ghaṭikā* (24 minutes) in Vaikuṇṭha. You hasten to the abode of the King.

52. In course of time Vṛṣadhvaja died on account of unavoidable and cruel destiny. Hamsadhvaja was his son. He also died deprived of prosperity.

53. Dharmadhvaja and Kuśadhvaja the most fortunate ones, were his sons. Those two great-devotees of Viṣṇu were bereft of prosperity on account of the curse of Sun.

54. They were deprived of the kingdom and prosperity. Both of them were devotees of Kamalā (lotus-born) (Lakṣmī). Goddess Lakṣmī would be born to their wives by means of digit-manifestation.

55. Then the two would be endowed with prosperity and become foremost kings. O Śambhu (Śiva) your devotee has died. You all go back.

56. Having spoken thus he disappeared along with Lakṣmī from the assembly. The gods returned to their abode with extreme delight and pleasure.

57. Śiva also hastily went away with fullness (of heart) in order to practise asceticism.

CHAPTER FOURTEEN

The Legend of Vedavatī

Nārāyaṇa said:

1. O Sage ! Those two pleased goddess Lakṣmī with severe penance. Each one of them obtained the favour of their choice.

2. By the grace of Mahālakṣmī both of them Dharmadhvaja and Kuśadhvaja became the rulers of the earth, wealthy and blessed with children.

3. In course of time, Mālāvatī, the chaste wife of Kuśadhvaja, gave birth to a pious girl.

4. She was endowed with knowledge on account of the contact with earth. (Soon after her birth) in the confinement room she stood up and recited the *vedas.*

5. Since that girl recited the *vedas* soon after her birth, she is called as Vedavatī by men.

6. Soon after birth she bathed and went to the forest for (doing) penance. Though she was prevented by all, she was earnestly devoted to Nārāyaṇa (Viṣṇu).

7. That ascetic girl performed intense penance for one *manvantara* (period) at Puṣkara sportively.

8. Inspite of that she was well nourished, not lean and endowed with a maiden form. She suddenly heard an invisible voice in the sky:

9. Hari (Viṣṇu) himself will be your husband in a different birth. O Beautiful one ! You will be getting a husband unattainable even by Brahmā and others.

10. After hearing this she was enraged and again practised penance on the Gandhamādana mountain at an uninhibited place.

11. After having performed penance for a long time she dwelt there in confidence. She beheld there the invincible Rāvaṇa in front of her.

12. Beholding him she offered him *pādya* (respectful water for washing the feet), besides sweet fruits, roots and cool water on account of devotion for the guest.

13. After partaking (the offering), that sinner stayed there near her. He then enquired her: O Auspicious one ! Who are you ?

14-15. Beholding her, a beautiful one, having stout and elevated breasts, having face like the autumnal moon, smiling, possessing beautiful teeth and chaste one, that wretched one (Rāvaṇa) afflicted by the love-shafts fainted. He attempted to ravish her by drawing her with his hand.

16. That chaste woman made him get paralysed with her wrathful look. His hands and feet paralysed, he was not able to speak.

17. Mentally he extolled the goddess, a part of Lakṣmī and having eyes resembling the lotus. Becoming pleased with that eulogy, she restored his (senses).

18. She then cursed him : You will die along with your kinsmen on account of me. Being touched by you passionately, I will discard (my life). Behold.

19. After having stated thus she discarded her body by means of ascetic practice. After placing her (body) on the Ganges, Rāvaṇa returned to his abode.

20. What wonderful thing I have seen ? What have I done today ? After having reflected thus he lamented again and again.

21. That pious woman was in course of time born as the daughter of Janaka, known as Sītādevī, on account of whom Rāvaṇa was killed.

22. That great ascetic woman attained Rāma as her husband, Hari, the complete form, on account of the penance (done) in her previous birth.

23. After having propitiated her lord, the master of the world, by means of her penance, that Rāma, the beautiful one, enjoyed the company of Rāma for a long time.

24. Remembering her condition in her former life, she had full knowledge about the course of her penance of the past. The happiness (of the present) obliterated all the (past) suffering and she got happiness.

25. That chaste one enjoyed different kinds of comforts for a long time after gaining that very handsome youth, virtues, connoisseur of taste, calm, well-dressed, outstanding and attractive for women as desired by her.

27. On account of the powerful destiny, the foremost among the Raghus, the truthful one, then went to the forest in order to honour the words of his father.

28. He remained near the ocean in the company of Sītā and Lakṣmaṇa. There that Hari beheld Fire-god who had assumed the form of a brahmin.

29. Beholding that Rāma was distressed, he also became unhappy. Then he, the truthful one, spoke some truth to that honest one.

Fire-god said:

30. O Fortunate one ! Listen to my words (about) that which has come on account of destiny. The time for the abduction of Sītā from you has come.

31. Destiny is inavoidable. There is nothing more powerful than the destiny. Having entrusted with me, the one originated from me, let the shadow be given to the demon now.

32. I will restore Sītā to you again at the time of the ordeal. I have been sent by the gods. I am not a brahmin, but I am Fire god.

33. After listening to those words and not revealing them to Lakṣmaṇa, Rāma accepted that at his own will with a distressed heart.

34. O Nārada ! The Fire god created an illusory Sītā resembling Sītā by means of his ascetic power. Then he entrusted her possessing the same attributes and form to Rāma.

35. Taking Sītā (with him) he went away concealing the matter not to be disclosed. Lakṣmaṇa not at all knew the matter relating to the concealed one.

36. In the meanwhile Rāma beheld a golden deer. Sītā induced him to strive for (getting) that one.

37. After having placed Lakṣmaṇa for guarding Sītā in the forest, he (Rāma) himself went in order to kill it and he struck it with an arrow.

38. After raising a cry 'Ah ! Lakṣmaṇa', that illusory deer discarded his life at once beholding Hari in front of it and remembering him.

39. After discarding the form of a deer and assuming a divine form he ascended the heaven in a car made of gem.

40. Among the two guardians, Jaya and Vijaya at the entrance to Vaikuṇṭha, Jaya was very powerful.

41. On account of the curse of Sanaka and others he had become a demon. Once again he attained the position at the entrance as the door-keeper.

42. After hearing the excited sound, 'Ah ! Lakṣmaṇa', Sītā sent away Lakṣmaṇa to the presence of Rāma.

43. After Lakṣmaṇa had gone to Rāma, the invincible Rāvaṇa took Sītā and went away to Laṅkā sportively.

44. Beholding Lakṣmaṇa Rāma was in despair. He went away quickly to his hermitage and did not find Sītā there.

45. He fell into a swoon and again lamented much for a long time. Again he wandered in the forest in search of her.

46. In course of time after gaining information about her from the vulture on the banks of the river, after making friendship with the monkey, Hari (Rāma) built a bridge across the ocean.

47. After reaching Laṅkā the foremost among the Raghus killed with a shaft Rāvaṇa together with the kinsmen and regained the grief-stricken Sītā.

48. Immediately he arranged for the fire-ordeal for her. At that time the Fire-god gave him the real Jānakī.

49. The fictitious Sītā spoke to the Fire-god and Rāma with humility: Tell me what shall I do.

Fire-god said:

50. O Respectable one ! You go forth to the merit-yielding Puṣkara for penance. There itself you will become goddess of fortune of the heaven.

51. After listening to those words she (reached) Puṣkara and performed penance for three lakhs of divine years. She then became Lakṣmī in the heaven.

52. In course of time she had her origin from the sacrificial pit by her penance. She was Draupatī, the daughter of Drupada and the spouse of the *pāṇḍavas.*

53. She was Vedavatī in the *kṛtayuga* as the auspicious daughter of Kuśadhvaja. In the *tretā* (*yuga*) she was Sītā, daughter of Janaka and the wife of Rāma.

54. Her shadow in the *dvāpara* is the venerable Draupadī, daughter of Drupada. She is stated to be *trihāyaṇī* (existing in the three periods of time) as she has existed in the three *yugas.*

Nārada said:

55. O Foremost among sages ! How there were five husbands for her ? O Great Lord ! You dispel this doubt from my mind.

Nārāyaṇa said:

56. O Nārada ! When Rāma attained the real Sītā at Laṅkā, the fictitious Sītā endowed with a beautiful form was much perturbed.

57-58. At the command of Rāma and the Fire-god she performed a penance and sought a boon from Śaṅkara (Śiva). Being excited with passion and intent on getting a husband, that chaste lady was requesting again and again five times : O Three-eyed one ! Give me a husband.

59. After listening to her request Śiva, the foremost connoisseur, smiled and blessed her with a boon: O Dear one! You will have five dear ones (spouses).

60. That is why there was a single spouse for the five *pāṇḍavas.*Thus I have described you everything. Listen now to (the narration about) the contextual matter.

61. After having regained the charming Sītā at Laṅkā, Rāma gave away Laṅkā to Vibhīṣaṇa and returned to Ayodhyā.

62. After having ruled over the kingdom in Bhārata for eleven thousand years, he went to Vaikuṇṭha with all the people.

63.Vedavatī, a part manifestation of Kamalā (Lakṣmī), re-entered Kamalā. I have described you the meritorious legend conferring good and destroying sins.

64. The four *vedas* are always embodied and present in her tip of the tongue. Hence she is known as Vedavatī.

65. I have described you briefly the legend of the daughter of Kuśadhvaja. I shall describe you now the legend of the daughter of Dharmadhvaja for your comprehension.

CHAPTER FIFTEEN

The Legend of Tulasī

Nārāyaṇa said:

1-3. The wife of Dharmadhvaja was known as Mādhavī. On account of passion she sported with the King in the Gandhamādana after having made ready the bed suited for amorous sports endowed with flowers and sandal. She had besmeared sandal paste over the entire body. The fragrance of flowers and sandal graced her. That gem of a woman had a charming form adorned with gems and ornaments. That passionate one, foremost among the connoisseurs had union with the master of connoisseurs.

4. There was no end for the amorous sports for both of them well-versed in the art of sexual science. They had no knowledge of the day and night. Hundred divine years had passed.

5. As she had the menstrual period he paused from his amorous sports. That lustrous woman did not have the satisfaction.

6. She became pregnant at once and the pregnancy lasted for hundred divine years. She was endowed with grace and it increased day by day.

7-14. At an auspicious moment on an auspicious day endowed with good *yoga*,[1] good *lagna* (point rising in the eastern horizon), good *aṁśa* endowed with good ownership of the houses (constellations), on the lunar day in Kārttika (November-December) falling on a Friday, she delivered a female child, a part manifestation of Lakṣmī, having the mark of lotus, charming, having red complexion in her hands and feet, *rājarājeśvari* (endowed with all prosperity), Lakṣmī (endowed with fortune), graceful in all her limbs, having the marks of the royal goddess of fortune, the presiding deity of the royal fortune, having the face like the autumnal moon, with eyes like the autumnal moon, lips red like the ripe bimba (fruit), smilingly looking at her house, having redness in her palm and sole, having a charming deep navel, having the three folds below that, having prominent and round buttocks, having a warm body during the winter and cold body during the summer, having dark complexion, having beautiful (locks of) hair, an excellent woman,[2] having the complexion of white *campaka* (flower) and outstanding among beautiful women. Men and women after beholding her beauty were not able to mention some one comparable to her. Hence those acquainted with the past refer to her name as Tulasī.

15. Soon after her birth on the earth that fitting person like Nature went to the Badarī forest for doing penance although forbidden by all.

16. She performed penance for a lakh divine years with a determination that Lord Nārāyaṇa should become her Lord.

17. She was bearing the five fires during the summer, standing in the water during the winter, exposed to the showers of rain and enduring it day and night.

18. She was partaking only fruits and water for twenty thousand years. That ascetic woman had only leaves as food for three thousands thousand years.[3]

19. That one with a slender bosom was consuming the wind only for forty thousand years. She remained without food for ten thousand years.

20. Beholding her standing on one foot and imperceptible, the Lotus-born (Brahmā) came to Badarikāśrama in order to confer a boon.

21. Beholding the four-faced one (Brahmā), one riding the swan, she bowed down. The creator of the world said to her.

Brahmā said:

22. O Tulasī ! You seek from me a boon that you may desire to have either devotion for Hari or liberation or indecrepitude or deathlessness.

Tulasī said:

23. O Sir ! Listen to me. I shall describe you what I desire. Why should I have any bashfulness in front of even the omniscient one ?

24. I am Tulasī, who was a cowherdess in the Goloka in the past. I was dear to Kṛṣṇa. (I was) his attendant, part manifestation and dear companion.

25. Once the goddess of dance (Rādhā) came and beheld me and fainted after having enjoyment with Govinda and unsatiated in the dance circle.

26. O Brahmā ! She rebuked Govinda and cursed me angrily thus : You be born as a mortal.

27. Then Govinda told me: By the favour of Brahmā you will attain the four-armed one (Viṣṇu), a past-manifestation of myself, after performing penance at Bhārata.

28. After having stated thus, the Lord of the celestials disappeared. Being afraid of the goddess (Rādhā), I discarded the body and was born on the earth.

29. I desire now to get Nārāyaṇa, the attractive and tranquil one, possessing a beautiful body. You confer on me this favour.

Brahmā said:

30. There was a cowherd known as Sudāmā born from the body of Śrī Kṛṣṇa. A lustrous part-manifestation of that person was born in Bhārata.

31. Now he had his origin in the line of Danu on account of the curse of Rādhā. He was known as Śaṅkhacūḍa in the three worlds. But he had no devotion.

32. Once he beheld you and his mind was agitated with passion. He was not able to get over that on account of the glory of Rādhikā.

33. He remembered his past birth. He did penance and desired to get you as a favour. You also remembered your past birth. O beautiful one! You know everything.

34. O Auspicious one ! You will now become his wife. Later on you will attain the attractive and tranquil Nārāyaṇa.

35. On account of the curse and the divine union of a digit of Nārāyaṇa, you will become a tree. You will be the sanctifier of the world.

36. You will be the foremost among all the flowers and dearer than the life of Viṣṇu. The worship of all without you will be fruitless.

37. As a tree at Vṛndāvana you will also be known as Vṛndāvanī. The cowherds and cowherdesses will worship Mādhava with your leaves.

38. In the form of the presiding deity of the tree you will always be sporting with Kṛṣṇa and the cowherd as you like, on account of my curse.

39. After listening to these words, she bowed down Brahmā with a smile and with delighted mind spoke a little.

Tulasī said:

40. O Sir ! I tell the truth. I do not have the desire towards the four-armed as I have towards the two-armed Kṛṣṇa, the beautiful black-complexioned one.

41. I am unsatiated with Govinda as my amorous sports with him was disturbed on account of fate. On account of the words of Govinda I request the four-armed one.

42. By his grace I will certainly obtain Govinda, the one difficult (to get) again. Kindly relieve me from the fear of Rādhā.

Brahmā said:

43. I will bless you with the sixteen syllabled formula of Rādhikā. You receive it. You will become equal to her life on account of my favour.

44. Rādhikā would command you two to have dalliance in secret. You will become favourite wife of Govinda as equal to Rādhā.

45-46. After having stated thus and imparted the sixteen syllabled formula to the noble lady, the creator of the world (imparted) her the hymn, excellent amulet, all the procedures for worship and the order of the preparatory rites. After bestowing on her good wishes he disappeared.

47. She also repeated the excellent formula that was favourite to her in the past birth, as instructed by Brahmā in the sacred Badarikāśrama.

48. She worshipped for twelve divine years. That noble lady attained perfection and got a declaration also for that.

49. After gaining perfection in penance and the formula, she gained the cherished favour and enjoyed the fortunate one, very difficult to be had in the universe.

50. That noble lady with delighted mind almost forgot the torments of penance. When the fruits are gained, grief becomes excellent happiness for men.

51. After having eaten, drunk and feeling delighted, she lied down on an attractive couch on which sandal (paste) and flowers had been strewn.

CHAPTER SIXTEEN

The Legend of Tulasī (Continued)

Nārāyaṇa said:

1. Tulasī was much delighted. She slept with a pleasant mind. She was endowed with a maiden form. That beautiful lady had been glorifying (Kṛṣṇa).

2-6. Then the God of love discharged the five shafts on her. Being tormented by the flower-weapon as she was adorned with flowers and sandal paste, she had horripilation all over her body. She was trembling. That red-eyed one became parched for a while, fainted for a moment, agitated at another time and felt lassitude leading to happiness at another time. At another moment she experienced burning sensation. One moment she felt intoxicated. For a while she regained consciousness. One moment she felt grief-stricken, at another moment she was getting up from the bed and at another moment she was going near. For a while she was wandering with agitation and at another moment put on her clothes. For a while she slept again on account of agitation.

7. That bed of flowers and sandal (paste) became (bed of) many thorns. Sweet (food) (became) poisonous food. Fruit having divine form (became) water.

8. The above (became) without shape. A fine cloth (became) fire. Vermilion mark (was) like a wound causing grief.

9-11. In her lassitude, that chaste one beheld for a while a well dressed, beautiful smiling young man and the lord of taste, besmeared with sandal all over the body, adorned with gems and ornaments, coming towards her, wearing a garland, looking at her lotus face, narrating her amorous stories, kissing her lips again, reclining on a bed of flowers and embracing her body.

12. (Beholding) the spring going and coming again she asked: O Dear one ! Where do you go? Stand here.

13. After regaining her consciousness, she lamented again and again. O Nārada ! She thus remained in the hermitage.

14-16a. The great ascetic Śaṅkhacūḍa obtained the charming formula of Kṛṣṇa from Jaigīṣavya and gained perfection at Puṣkara after reading always the most auspicious amulet. After gaining the cherished desire from Brahmeśa, he (Śaṅkhacūḍa) also arrived at Badarī by the command of Brahmā.

16b-20. O Sage! Tulasī beheld Śaṅkhacūḍa who was coming, endowed with a youthful form, possessing a lustre as that of Kāmadeva, having the hue of white *campaka* (flower), adorned with gem-studded ornaments, face resembling the autumnal moon, possessing eyes like the autumnal lotus, riding a charming car adorned with a cluster of valuable gems, shining with the cheeks endowed with a pair of gem-studded ear-rings, wearing a garland of *pārijāta* flowers, smiling, shining with a fragrant mark of musk and saffron.

21-23a. Beholding him in her presence, she covered her face with a cloth, smiled and looked at him again and again with her side-glances. She had her head bent down on account of bashfulness due to association with a new person. She was passionate, afflicted with the shafts of the God of Love and had horripilation. She was always drinking with her eyes (the beauty) of that lotus face.

23b-36. Śaṅkhacūḍa also beheld that girl in the hermitage, on the bed of flowers and sandal, wearing good dress, looking at his face always with a smile, charming, having stout and hard hips, having stout and elevated breasts, having a row of teeth humiliating the lustre of a row of pearls, having the lips like the *bimba* fruit, having a beautiful nose, beautiful and outstanding, possessing the complexion of heated gold, having the lustre of autumnal moon, encompassed by her own lustre, charming and pleasant to behold, the region below the *sīmanta* (parting of the hair on the head) always radiant with the dot of saffron together with the dots of musk and sandal, having a low and deep navel with three folds below that, the palms red as the lotus and adorned with the nails (like the) moon, possessing the lotus feet excelling the grace of the land lotus, red in colour, tender and having the lustre of red dye, adorned with the land lotuses, lotuses and rubies, shining with the flood of splendour of a single moon in the hail humiliating the autumnal moon, well adorned with red dye mixed invaluable gems, having jingling charming anklets studded with excellent gems, bearing the beautiful locks of hair together with a garland of the *mālatī* (flowers), rendered beautiful by the charming ear-rings studded with invaluable gems and of the shape of a crocodile, radiant with the graceful breasts and waist and gem-studded pearl necklace, adorned with gem-studded bracelet, armlet and conch and endowed with a row of fingers adorned with the gem studded rings. Beholding that graceful, beautiful, virtuous and chaste woman with well-formed teeth, he sat by her side and spoke to her sweet words:

Śaṅkhacūḍa said:

37-39. Who are you? Whose daughter are you? O Fortunate one ! Respectable one among women ! O Lovely woman !

Who are you ? O Auspicious one ! Conferrer of all goodness ! A necklace in the pleasure garden on the river of emancipation and enjoyment ! The essence in the cleft of mundane existence ! The support of illusion ! Charming one ! The paragon of beauty! Emaciated one ! One stupefying the ascetics ! O Beautiful one ! You shed your silence and talk to me as a servant.

40. After listening to these words, the lustful and charming eyed lady spoke to him smilingly and passionately with bent head.

Tulasī said:

41. I am the daughter of Dharmadhvaja. I am an ascetic doing penance in the penance grove. Who are you ? You go as you desire.

42. It is stated in the scriptures that a person born in a noble family does not ask thus in secret a beautiful and noble woman born in a noble family.

43-47. A libidinous, lustful person who has not known the sense of the scriptures and who was born in a vile family and is bereft of the sense conveyed by texts on religious law, would desire for a beautiful woman, sweet at the first instance and killer of man in the end, having a form like a pitcher with poison and always having a nectarine countenance, similar to the edges of a razor speaking always sweet, always bent on achieving her goal, submissive to her husband in order to gain her object, but not submissive otherwise, vile in heart and having a pleasant countenance. Which wiseman, as if he is ignorant would trust a person whose life account has not been described in the scriptures and the *purāṇas* ?

48-61. Who is an enemy or a friend for such women making entreaties to new person every time, beholding a well-dressed person desiring for a person in her heart, publishing her chastity outwardly with great effort, always lustful, beautiful, a receptacle for passion, charming, outwardly deceptive concealing her desire for sexual union, swallowing the spouse secretly but extremely bashful outwardly, irritated, angry and quarrelsome in the absence of sexual union, dreading excessive intercourse and distressed in having little copulation, mentally desiring for cooked food and cool water, always (desiring) a beautiful, virtuous and beautiful youth who is a connoisseur, more affectionate towards the person indulging in coitus than her son, showing more affection than her own life to a dear one well-versed in the art of sexual union, looking at an old man or a person incapable of copulation like an enemy, quarrelling with him always, much irascible, devouring him with arguments like Kīnāśa,[1] the minute particle, an embodiment of rashness, always the abode of all blemishes, always an embodiment of conceit, abode of all blemishes always, unavoidable by Brahmā, Viṣṇu, Śiva and others, an embodiment of delusion, always an impediment for ascetic practices, a door for the entrance to emancipation, devoid of devotion to Hari, an abode of all delusions, always of the form of a fetter in the prison house of mundane existence, a sorcerer, a personification of falsehood, apparently exhibiting beauty but inwardly much vile as an abode of all impurities such as urine, ordure, pus etc., foul-smelling, endowed with defects and blood and unrefined, an embodiment of illusion for conjurers created by Brahmā in the past and a personification of poison, never to be beheld by the aspirants of emancipation.

62. After saying him thus Tulasī stopped talking. Śaṅkhacūḍa began to speak to her with a smile.

Śaṅkhacūḍa said:

63. O Noble lady ! All that you have told me are false. It is partly true and partly false. You listen to me.

64. Brahmā has created two types of women— one infatuating and be seduced and the other chaste that is commendable. (The first one) is condemned.

65. Lakṣmī, Sarasvati, Durgā, Sāvitrī, Rādhikā and others are the forms of the process of creation. They have been the first creations of Brahmā.

66. The form of chaste woman is known to be their part-manifestations. It is commendable. It is of the form of fame and is the cause of all auspiciousness.

67-72. Śatarūpā, Devahūti, Svadhā, Svāhā, Dakṣiṇā, Chāyāvatī, Rohiṇī, Varuṇānī, Śacī, the wives of Kubera and Vāyu, Aditi, Diti, Lopamudrā, Anasūyā, Kaiṭabhī, Tulasī, Ahalyā, Arundhatī, Menā, Tārā, the excellent Mandodarī, Damayantī, Vedavatī, Gaṅgā, Yamunā, Puṣṭi, Tuṣṭi, Smṛti, Medhā, Kālikā, Vasundharā, Śaṣṭhi, Maṅgalacaṇḍī, the consort of Dharma, Svasti, Śraddhā, Kānti, Tuṣṭi, Śānti, Nidrā (sleep), Tandrā (lassitude), Kṣut(hunger), Pipāsā(thirst), Sandhyā (twilight), Rātri (night), Dināni (days), Sampatti (prosperity), Vṛtti (livelihood), Kīrti (fame), Kriyā (act or rite), Śobhā(beauty) and Prabhā(lustrous) are the commendable forms born in different *yugas*.

73. The seductive ones are the heavenly nymphs, courtesans and others. These are censurable ones. They are of the forms of libidinous women in the universe.

74. The form having the *sattva* (goodness) quality predominant is by nature pure. That is outstanding in the universe. That pious form is commended.

75. The wise proclaim that form to be the real one. Among the wanton women there are two kinds (of) the forms of *rajas* (haughty) and *tamas* (ignorant).

76-77. O Beautiful one ! For want of a place or moment or opportunity and on account of physical pain or disease or on account of contact with virtuous men or surrounded by an assembly of men or the fear of an enemy king, the form of *rajas* gets transformed into a pious one.

78. The wise men declare this as the middle form. The wise men know the form of *tamas* as irresistible and the lowest one.

79. A learned person born in a noble family does not speak to other women in a solitary place or in the assembly of the wicked or in secrecy.

80. At the command of Brahmā I have come to your presence now. O Beautiful one ! I will marry you by the *gandharva* (form of) marriage.

81-82. I am Śaṅkhacūḍa, the conqueror of the *devas*, born in the line of Danu on the earth. I am Sudāmā in the city of Hari. Among the eight cowherds in the assembly of cows and cowherdesses. Now I am the chieftain of the demons on account of the curse of Rādhikā.

83. On account of the glory of the formula of Kṛṣṇa I remember my former birth. Similarly you remember yourself as Tulasī in your former birth closely connected with Hari in the past.

84. You yourself were born in Bhārata on earth on account of the wrath of Rādhikā. I was desirous of having sexual union with you. But I could not do on account of the fear of Rādhā.

85. O Great Ascetic ! After having stated thus he stopped talking. The delighted Tulasī smilingly commenced speaking.

Tulasī said:

86. Such a wise man is commended among the wisemen in the universe. A loving woman desires always such a husband willingly.

87. I have been truly defeated by you now by your arguments. Whichever man is conquered by a woman is censured and impure.

88. The manes, gods and kinsmen despise a person conquered by a woman. The father and brother of a person conquered by a woman censure mentally and verbally.

89-90. A brahmin gets free from pollution due to birth or death in ten days, a king in twelve days, a trader in fifteen days and a *śūdra* after a month. A person born in a mixed caste, (the purification) is as per (the caste of) the mother. An impure person conquered by a woman gets purified only after cremation.

91. The manes do not like to accept the oblations of rice balls and water and the gods do not like to receive the flowers, water etc., from such a person.

92. What is the use of learning, ascetic practices, repetition (of formulae), oblations in fire, worship, knowledge and fame for such a person whose mind has been seized by women.

93. You have been examined by me in order to know the glory of your knowledge. After testing a lovely person, a lovely lady chooses a husband.

94-96. Whoever gives away his daughter to a person devoid of virtues, old, ignorant, indigent, stupid, sick, despised, much wrathful, extremely ugly, lame, deformed, blind, deaf, dull, dumb and one equal to an eunuch, such a person would incur the sin of killing a brahmin.

97. Whoever gives his daughter to a tranquil, virtuous, learned *vaiṣṇava* youth, such a person would gain the fruits of ten horse-sacrifices.

98-100. If a person after protecting his daughter sells her on account of a calamity and greedy of getting money, such a person would go to (the hell) *kumbhīpāka*. That sinner would consume there the urine and odure of a girl, being bitten by insects and crows for a period of fourteen Indras. In the end he would certainly be born to a hunter and he would carry the burden of flesh day and night and sell.

101. After having stated thus Tulasī stopped talking. In the meanwhile Brahmā came to them.

102. O Nārada ! Tulasī and Śaṅkhacūḍa saluted him. The Lord of the gods stayed there and spoke to them beneficial words.

103. O Śaṅkhacūḍa ! What discussion you are having with her ? You marry her by means of *gandharva* marriage.

104. You are a gem among men. This chaste one is a gem among women. The union of the gallant woman with a gallant person will be meritorious.

105. O King ! Who will reject happiness indisputable and difficult to get ? Whoever abandons indisputable happiness is no doubt an animal.

106. O Chaste one ! Do you disregard such a virtuous and attractive person who is the conqueror of the gods and demons ?

107-112. Just as Lakṣmī in the master of Lakṣmī, Rādhikā in Kṛṣṇa, Sāvitrī in me, Bhavānī in Bhava (Śiva), Dharā (Earth) in Varāha (Boar manifestation of Viṣṇu), Menā in Himavān,

Anasūyā in Atri, Damayanti in Nala, Rohiṇī in Candra, Rati in Kāma, Diti in Kaśyapa, Arundhatī in Vasiṣṭha, Ahalyā in Gautama, Devahūti in Kardama, Tārā in Bṛhaspati, Śatarūpā in Manu, Dakṣiṇā (sacrificial fees) in Yajña (sacrifice), Svāhā in Hutāśana (Fire god), Śacī in Mahendra, Puṣṭi in Gaṇeśvara, Devasenā in Skanda and Satī in Dharma, you be prosperous and dear to Śaṅkhacūḍa.

113. O Beautiful One ! You always sport with this beautiful one for a long time at different places as you like.

114. You will again attain Govinda in Goloka. After the death of Śankhacūḍa you will attain the four-armed one (Viṣṇu) in Vaikuṇṭha.

115. After having blessed, Brahmā returned to his place. The demon married her by *gandharva* form of marriage.

116. Then there was (the sound of) the drum in the heaven and a shower of flowers. He sported with her in a charming abode.

117. Tulasī fainted on account of the pleasure of the new union. That pious one was immersed in the pleasure of sexual union in that lonely place.

118-119. That connoisseur engaged in all happy pleasures of sixty-four kinds described in the science of erotics as desired by the connoisseurs, by the conjunction of the different parts of the body that attracts the women.

120-122. There was no end for sexual enjoyment for those two well-versed in sexual union in a much attractive place devoid of all beings on a couch of flowers and sandal or with the fragrance of flower and sandal or in a flower garden or on the banks of a river abound with flowers and sandal taking that beautiful one adorned with flower, sandal and all ornaments and very attractive.

123. Tulasī sportively attracted the mind of her husband. The connoisseur of art deprived her of her consciousness.

124. She took away the sandal on the chest and the marks on the arms. He took away the vermilion mark from her (forehead).

125. He made nail marks on her chest with delight. She impressed the marks of the ornaments of her hand on his left shoulder.

126. The king bit her lips. She gave that on his pair of cheeks four times that.

127. After their sexual union had concluded they both stood up and mutually dressed each other as they desired.

128-130. She made a mark of sandal mixed with saffron (on his forehead). She besmeared his beautiful body. She gave him fragrant betel, clothes as pure as fire, a beautiful garland of *pārijāta* (flowers), an excellent ring made of invaluable gems and a foremost gem very difficult to obtain in the three worlds.

131. She repeatedly said: I am your slave. Then she saluted her master, the virtuous one, with great devotion.

132. With a smile, she drank again (the beauty of) his lotus face with her unwinking eyes and beautiful side-glance.

133. He drew her near and made that dear one (seated) on his chest. Smilingly he looked at her lotus face covered by a cloth.

134. He kissed again her hard cheeks and red lips. He gave her a pair of robes brought from Varuṇa and the necklace brought by him and glorified in the three worlds.

135. He gave her a pair of anklets taken from Svāhā, bracelet of Chāyā and ear-ring belonging to Rohiṇī.

136. (He also presented her) with a ring and gem, the excellent ornaments of Rati, brilliant and charming given away by Viśvakarmā.

137. After having offered her multitudes of attractive pedestals, bed, rare to get, and ornaments, he abandoned.

138-139. After having set her braids of hair together with the garland, he made beautiful marks of leaves on her cheeks resembling signs of victory together with three streaks of the moon with fragrant sandal encircled by dots of bright saffron.

140-142a. He then made a vermilion mark resembling the glowing fire. He besmeared with bright lac-dye the toe-nails on the pair of lotus feet humiliating the land lotuses.

After placing her lotus feet on his chest passionately again, he repeatedly stated : O Noble lady ! I am your slave. Then the king placed her on his chest and left the hermitage for a different place riding a car made of gems.

143b-151. That passionate one indulged in amusing with that lustful (woman) with passion in extremely beautiful places, flower gardens, most lonely places, caves, on the banks of the ocean, beautiful forest, on the banks of the river Puṣpabhadrā, in charming water and breeze, on the sands, on the masculine and feminine rivers, in the honey of the honey bees resounding with sweet notes, in the gently flowing breeze, in the garden, on the Gandhamādana, in divine gardens, in divine forests, in sandal forest, in the bowers of *campaka, ketakī, mādhavī, mādhava, kunda* (jasmine), *mālatī, kumuda* (lily) and *ambhoja* (lotus), in the *kalpavṛkṣa* (wish-yielding tree), *pārijāta* garden, in uninhabited golden region, in auspicious golden mountain, Kāñcī forest, in the shining little golden mines, on the beds of flowers and sandal, in the region reverberating with the notes of the cuckoos, endowed with flower and sandal with (the fragrance of) flower and sandal (carried) by the wind. She and the demon did not get satisfaction.

152-153. Their passion increased like the fire by ghee. After returning to his abode along with her, the demon king set up an attractive place for amusement and sported there again. The glorious Śaṅkhacūḍa thus enjoyed the kingdom.

154-156. That powerful king of kings (ruled) for a whole *manvantara*. He held his sway over the gods, demons, descendants of Danu, *gandharvas, kinnaras* and *rākṣasas*. The gods being deprived of their authority wandered like mendicants. He forcibly seized the offerings of worship and oblations intended for them, their abodes, authority, weapons, missiles and ornaments etc.

157. All the gods were like painted images without diligence. They all were dejected and went to the court of Brahmā.

158. They narrated (him) the events (taken place) and wept repeatedly. Then Brahmā repaired to the abode of Śaṅkara (Śiva) together with the gods.

159-160. Brahmā narrated all the matter to Candraśekhara (god with crescent on the head) (Śiva). Brahmā and Śiva went along with them to Vaikuṇṭha, very difficult to be attained, and supreme place that removes old age and death. They reached that excellent door-way of the hermitages of Hari.

161-163. They beheld there the door-keepers seated on royal thrones made of gems, clad in yellow robes, adorned with gems and ornaments, wearing garlands of wild flowers, all having black and beautiful bodies, wielding conches, discs, maces and lotuses and four arms and smiling lotus faces with charming lotus eyes. Brahmā told them the episode and the purpose of his visit.

164-174a. They gave him permission. He entered it with their permission. The lotus-born (Brahmā) beholding thus sixteen door-ways crossed them with the gods and entered the court of Hari. It was attended by gods and sages and courtiers having four arms, all being forms of Nārāyaṇa adorned with *kaustubha*, shaped as the orb of the full moon, four-sided and charming, made of excellent gems and made beautiful with foremost diamonds studded with invaluable gems and set by the free will of Hari (Viṣṇu), endowed with multitudes of garlands made of rubies, adorned with rows of pearls, decorated with millions of gemmed mirrors of the shape of a circle, made beautiful with different pictures drawn with different pictorial designs, with artificial lotuses set with foremost emeralds, endowed with hundreds of steps made of symantaka (a king of valuable gem) gems, having charming sprouts of sandal, cloth, threads and knots, exquisitely beautiful encircled by pillars of blue sapphire gems, endowed with a collection of pitchers filled with excellent gems, shining with a collection of garlands of the *pārijāta* flowers, decorated all around with fragrant liquid sandal mixed with musk and saffron and made fragrant by fragrant wind, charming with the music of multitudes of Vidyādhara (a class of semi-divine beings) women, extending to thousand *yojanas* and abound with attendants.

174b-182. Along with Śaṅkara (Śiva) and the gods, Brahmā beheld there Śrī Hari (Viṣṇu) staying at the centre just like the moon surrounded by the stars, seated on variegated royal throne set up with invaluable gems, wearing a crown and a pendant, adorned with garland of wild flowers, holding a conch, disc, mace and lotus, having four arms, black like a fresh cloud, beautiful, attractive, adorned with all the ornaments made of invaluable gems, besmeared with sandal (paste) all over the body, holding a sportive lotus, beholding smilingly with delight the dance music in front of him, tranquil, that consort of Sarasvatī, the person whose lotus feet was being massaged by Lakṣmī, partaking the fragrant betel offered by the devotees, being served with the white chouries by Gaṅgā with extreme devotion and being extolled by all with their heads bent on account of devotion. After beholding that exquisite lord, the composite one, Brahmā and all other gods then saluted and extolled him with horripilation on their bodies, with tears in their eyes and choked throat, with supreme devotion, the devotees being afraid and having head bent down.

183-184. Brahmā, the creator of the world, holding his palms folded and held together narrated the events with humility in front of Hari. The omniscient knower of the feelings of all, (Lord) Hari, heard those words and smilingly told Brahmā the secret that is attractive.

The Lord said:

185. O Lotus-born ! I know all the episode of Śaṅkhacūḍa, a shepherd devotee, most lustrous one.

186. O Gods ! You listen to me for all that old episode. That anecdote is destroyer of sin and the cause of merit like the Goloka.

187. There was a shepherd named Sudāmā, foremost among my courtiers. He obtained the birth as a *dānava* (demon) on account of the terrible curse of Rādhā.

188. There once I had come to the dance-circle from my abode after leaving the proud Rādhā, most dear to me than life.

189. She learnt from her servant maid that I was with Virajā, came angrily to me and found me there.

190. (Finding) Virajā in the form of a river and knowing me as having disappeared, she again returned with wrath to her place along with her companions.

191. The goddess after having beheld me in the abode in the company of Sudāmā, she rebuked me much as I was standing silent and firm.

192. Hearing that, the great Sudāmā was angry. He rebuked her with wrath in my presence.

193. Having heard that she with her eyes ruddy on account of wrath ordered him to be expelled, getting excited in my presence.

194. A lakh of her companions rose up and quickly expelled that irresistible one glowing with radiance and murmuring repeatedly.

195. She heard his words and cursed him with wrath, the terrible words : You go away and attain birth as a *dānava* (demon).

196-197. As he was going away, cursing and weeping after saluting me, she felt pleased and weeping overwhelmed with compassion began preventing him (with the words): O Child! Stop. Do not go. Where do you go ? Having stated thus repeatedly, she was surprised.

198. The cowherdesses wept. All the cowherds were grief-stricken. Rādhikā and all of them were then advised by me.

199. Sudāmā will return in half a moment after honouring the curse. Sudāmā ! You come back. After stating thus she was prevented.

200. O Creator of the world ! Half a moment of Goloka will be a Manu-period on the earth. These words are certain.

201. Hc is that Śaṅkhacūḍa. He will go back there. He is very powerful, adept in yoga (asceticism). He is an expert in all kinds of tricks.

202. You take my spear and go away to Bhārata quickly. Let Śiva kill the demon with my spear.

203. That demon always wears my amulet that is most auspicious on his throat.

204. O Brahmā ! As long as that amulet remains on his throat, no one is capable of hurting him. (Assuming) the form of a brahmin, I will make a request to him.

205. You have conferred a boon on him that he will have his death when there shall be a violation of the chastity of his wife.

206. I will certainly impregnate his wife. There is no doubt that he will have his death at that moment itself.

207. Then she will discard her body and become my dear. After having told thus, the lord of the world delivered the spear to Hara (Śiva).

208. After giving the spear, Hari quickly went inside with delight. The gods led by Brahmā, Rudra and others went to Bhārata.

CHAPTER SEVENTEEN

The Dalliance of Tulasī and Śaṅkhacūḍa

Nārāyaṇa said:

1. O Great sage ! After having deputed (Lord) Śiva for the destruction of the demon, Brahmā duly went back quickly to his place.

2. Mahādeva (Śiva) stationed at the root of the banyan tree on the banks of the Candrabhāgā river for the sake of the rescue of the gods.

3. After appointing Puṣpadanta, the Lord of the Gandharvas, as the desired messenger, he despatched him to Śaṅkhacūḍa with delight.

4-16. O Sage ! He too at the command of the Lord repaired hastily to that city surpassing the city of Mahendra (Lord of the gods), more excellent than the mansion of Kubera (Lord of wealth), five *yojanas* in extent and twofold that in its length, encircled all around by gems resembling the crystals, endowed with seven impassable moats, always adorned with several gems resembling glowing fire, containing hundreds of roads with gem pedestals, with a host of merchants shining with different articles, endowed with hundred crores of hermitages adorned with exquisite decorations and set up with gems resembling the red lead. After reaching there he beheld there the excellent abode of Śaṅkhacūḍa at the centre. It was perfectly circular resembling the orb of the moon-surrounded by four moats with glowing flames of fire, impassable for the enemies, inaccessible for others, comfortable, surrounded by gemmed walls rising high touching the sky, shining with twelve doors having the guardians, adorned with artificial lotuses made of gems, adorned with gemmed mirrors beautiful with a lakh mansions studded with excellent gems, beautiful with gemmed steps, radiant with gemmed pillars, with gemmed and variegated door panels and gem-studded pitchers, made shining by rows of excellent gems of different kinds, always guarded all around by hundred crores of valorous, strong, beautiful, well-dressed and well-adorned demons holding splendid weapons. Beholding them Puṣpadanta also had a view of the excellent entrance. (He also beheld) the person guarding the entrance holding a spear, smiling and standing, terrible, having reddish brown eyes and red complexion.

17. He narrated the episode and went with his permission. After crossing the nine entrances he went inside the city.

18-19. The messenger was not prevented by anyone since he had the form as a messenger. After having gone to the inner entrance he told the guardian at the entrance all the episode relating to the battle to be conveyed to the master. He (the guard) after having informed him (the master) asked the messenger to go (inside).

20-24. He went in and beheld that beautiful Śaṅkhacūḍa at the centre of the dance-circle seated on a golden royal seat studded with gems and endowed with an excellent gemmed staff always beautiful and glorified with artificial flowers made of gems, an attractive golden umbrella being held over him with the hand by the servant being served by host of attendants with fans and white chowries, dressed well, beautiful, adorned with charming gemmed ornaments, besmeared with unguents, wearing a fine dress, surrounded by three crores of foremost demons and hundred crores of other wandering bearing weapons.

25. Puṣpadanta beheld him with wonder as described above. He told him the matter relating to the battle as spoken by Śaṅkara (Śiva).

Puṣpadanta said:

26. O Foremost King ! I am a messenger of Śiva known as Puṣpadanta my lord. You listen to me. I shall tell you what ?

Śaṅkara said:

27. Return the kingdom to the gods now. The gods have sought refuge at the lord of the gods, Lord Hari the supreme.

28. Śiva has been sent to you by Hari after giving a trident. The three-eyed one (Śiva) is stationed at the root of the banyan tree on the banks of the river Candrabhāgā.

29. Either you return them their property or prepare for a fight. You may tell me what I shall tell Śambhu (Śiva) after returning to him.

30. After listening to the words of the messenger, Śaṅkhacūḍa smiled and said : I will come in the morning. You go back.

31. He returned quickly to the lord stationed at the root of the banyan tree and (told him) the words of Śaṅkhacūḍa and (described) his paraphernalia.

32-38. In the meanwhile Skanda[1] came near Śiva. Vīrabhadra,[2] Nandi, Mahākāla, Subhadraka, Viśālākṣa, Bāṇa, Piṅgalākṣa, Vikampana, Virūpa, Vikṛti, Maṇibhadra, Bāṣkala, Kapilākṣa, Dīrghadaṁṣtra, Vikaṭa, Tāmralocana, Kālaṅkaṭa, Balībhadra, Kālajihva, Kuṭīcara, Balonmatta, Raṇaślāghī, Durjaya and Durgama, the eight terrible Bhairavas, the eleven Rudras, Vāsava and other Vasus, the twelve Ādityas, Hutāśana (Fire-god), Candra(moon), Viśvakarmā, the two Aśvins, Kubera,

Yama, Jayanta, Nalakūbara, Vāyu, Varuṇa, Budha, Maṅgala, Dharma, Śani, Īśāna, Kāmadeva, the valorous one, Ugradaṁṣṭra, Ugracaṇḍā, Koṭṭarī and Kaiṭabhī (also came).

39-45. The hundred armed goddess Bhadrakālī, the terrible one, was seated on an aerial car studded with excellent gems. She was clad in red dress. She had (her body) besmeared with red unguent. She was dancing, laughing and singing fine notes with delight. She was offering protection to the devotee and that fearless only fear to the enemies. She was having a formidable tongue, rolling and extending to a *yojana*. She had a circular and lofty skull extending to a *yojana*. She had a trident touching the sky, and dart extending to a *yojana*. She had a conch, wheel, mace, lotus, arrows, bow that is frightening, mallet, mace, thunderbolt, sword, shining plank, the missiles *vaiṣṇava, vāruṇa, āgneya, nāgapāśaka, nārāyaṇa, brahmā, gandharva, garuḍa, pārjanya, pāśupata, jhṛmbhaṇa, pārvata, māhesvara, vāyavya, daṇḍa* and *sammohana*. (She had) different kinds of weapons and hundred excellent missiles.

46-47. She came and stood there along with three crores of *yoginīs*,[3] three crores of formidable *ḍākinīs, bhūtas, pretas, piśācas, kūṣmāṇḍas, brahmarākṣasas, vetālas, yakṣas, rākṣasas* and *kinnaras*.

48. Along with them Skanda made obeisance to Candraśekhara (Lord Śiva with crescent on the head) and sat besides his father in the assembly on the command of (Lord) Śiva.

49. After the messenger had gone, the powerful Śaṅkhacūḍa went inside the harem and conveyed the news to Tulasī.

50. After hearing the news about the battle, that pious lady spoke sweet words to him with parched throat, lips and palate with remorse.

Tulasī said:

51. O Dear Lord ! O Kinsman ! Stay a while on my chest. O Presiding deity of my life! Protect my life for a moment.

52. Enjoy the pleasures of this birth desired by you in your mind. Let me look at you for a while with my thirsty eyes.

53. My vital forces are swinging. My mind is always getting burnt. I had a bad dream in the last part of the night.

54. After listening to the words of Tulasī, the foremost king, the wise man, ate and drank and spoke befitting words true and beneficial.

Śaṅkhacūḍa said:

55. All actions are associated with time for reaping the fruits such as auspicious events, rejoice, happiness, grief, fear, sorrow and inauspicious events.

56. The trees grow branches, bear flowers and fruits in course of time according to time.

57. Their fruits become ripe in course of time. They all become bearers of fruits and get destroyed in course of time.

58. The beings are born as per time and get destroyed according to time. O Beautiful one! The universes are born and get destroyed as per time.

59. The creator creates according to time. The protector protects as per time. The destroyer destroys as per time. They all move about in order.

60-62. (Lord Kṛṣṇa) is the lord of Brahmā, Viṣṇu and Śiva and superior to Nature. (He is) the creator, protector and the destroyer with his whole form always. According to time the lord creates the Nature by his free-will. He creates the movable and immovable things of primordial nature in the universe. All the objects from Brahmā to a clump of grass are artificial. They come into being and get destroyed as per time.

63. You always worship that Supreme Brahman, the lord of Rādhā, beyond the three qualities, lord of all beings, form and soul of all the beings and lord.

64. You always adore that Lord Kṛṣṇa who creates water with water, protects water with water and destroys water with water.

65-68. You seek refuge from one by whose command the wind blows and always moves swiftly, the sun shines in time, Indra rains in time, (the god of) death moves around the beings, fire burns in time and the moon wanders like one afraid. He is the root of death and of time. He is the supreme (god of) death for (the god of) death. He is the creator of the creator, protector of the protector and the destroyer of the destroyer. O Dear one! You adore that kinsman and of whom all are kinsmen.

69. Who am I and who are you? By fate we have been united in the past. (I) have been united with you by the deed by him.

70. An ignorant person gets distressed in grief and calamities, but not a wise man. Pleasure and pain revolve like the rim of a wheel.

71. You will certainly attain (Lord) Nārāyaṇa, the lord of all beings, as lord, for which purpose you had performed a penance at the Badarikāśrama in the past.

72. You have been gained by me by penance by the grace of Brahmā. Your penance is for getting Hari. My dear ! You will get Hari.

73. You will get Govinda at Vṛndāvana and Goloka. I will discard my body as a demon and reach that world.

74. You will behold me there and I will behold you there always. On account of the curse of Rādhā, I reached Bhārata, difficult to be attained.

75-76a. O Dear one ! Listen to me. I will again go there itself. What grief for me ? After discarding your body and assuming a divine form you will attain Hari then itself. O Dear one ! You do not get distressed.

76b-78. After having stated thus he slept at the end of the day on a beautiful and attractive bed decorated with flowers and sandal. He wandered in gemmed mansion endowed with all kinds of riches. The king spent the night in the company of that excellent woman (in the mansion) endowed with gemmed lamp in auspicious amusements.

79-80. Aftcr holding her close to the chest, the king, an adept in realities, consoled again with the divine knowledge and foremost truth that was imparted by (Lord) Kṛṣṇa in the past under the fig-tree; the weeping spouse, extremely grief-stricken, emaciated, abstaining from food and drowned in the ocean of grief.

81-82a. And then he imparted her that excellent (knowledge) capable of removing all grief. After gaining that knowledge that lady with a smiling countenance sported with delight after considering everything as extremely perishable.

82b-83. O Sage ! The couple were exhausted in their amorous sports and immersed in the ocean of bliss, with horripilation on all their limbs and fainted in an uninhabited place. They were in close embrace, much pleased and intent on having sexual union.

84. Those two had almost a single body like the Ardhanārīśvara![4] Tulasī considered her dear lord superior to her own life.

85. The most powerful king considered her more than his life. Both of them remained in a pleasant sleep.

86-87. They both were well-dressed, beautiful and motionless on account of pleasant amorous union. For a while they were conscious and were narrating sweet, divine and charming legends. They were again laughing for a while. They had partaken betel leaf offered by the other.

88-90. Both were serving each other with white chouries with affection. For a while they were reclining with pleasure. For a while they remained engaged in amorous sports coupled with feelings of emotion. For those two well-versed in that matter, there was no end for their amorous sports. They were always engaged with success and (they) had no defeat even for a while.

CHAPTER EIGHTEEN

The Dialogue between Śiva and Śaṅkhacūḍa

Nārāyaṇa said:

1-3. After having contemplated mentally (Lord) Śrī Kṛṣṇa, the king, devoted to (Lord) Kṛṣṇa, woke up in the *brāhmamuhūrta* (before dawn) from the charming bed of flowers, discarded the night dress, bathed in auspicious water, wore washed garments, wore shining dot (on the forehead) and performed the daily rites as well as the favourite worship of the preceptor. He perceived the auspicious articles such as curd, clarified butter, honey and parched grains.

4. O Nārada ! He gave away excellent gems, quality jewels, outstanding clothes and gold with devotion to brahmins as usual.

5. For the sake of an auspicious journey, he gave away some invaluable gems such as pearls, rubies and diamonds to the brahmin preceptor.

6. For the sake of welfare, he gifted to a poor brahmin an excellent elephant, an outstanding horse and a foremost cow all quite charming.

7. He gifted with pleasure thousands of treasury, three lakhs of cities and hundred crores of villages to brahmins.

8-9. After installing his son as the foremost king, as a moon among the demons and entrusting to his son his wife and his kingdom endowed with all riches, hosts of subjects, treasury, vehicles etc. he armed himself for the battle holding a bow etc.

10-14. O Nārada ! With the help of his attendants the demon duly gathered his mighty army three lakhs horses, five lakhs elephants, ten thousands chariots, three crores archers, three crores with shields and three crores with spears. The Commander-in-Chief of this army was Mahāratha, proficient in the science of warfare, and foremost among the warriors in battle. After having made him the commander of the three lakhs of *akṣauhiṇi*,[1] the king arranged for thirty *akṣauhiṇī* of drum-beaters. Contemplating Lord Hari mentally, he remained outside the camp.

15. He rode an excellent aerial car studded with outstanding gems. After having placed his preceptors at the front, he went towards (Lord) Śiva.

16. In Bhārata on the banks of the river Puṣpabhadrā, there is an undecaying banyan tree. It is an excellent hermitage of

accomplishment known as *siddhikṣetra* for the accomplished souls.

17-18. It is the holy place of penance of (the sage) Kapila in Bhārata. It is on the east of the western ocean, west of Malaya (mountains), north of Śriśaila and south of Gandhamādana, five *yojanas* wide and hundred times long. The sacred river Puṣpabhadrā is perennial.

19. The dear wife of the salt ocean is always endowed with good fortune. It has the hue of pure crystal and is the conferrer of merits in Bhārata.

20. It had its origin from the Himālaya and is joined by (the river) Sārāvatī. Having Gomanta on its left it enters the western ocean.

21-28a. After having gone there Śaṅkhacūḍa had the sight of Candraśekhara (Lord Śiva with the crescent moon on the head) seated at the root of the holy fig tree in a meditative posture, with *mudrā* (posture of hand), radiant like a crore suns and smiling, bright like pure crystal, effulgent with the lustre of Brahman, wielding the trident and axe, clad with the tiger-hide, having a matted hair possessing the hue of heated gold, having three eyes and five faces and wearing the snake as the sacred thread (over the left shoulder), the conqueror of deaths, the death of death and the destroyer of the world, the remover of the death of the devotees, tranquit, the consort of (goddess) Gaurī, charming, conferrer of the fruits of penance, the bestower of all prosperity, one that gets pleased quickly, having a smiling countenance, the cause of blessing the devotees, the Lord of the universe, the form of the universe, the root of the universe, the source of the universe, the sustainer of the universe, the foremost in the universe, the cause of the destruction of the universe, the cause of all causes, the rescuer from the ocean of hell, the conferrer of knowledge, the cause of knowledge, the bliss of knowledge, and the eternal.

28b-29. After getting down from the vehicle, the king of demons looked at Lord (Śiva) with Bhadrakālī on the left and Skanda remaining in the front and bowed down with bent head and devotion along with others.

30. Goddess Kālī, Skanda and Śaṅkara blessed him. Nandīśvara and all others (attendants) stood up on beholding the demon.

31. They all conversed with each other then. The king spoke to them and stayed in the presence of (Lord) Śiva.

32. The foremost god got pleased and said to him:

Sri Mahādeva said:

33. (Lord) Brahmā is the creator of the world. That knower of piety is the father of piety. (Sage) Marīci was his son, a pious devotee of (Lord) Viṣṇu.

34. (Sage) Kaśyapa was his son, a patriarch deep-rooted in piety. Dakṣa gave him with pleasure and devotion his thirteen daughters.

35. One among them was the noble Danu, brought up with his prosperity. Danu had forty sons known as *danavas*, effulgent with radiance.

36. One among them was the strong and valiant Vipracitti. The pious Dambha was his son. He was a devotee of (Lord) Viṣṇu and had controlled his senses.

37. He repeated the supreme formula of Lord Kṛṣṇa for a lakh years at Puṣkara having Śukracarya as his preceptor.

38. He then obtained you as his son, much devoted to (Lord) Kṛṣṇa. In the past you were the most pious among the eight cowherds of Kṛṣṇa.

39. You have been born as a Lord of the demons on account of the curse of Rādhā. A devotee of (Lord) Viṣṇu regards every thing from Brahmā to clump as delusion.

40. The devotees of (Lord) Viṣṇu do not accept the identity with Lord Viṣṇu in regard of location, oneness, form and proximity that is offered, except service (to Lord).

41. A devotee of (Lord) Viṣṇu considers the positions of Brahmā or the gods as insignificant. They do not even reckon the positions of Indra (Lord of celestials) or Kubera (Lord of wealth).

42. Why should there be any delusion for you, a devotee of (Lord) Kṛṣṇa, in matter relating to the gods ? O King ! You give away the kingdom to the gods and please me.

43. You remain happily in your kingdom and let the gods remain in their domain. Enough with your enmity to your brothers. All of you were the descendants of (patriarch) Kaśyapa.

44. All sins such as the killing of a brahmin, are not par with a sixteenth part of doing harm to one's kinsman.

45. O Foremost king ! If you are afraid of harm to your prosperity, who indeed would have stable state always ?

46. When there is absolute dissolution, Brahmā disappears. His reappearance is at the will of the Lord.

47. It is certain that the knowledge, intellect and memory of the people are by penance. Brahmā creates by means of wisdom in order.

48. In the *satyayuga*, piety is complete and it is always based on truth. In the *tretāyuga* it is three forth and half in the *dvāparayuga*.

49. It is one-fourth in the *kaliyuga* at the beginning and declines gradually. At the end of the Kali it is only a digit (one-sixteenth) similar to the digit of the moon on the New moon day of the dark fortnight.

50. The Sun does not have the same lustre in the winter as in the summer. It does not have the same (radiance) in the morning or evening as at midday.

51. The Sun rises in time, gradually gains warmth, becomes hot thereafter and sets in time.

52. On a bad day of rain it gets concealed. When it is seized by Rāhu, it becomes shaky and manifests again.

53. The Moon does not have the same lustre always as on the full-moon day. It decreases every day.

54. It gets its strength again on the day after New moon. It is endowed with lustre during the bright fortnight and becomes emaciated with disease in the dark (fortnight).

55. It is emaciated when seized by Rāhu and on a bad day of dense clouds. In course of time the Moon becomes pure and deprived of lustre at the adverse period.

56. Indra deprived of his prosperity in the heavens now would become strong. The earth (would be) in due course

abundant with grains, support of all beings and the abode of all fortune.

57. It is only because of time she is submerged in the water and has disappeared beset with misfortune. The whole universe gets destroyed in course of time and flourish because of time.

58. The movable and immovable things get destroyed in course of time and flourish. It is only for the Supreme soul (Lord) Kṛṣṇa, same condition prevails.

59. Because of him I am the conqueror of death and I repeatedly witness the innumerable dissolutions which could not be perceived.

60. He is of the form of nature and he is known as the first being. He is the soul of all the beings and the supreme person assuming manifold forms.

61. One who repeats the glory of his name would conquer time, death, birth, disease, decrepitude and apprehension.

62. He has made Brahmā as the creator in this world and Viṣṇu as the protector. I have been made as the destroyer. We are resourceful because of him.

63. O King ! After having directed Kālāgnirudra for destruction, I am always engaged in the repetition of the glory of his name.

64. Hence I am the destroyer of death. I am fearless on account of this knowledge. Death goes away afraid of me similar to serpents (seeing) Vainateya (Garuḍa, vehicle of Viṣṇu).

65. O Nārada ! After having stated thus that omniscient Lord of all beings present in the beings paused in that assembly.

66. Having listened to these words, the king praised repeatedly and spoke with modesty to that beautiful Lord.

Śaṅkhacuḍa said:

67. What all has been stated by you is truth and not false. Still listen to me for some truth that I am letting you know.

68. You have uttered thrice now that (there is) great sin in being unfaithful to one's kinsman. Then after confiscating all his wealth, how Bali had been established ?

69. By my valour I have lifted up all wealth from *sutala* (nether world) which the wielder of the mace (Viṣṇu) could not do.

70. Why the gods killed their brother Hiraṇyākṣa? Why were the demons Śumbha and others killed by the gods ?

71. At the time of churning of the ocean in the past, the gods drank the nectar. While they gained all the fruits, we had to experience pain only.

72. This universe is a sporting ground for the Supreme Being, Lord Kṛṣṇa. One gains fortune when he (Lord Kṛṣṇa) bestows on him.

73. The dispute between the gods and demons had always been conditioned by time. Defeat and success for them and for us occur in order.

74. Your interference in our quarrel is fruitless, especially because of the relationship between you, the Supreme Being and myself.

75. The contest with us now brings you great shame, more so when there is fame in victory in battle and infamy in defeat.

76. After listening to the words of Śaṅkhacūḍa, the three-eyed Lord (Śiva) spoke with a smile appropriate and pleasing words to that fierce demon king.

Śrī Mahādeva said:

77. O King ! What shame or infamy in defeat in battle with you born in the family of (Lord) Brahmā ?

78. O King ! At first there was a fight between Viṣṇu, Madhu and Kaiṭabha, then with Hiraṇyakaśipu and then with you.

79. Then again there was the fight with Hiraṇyākṣa and the wielder of the mace (Viṣṇu). I have also fought in the past with (the demons of) the Tripura (the three cities).

80. There had been a wonderful battle with Śumbha and others by omnipotent mother goddess *prakṛti* (Nature).

81. You are the outstanding attendant of (Lord) Kṛṣṇa, the Supreme Being. None of those who were killed (as mentioned above) is equivalent to you.

82. O King ! What shame is there in my fight with you, when I have been deputed by Lord Hari, whom the gods had sought for protection.

83. You return the kingdom to the gods. What use in wasting dialogue ? My confirmed words are that you do not fight with me.

84. O Nārada ! After having spoken thus, Lord Śaṅkara gave a pause. Śaṅkhacūḍa also immediately rose up with his ministers.

CHAPTER NINETEEN

The Fight between Śaṅkhacūḍa and the Gods

Nārāyaṇa said:

1. The valorous demon king after saluting (Lord) Śiva boarded immediately the chariot along with his ministers.

2-4. They became agitated being struck by the missiles of (Lord) Skanda. Drums sounded in the heaven. Shower of flowers fell on Skanda in that terrible battle. After having witnessed the wonderful fight of Skanda that brought ruin in the ranks of the demons just like the destruction at the time of the dissolution, the King mounted his vehicle and made a shower of arrows.

5. The shower of arrows of the King was like a heavy downpour. There was a terrible darkness with occasional rise of flames.

6-7. All the gods, Nandīśvara and others fled away. Kārttikeya alone remained on the battle-field. There was an unbearable and terrible shower of mountains, serpents, stones and trees.

8. The son of Lord Śiva was covered by the shower of arrows of the King, just as the Sun is covered by the moist rain-bearing clouds.

9. (The demon) broke the invincible and terrible bow of Skanda, broke the divine chariot and cut to pieces the steeds of the chariot.

10. With divine weapon he shattered the peacock. Then he threw his spear, radiant like the Sun, and capable of piercing his breast.

11-12. After being unconscious for a while, Kārttikeya regained his consciousness, took hold of another divine bow given to him by (Lord)Viṣṇu in the past, mounted a chariot studded with excellent gems, took possession of weapons of different kinds and resumed his fight.

13. The angry son of (Lord) Śiva split into pieces, with his divine missiles, the serpents, mountains, trees and stones (thrown by the demon).

14-15. Guha (Skanda) obstructed the *āgneya* (missile) (fiery one) with the missile of *varuṇa.* He sportively cut to pieces the chariot and bow of Śaṅkhacūḍa, together with the steeds, the charioteer and the radiant crown and threw the spear, effulgent like meteor on the chest of the demon king.

16. The King became unconscious and regained his consciousness. He mounted another vehicle and wielded the bow quickly.

17. O Nārada ! That one proficient in magical warfare created a network of arrows by magic and covered Guha in the battle-field with a net of arrows.

18. He wielded the spear that never becomes fruitless, that has the radiance of hundred Suns, that is of the form of the flame at the time of the deluge and that which is endowed with the lustre of (Lord) Viṣṇu.

19. He threw it at Kārttikeya swiftly with rage and it fell on the body (of the latter) like a glowing mass of fire.

20. The powerful Kārttikeya fainted (on being struck) by the spear and was taken by Kālī on her lap to the presence of Lord Śiva.

21. Lord Śiva revived him sportively by his mere looks and endowed him with enormous strength. That valorous one stood up.

22. (Lord) Śiva at once despatched his warriors and the gods. They ensued the battle with the King of demons and his forces.

23-28. Mahendra fought with Vṛṣaparvan, Sun with Vipracitti, Moon a great battle with Dambha, Kāla with Kāleśvara, Fire-god with Gokarṇa, Kubera with Kālakeya, Viśvakarman with Maya, Mṛtyu (Death) with Bhayaṅkara, Yama with Saṁhāra, Varuṇa with Kalaviṅka, Samīraṇa with Cañcala, Budha with Dhṛtapuṣṭa, Śaniścara with Raktākṣa, Jayanta with Ratnasāra, Vasus with the hosts of Varcas, the pair of Aśvins with Dīptimat, Nalakūbara with Dhūmra, Dharma with Dhanurdhara, Maṅgala with Maṇḍūkākṣa, Īśāna with Śobhākara, and Manmatha with Piṭhara.

29-30. The (twelve) *ādityas* fought with Ulkāmukha, Dhūmra, Khaḍga, Dhvaja, Kāñcīmukha, Piṇḍa, Dhūmra, Sahanandin, Viṣva and Palāśa. The eleven *rudras* fought with eleven terrible (demons).

31-32. Mahāmārī fought with Ugradaṇḍa and others, Nandīśvara and all others fought with the hosts of *dānavas* in that great battle frightful (like the) deluge. Lord Śambhu (Śiva) stood at the foot of the holy fig tree with (goddess) Kālī and his son.

33-34. O Sage ! Both the armies fought continuously. Śaṅkhacūḍa was seated on a charming gem-studded throne being surrounded by a crore of demons and adorned with gem-studded ornaments. All the warriors of (Lord) Śaṅkara were defeated in the battle.

35. All the wounded gods ran away out of fear. Skanda became enraged and offered protection to the gods.

36. He multiplied the strength of his forces by dint of his lustre. Alone he fought with the hosts of demons.

37-38. He killed hundred *akṣauhiṇī*[1] warriors in the battle. The lotus-eyed (goddess) Kālī filled the skull with the blood of the demons angrily and drank hundred skulls of blood of ten lakhs of elephants and hundred lakhs of horses.

39. O Sage ! She collected the trunks of thousands of the dead and threw sportively on the face (of the demon) and danced in the battle.

40. The demons were wounded by the shower of arrows of Skanda. All those powerful and valorous (warriors) fled away with fright.

41. Vṛṣaparvā, Vipracitti, Dambha and Vikaṅkane fought in order with Skanda.

42. Kālī went to the battle-field and (Lord) Śiva guarded Kārttika. Nandīśvara and other warriors followed her.

43. All the gods, *gandharvas, yakṣa, rākṣasa* and *kinnaras,* manifold royal utensils and hundred crores of commanders[2] (followed her).

44. After going to the battle-field she roared like a lioness. The demons got frightened on hearing the roar of a lioness (made) by the goddess.

45. She repeatedly made a hideous laugh portending evil, drank honey with rejoice, and danced on the battle-field.

46. (Then) Ugradaṁṣṭrā, Ugracaṇḍā, Koṭṭarī and hosts of *yoginīs, ḍākinīs* and gods also drank honey.

47. Beholding Kālī, Śaṅkhacūḍa came quickly to the battle-field. He offered protection to the demons who were frightened.

48. Kālī threw (the missile) *āgneya* resembling the flame of the fire at the time of deluge. The King sportively arrested it with (the missile of) Vāruṇa.

49. She then discharged the most wonderful and potential Vāruṇa. The King of the demons sportively pierced it with the Gāndharva.

50. Then Kālī discharged the Māheśvara, resembling the flame of the fire. The King sportively rendered it ineffective quickly with the *vaiṣṇava.*

51. Then the goddess discharged the *nārāyaṇa* missile preceded by (the recitation of) the formula. Beholding that the King got down from the chariot and fell prostrate.

52-55. That missile rose upwards like the destructive fire at the deluge. Śaṅkhacūḍa also fell down with devotion on the earth like a flagstaff. She then discharged the *brahmā* missile with effort preceded by (the repetition of) the formula. The King prevented the *brahmā* missile. Then the goddess discharged a might celestial weapon preceded by the mystic formula and the King successfully averted it. Then the goddess threw the spear extending to a *yojana* (a distance of eight or nine miles) with effort. The King pierced it into hundred pieces with a network of sharp missiles. The angry goddess then seized the (missile) *pāśupata* preceded by (the repetition of) the formula.

56-58. She was prevented from discharging (the missile) by a voice in the sky (stating that) there is no death for the great King by means of the *pāśupata*. As long as the amulet of (Lord) rests or his neck and chaste remains in the wife of the King, till then he will neither have old age nor death. That is the boon (conferred on him) by (Lord) Brahmā. Having heard that, (goddess) Mahākālī, the chaste woman, did not throw that (missile).

59. The angry one seized one hundred lakh of demons sportively and that frightful one hastened to devour Śaṅkhacūḍa.

60. The demon prevented her by means of sharp divine missiles. Then the goddess threw the sword resembling the sun of the summer.

61. The King of the demons made it into hundred pieces by means of divine weapons. Again the goddess hastened to devour him.

62-63. Then the proficient one, the King of the demons grew up in size and being an adept effectively prevented her. Then the enraged and frightful Kālī quickly broke his chariot with her fist. The chaste lady killed his charioteer. Then she discharged the spear resembling the flame of the destructive fire at the time of the deluge.

64. Śaṅkhacūḍa sportively seized it with his left hand. The goddess stuck him with her fist with great wrath and speed.

65. The demon reeled with pain and fainted for a while. The valorous one regained his consciousness after a while and stood up.

66. He did not engage in physical fight (with her) and he saluted her. He pierced the missiles of the goddess and seized them with his radiant power.

67. On account of derision that she was the mother and that he was a *vaiṣṇava* (a devotee of Lord Viṣṇu)he did not discharge any missile.

68. The goddess seized the demon and repeatedly revolved him and threw him upwards with great speed and anger.

69-70. The glorious Śaṅkhacūḍa fell down with speed. After falling down, he stood up, bowed to Bhadrakālī and mounted a charming gem-studded chariot with delight without any fatigue in that great battle.

71. After having eaten the flesh of the hoots of wounded demons and drank (the blood), Bhadrakālī repaired to (Lord)Śaṅkara.

72. She described the details of the battle in the sequence of its occurrence. After having heard about the death of the demons, (Lord)Śambhu smiled.

73-74. The goddess said : A lakh of foremost demons still remain in the battle-field now and are ready to fight along with the King. The rest I have devoured, O Lord ! I was not able to kill the King of the demons with the *pāśupata* (missile). There was a voice in the heaven: The King cannot be killed by you.

75. The King was a wise man having prowess and valour. He did not discharge a missile at me. But he cut off my weapons.

CHAPTER TWENTY

The Death of Śaṅkhacūḍa

Nārāyaṇa said:

1. O Nārada! After listening to the true nature of events, (Lord) Śiva, proficient in the insight into nature of things, himself went to the battle-field accompanied by the attendants.

2. After beholding (Lord Śiva), Śaṅkhacūḍa got down from the chariot fell down prostrate on the earth like a flagstaff and saluted with great devotion.

3. After having bowed to him, he hurriedly mounted the chariot. (The demon) quickly gathered the forces and held the unwieldy bow.

4. The battle between (Lord) Śiva and the demon lasted for one whole year. O Brahman ! there was no victory or defeat for both of them.

5. The Lord was endowed with the weapons and the demon was well-equipped with the missiles. Śaṅkhacūḍa was mounted on the chariot and the Lord with the banner of bull (Śiva) rode the bull.

6. Only a hundred demons were left behind. Those who were dead on the side of (Lord) Śambhu, were revived by the Lord.

7. Then Viṣṇu, an adept in conjuring, took the form of an old brahmin, came to the battle-field and told the King of the demons.

The old brahmin said:

8-9. O King ! Now give alms to me, a brahmin. You are the bestower of all riches that I may desire. I am an old man and I have not partaken food or water and am anxious to get. I will let you know the truth later. You give me a promise first.

10. The King said yes with a cheerful face on account of illusion. (Viṣṇu) said : I am seeking your armour.

11. After having heard him, the foremost demon gave away the excellent armour. Hari went away after having received the divine armour.

12. He went to Tulasī in the guise of Śaṅkhacūḍa and by illusion impregnated her.

13. Then Lord Śambhu took up Hari's spear resembling the radiance of hundreds of midday suns of the summer in order to strike the demon.

14-17. That spear was presided over by (Lord) Nārāyaṇa in the tip, by Brahmā in the middle, by Śiva at the root and by Kāla (death) at the edge. It was endowed with a row of rays, resembling the flame of the fire at the time of the deluge. It could not be obstructed and restrained. It was not purposeless. It was capable of killing the enemy. In its lustre it was equivalent to the disc. It was capable of destroying all the weapons. It was frightful and could not be wielded by anyone other than Siva and Keśava (Viṣṇu). It was thousand bows in its length and hundred arms in its breadth. This animate one of the form of Brahmā and eternal was not created (by anyone).

18. O Nārada ! He (Śiva) revolved and threw at Śaṅkhacūḍa (that spear) capable of destroying by divine sport the whole universe.

19. The King discarded the bow and assuming the *yogāsana* posture meditated with devotion the lotus feet of Śrīkṛṣṇa.

20. The spear revolved and fell on the demon. It sportively reduced him to ashes together with his chariot.

21. The King (after death) assumed the divine form of a young cowherd with two hands and the flute in the hand and adorned by different gems.

22. The King mounted a vehicle that had come from the Goloka and went away to that place surrounded by a crore cowherds adorned with different gems and exquisite attire.

23. O Sage ! He went and bowed down with his head with devotion the lotus feet of Rādhā and Mādhava in the dance-circle in Vṛndāvana. Beholding Sudāman the two had a pleasant countenance.

24. Becoming overwhelmed with affection they then made him sit on the lap. Then the spear returned quickly to the hand of Śūlin (bearer of spear, Lord Śiva).

25-26. Then (Lord) Sankara despatched with love the heap of bones of the demon to the salt ocean with the spear. The bones of Śaṅkhacūḍa became species of conches.

27. They were of different forms, exquisite and sacred for the worship of the gods. The water (held) in the conch is commended and it gives the gods great satisfaction.

28. It is holy like the water of a sanctified place, except for (the worship of) Śaṅkara. Wherever the word 'conch' is present, (goddess) Lakṣmī is permanently manifest.

29. Whoever bathes with the water (held) in a conch is deemed to have bathed in all the sacred waters. Conch is the abode of (Lord) Hari. Hari is present there, where the conch is.

30. Goddess Lakṣmī (is manifest) therein always and all inauspiciousness are driven away. But goddess Lakṣmī deserts the place with fright and anger to another place when the conches are sounded by women and especially, the *śūdras.*

31. After killing the demon, Lord Śiva also returned to Śivaloka (the abode of Śiva) with delight riding the bull and being surrounded by his attendants.

32. The gods regained their property and were much delighted. The drums sounded in the heaven and the *gandharvas* and *kinnaras* (semi divine beings) sang.

33. There was a continuous shower of flowers on (Lord) Śiva. The gods, foremost sages and others commended him.

CHAPTER TWENTY-ONE

The Legend of Tulasī

Nārada said:

1. You are fit to explain me with which form Lord Nārāyaṇa impregnated Tulasī.

Lord Nārāyaṇa said:

2. For the sake of the gods Lord Nārāyaṇa assumed the form of Śaṅkhacūḍa and cohabited with that beauty (Tulasī).

3. After having received the armour of Śaṅkhacūḍa, Lord Hari assumed his form by magical power and went to the house of Tulasī.

4. He played the drum at the entrance to the house of Tulasī. He announced to that beautiful lady (his arrival) by means of sounds of victory.

5. After having heard that, the pious lady looked through the window at the royal path with great delight.

6. She arranged for auspicious (celebrations) by giving gifts to brahmins. She gave away riches to the bards, mendicants and soothsayers.

7. The Lord got down from the chariot and went to the beautiful and charming abode of the lady built with invaluable gems.

8. Beholding her husband in front of her she was delighted. She washed his feet, bowed down and wept.

9. The passionate one made him seated on an attractive gem-studded throne. She offered him betel made fragrant with camphor etc.

10. (She said:) My birth has been fruitful today. My actions have been regarded today. After beholding the dear lord returned home from the battle (she spoke).

11. She enquired him the details relating to the battles in a sweet voice endowed with a smile, side-glances, passion and horripilation.

Tulasī said:

12. O Lord ! You had the battle with the destroyer of innumerable universe. O Ocean of compassion ! Describe me how you were victorious.

13. After having heard the words of Tulasī, the consort of Kamalā (Lakṣmī) smiled and in the guise of Śaṅkhacūḍa told a lie.

Śrī Hari said:

14. O Dear one ! The battle between us lasted for a year. O Passionate one ! All the demons were destroyed.

15. (Lord) Brahmā himself favoured us both. Brahmā had given the authority to the gods as before.

16. I have returned to my abode and (Lord) Śiva has gone to Śivaloka (world of Śiva). After having spoken thus, the Lord of the world lied down.

17. O Nārada ! The consort of Ramā(Lakṣmī) enjoyed the company of that beauty. That pious lady suspected the bonafides of the person because of the difference in the method of intercourse. Then she asked : Who are you ?

Tulasī said:

18-19a. O Conjurer ! You tell me who you are. You have enjoyed me by conceit. My chastity has been lost. Otherwise I will curse you.

19b-20a. O Brahman ! After hearing the words of Tulasī, (Lord)Hari, being afraid of the curse, assumed sportively his original charming form.

20b-21. The lady beheld in front of her the Lord of gods, eternal one, dark like the fresh rain-bearing clouds, eyes resembling the autumnal lotus, sportive like a crore of god of love, adorned with gem-studded ornaments, smiling gently, having a pleasing countenance, and beautiful with the yellow garment.

22. Beholding him the beautiful lady fainted on account of lust, but regained consciousness on account of divine sport and spoke to him again.

23-27. O Lord ! You are like a stone and do not have any compassion. By fraudulent means and violating righteousness my lord has been killed by you. O Lord ! Because you are like a stone and bereft of compassion, you attain the form of a stone now. There is no doubt that those who glorify you as the ocean of compassion are deluded. Why have you killed a faultless devotee for the sake of others ? Your conduct is bad. Although you are omniscient, you do not know the pain of others. Hence when you make a manifestation, you forget yourself. After having spoken thus that great pious one fell down at the feet of (Lord)Hari and wept bitterly with grief. She lamented repeatedly.

28. Beholding that pitiable one, (Lord) Nārāyaṇa, the consort of Kamalā (Lakṣmī), the embodiment of ocean of compassion, spoke to her in order to make her realise.

The Lord said:

29. O Pious one ! In Bhārata you have done penance for a long time for my sake (i.e. in order to get me). In order to get you, Śaṅkhaçūḍa had performed penance for a long time.

30. That passionate one made you his wife and enjoyed your company as its consequence. Now it is befitting to confer on you the fruits of your penance.

31. You discard your body, assume a divine body and become like Ramā (Lakṣmī) in the dance-circle along with Ramā.

32. Let this (discarded) body assume the form of a river well-known as Gaṇḍakā in Bhārata, sanctified, merit-yielding and meritorious for men.

33. May your tresses of hair become a holy tree, well-known as Tulasī on account of its origin from the hair of Tulasī.

34. O lady with a beautiful face ! Tulasī would be the foremost among the flowers and leaves in the worship of gods in the three worlds.

35. O Beautiful one ! May Tulasī plant be superior among flowers in the heaven, earth, nether world, Vaikuṇṭha and in my presence.

36-37. May the meritorious plants grow in Goloka, on the bank of Virajā (Yamunā), in the dance-circle at Vṛndāvana on earth, in the holy Indian fig tree, in the beautiful *campak* forest, sandal forest, groves of Mādhavī, Ketakī, Kunda, Mallikā and Mālatī in the place of the flowers.

38. All the sanctified places would have their abode in the meritorious and auspicious place at the root of the Tulasī plant.

39. O Fair lady ? Wherever the Tulasī leaves fall, those places, in general, would become the abodes of all gods.

40. Whoever anoints with water together with the Tulasī leaf, such a person would be deemed to have bathed in all the holy waters and initiated in all the sacrifices.

41. Even (Lord) Hari will not have such a satisfaction (by being anointed) with a thousand of pitchers of ambrosia, as the satisfaction derived by men by being given the Tulasī leaf.

42. One would derive the benefit of giving ten thousand cows at once by making a gift of the Tulasī leaf.

43. Whosoever gets the water with the Tulasī leaf at the time of his death, such a person would be freed from all his sins and would attain the world of Viṣṇu.

44. A person, who partakes of the Tulasī water daily with devotion, such a person would be liberated while alive and would gain the merits of bathing in the Ganges.

45. A person who would worship me daily offering Tulasī, would no doubt gain the benefit of (performing) a lakh horse sacrifices.

46. Whoever holds the Tulasī in his hand or has it on his body and discards his life at the sanctified spots, such a person would reach the world of Viṣṇu.

47. One that wears the garland made of Tulasī stem, would attain the fruits of (performing) the horse sacrifice at each step.

48. Holding the Tulasī in the hand, one that does not maintain his vow, would go to hell till the moon and sun shine.

49. One that swears the lie with the Tulasī, would go to (the hell) *kumbhīpāka* till (the period of) the fourteen Indras.

50. One that gets the Tulasī water at the time of his death, would mount the gem-studded vehicle and proceed to Vaikuṇṭha (world of Viṣṇu).

51-52. Those who cut the Tulasī on the full-moon day, new-moon day, twelfth day (of a fortnight), transit of the sun (from one constellation to another), at the time of anointing one's body with oil, without bathing, at noon, at night, at the two twilight periods, at the time of pollution, when impure or wearing the night dress would (be deemed to) cut the head of (Lord) Hari.

53. Such a leaf kept up for three nights would become pure and can be used for ceremonies, vows, making gifts, for installation (of images) and in the worship of gods.

54. The Tulasī leaf that had fallen on the ground or fallen into the water would be pure if offered to (Lord) Viṣṇu and by washing for other purposes.

55. The presiding goddess of the plant would sport secretly with (Lord) Kṛṣṇa daily at the Goloka without any sickness.

56. The presiding goddess of the river, most meritorious in Bhārata, would become the consort of the salt-ocean, a part-manifestation of myself.

57. You yourself would no doubt be most pious in my presence at Vaikuṇṭha on par with Ramā (Lakṣmī) in the dance-circle.

58. On account of your curse, I would preside over the form of a stone in the vicinity of the banks of (river) Gaṇḍakī in Bhārata.

59. The insects known as Vajrakīṭa (possessing strong teeth) would make the marks of my disc inside the stones there.

60. The stone having a mouth, four discs, adorned with the wild flowers, and dark-coloured like the fresh cloud is called Lakṣmīnārāyaṇa.

61. That with a mouth, four discs and having dark complexion like the cloud without being adorned by the garland of wild flowers is known as Lakṣmī Janārdana.

62. Four discs at the mouth and (the mark) of a Goloka (world of cows) without the garland of wild flower is known as Raghunātha.

63. That one very small having two discs and resembling the hue of fresh cloud is known as Dadhivāmana conferring happiness on the householders.

64. That one very small having two discs and adorned with a garland of wild flowers is known as Śrīdhara always bestowing wealth on the householders.

65. It is known as Dāmodara, if it is big, circular and not adorned with garland of wild flowers, having two discs and well-manifest.

66. The mediocre one of circular shape, having two discs, injured by arrows and possessing arrows and quiver is known as Raṇarāma.

67. The mediocre one possessing seven discs, umbrella and quiver is known as *rājarājeśvara* conferring the opulence of kings on men.

68. That one big having the hue of fresh cloud and fourteen discs is known as Ananta conferring the benefits of the fourfold human goals.

69. That one shaped like a disc, with two discs graceful, resembling the hue of a cloud, with a (mark of) cow hoof and medium (in size) is called Madhusūdana.

70. Sudarśana (variety) is known to have one disc, Gadādhara with concealed disc, and Hayagrīva with two discs and resembling the face of a horse.

71. It is known as the Narasiṁha, if it has a wide face, two discs, and hideous, conferring detachment on men at once.

72. That one having a wide face endowed with a garland of wild flowers is known as Lakṣmīnṛsiṁha bestowing happiness on the householders always.

73. That one having two discs at its mouth, growns, even and well manifest, is known as Vāsudeva, conferring the fruits of all desires.

74. The Pradyumna has a subtle disc, hue of fresh cloud and many holes at its mouth conferring happiness on the householders.

75. That one having two discs united, a lotus mark on its back is known as *saṅkarṣaṇa*, conferring happiness on the householders always.

76. Aniruddha is yellow-coloured, circular and quite charming. People declare that it yields happiness for the householders.

77. Wherever the *śālagrāma* stone (exists), Lord Hari is present there. Goddess Lakṣmī resides therein and it is endowed with all the sanctified places.

78. All sins such as the killing of a brahmin, get destroyed by the worship of the *śālagrāma* stone.

79. The stone of the shape of an umbrella bestows a kingdom, circular one great wealth, and the shape of a cart brings about certain death at the tip of the spear.

80. If the face is deformed (it confers) poverty, and brown (coloured one) misfortune. If the disc is joined (it would cause) illness and if broken, death is certain.

81. It is commendable to perform austerities, make gifts, do installation (of deities), perform ceremonies and worship of gods in the presence of the *śālagrāma* stone.

82. One that performs the anointment with the water sanctified by the *śālagrāma*, is deemed to have bathed in all the sacred waters and initiated in all the sacrificial rites.

83. The merits accruing in all gifts, by the circumambulation of the earth, in all the sacrificial rites, in all the sacred spots, in austerities and fasting (would accrue to him).

84. All the sacred spots would desire to be touched by him. There is no doubt that he would be liberated while living and much purified.

85. One would certainly gain the merits of reading the four *vedas* and the practice of penance by worshipping the *śālagrāma* stone.

86-87. A person that drinks daily the water sanctified by the *śālagrāma*, would gain the desired favours from the gods and would be free from birth, death and decrepitude. All the sacred water would desire to have his touch. He gets liberated while alive, much purified and reaches the place of (Lord) Hari finally.

88. Remaining there itself with (Lord) Hari, he witnesses innumerable primary dissolutions as an attendant bereft of the actions of servitude.

89. Sins such as the killing of a brahmin would fled away out of fear on beholding him like the serpents (at the sight of) Vainateya (Kite).

90. The earth gets sanctified at once by the dust from his lotus feet. A lakh men and his ancestors would get liberated on account of his birth.

91. One that gets the water sanctified by the *śālagrāma* at the time of his death, would attain the world of (Lord) Viṣṇu becoming freed from all sins.

92. He gains liberation from renunciation and gets free from enjoying the fruits of action. There is no doubt that he gets absorbed in the feet of (Lord) Viṣṇu.

93. One that utters a lie holding the *śālagrāma* stone, would go to (the hell) *kūrmadaṁṣṭra* (jaws of tortoise) for a period of the life of Brahmā.

94. One that breaks his pledge after touching the *śālagrāma* stone, would go to (the hell) Asipatra (leaves like the edges of sword) for a duration of lakh Manu periods.

95. One that separates the holy basil from the *śālagrāma*, would be separated from his wife in his next birth.

96. One that separates the holy basil from the conch, would be deprived of his wife and would be sick for seven births.

97. One that keeps together the *śālagrāma*, holy basil and the conch at a place and maintains them, would become a great wise man and dear to (Lord) Hari.

98. It would be a painful separation for both, if one has impregnated his beloved only once.

99. You were the beloved of Śaṅkhacūḍa for a period of one *manvantara*. It is painful for you to have separation from Śaṅkha (cūḍa).

100. After having spoken to her thus (Lord) Hari stopped with respect. He (Śaṅkhacūḍa) also discarded his body and assumed a divine form.

101. Just like (goddess) Śrī (Lakṣmī), she (Tulasī) also rested on the chest of (Lord) Hari. The consort of Kamalā (Lakṣmī) repaired to Vaikuṇṭha along with her.

102. O Nārada ! Lakṣmī, Sarasvatī, Gaṅgā and Tulasī all the four became dear to Lord Hari.

103. The river Gaṇḍakī spontaneously produced from his body and the stone as a part manifestation of the Lord on its banks are meritorious for men.

104. O Sage ! The insects make many (marks) on the stones there. Those which fall into the water would certainly resemble the colour of the clouds.

105. Those on the ground should be known as tawny on account of the heat of the Sun. I have thus described you everything. What else would you like to hear ?

CHAPTER TWENTY-TWO

Mode of Worship of Tulasī

Nārada said:

1. Tulasī, the holy and dear one of (Lord) Nārāyaṇa, has become an object of worship. I have not heard the mode of her worship and hymn on her.

2. O Sage ! In the past who worshipped and glorified her first ? Indeed you deserve to tell me how she became an object of your worship.

Sūta said:

3. After listening to the words of Nārada, Garuḍadhvaja (the Lord with the kite in the banner) (Viṣṇu) smiled and began to describe the sacred old legend.

Nārāyaṇa said:

4. After gaining Tulasī, (Lord) Hari enjoyed her company and honoured her on par with Ramā (Lakṣmī).

5. Lakṣmī and Gaṅgā bore this new union. But Sarasvatī did not bear the fortune and honour (bestowed on Tulasī) on account of wrath.

6-7. Once the respectful Sarasvatī assailed her in a quarrel in front of (Lord) Hari. That accomplished lady wise and adept in *yoga* disappeared on account of shame and disgrace. On account of wrath she became invisible everywhere and to (Lord) Hari also.

8. Not finding Tulasī, (Lord) Hari informed Sarasvatī, obtained her permission and repaired to Tulasi grove.

9-10. After reaching there and bathing, he worshipped the chaste Tulasī with holy basil. After meditating her he glorified her with devotion with the mystic formula of ten syllables preceded by germinating letters relating to Lakṣmī, Māyā, Kāma, Vāṇī and Vṛndāvanī concluding with '*na*' (dedication) and Svāhā (oblation).

11-12. O Nārada ! One should worship with the wish-yielding mystic formula *śrīm, hrīm klīm, aim,* oblations to Vṛndāvanī as laid down. O Nārada ! One would accomplish everything by the offer of lamp (lit)with ghee, incense, vermilion, sandal, offerings (of eatables), flowers and presents (to Tulasī).

13. Being pleased with the eulogy of Hari, she manifested from the plant and sought refuge at the lotus feet of the Lord with devotion.

14-15. (Lord) Viṣṇu conferred a boon on her : Be adored throughout the world. I will hold you on my head and chest. All the people, the gods and others would hold you on their heads. After stating thus, the Lord took her and repaired to his abode.

Nārada said:

16. O Fortunate one ! You deserve to describe me the mode of meditation, glorification, and mode of worship of Tulasī.

Nārāyaṇa said:

17. After she had disappeared, Hari went to the Tulasī grove afflicted by separation and worshipped Tulasī and glorified her.

The Lord said:

18. Wherever there are trees of the form of Vṛndā, the wise knew her as Vṛndā, my dear. I worship her.

19. In the past she was in the Vṛndāvana and hence she is known as Vṛndāvanī. I adore that fortunate one.

20. I adore that one worshipped all over the world known as *viśvapūjitā* since she has been worshipped always in innumerable universes.

21. I remember that goddess, the sanctifier of the universe, on account of separation, by whom the universes have always been sanctified.

22. Being grief-stricken I desire to see that pure essence of the flowers, without whom the gods do not get pleased with the (other) collection of flowers.

23. She would be my dear known as Nandinī (causing delight), on account of gaining whom by devotion one would have joy certainly.

24. I seek refuge at that dear one known as Tulasī since she has no one equal to her in the entire world.

25. May she protect my life. She is known as Kṛṣṇajīvanī because she is of the form of the life of Kṛṣṇa, always dear and chaste.

26. After having eulogised thus, the consort of Ramā, stood there and beheld chaste Tulasī, herself bowing at his lotus feet.

27. Beholding that respectful dear one weeping, he held her quickly on his chest with affection.

28. After obtaining the permission from Bhāratī (Sarasvatī), (Lord) Hari went to his abode, and at once pleased her (Tulasī) along with Bhāratī.

29. (Lord) Viṣṇu conferred on her the boon to be worshipped in the universe, to be held by all on the head, worshipped and honoured by him.

30. The goddess was pleased with the boon (conferred) by Viṣṇu. Sarasvatī embraced her and made her seated in her presence.

31-32. O Nārada ! Lakṣmī and Gaṅgā embraced her with a smile and took that chaste one, Vṛndā, Vṛndāvanī, Viśvapāvani, Viśvapūjitā, Puṣpasārā Nandinī and Tulasī into the abode with modesty.

33. One that repeats these eight names and the hymn containing these eight names after worshipping her would obtain the benefits of the horse sacrifice.

34. Tulasī had her auspicious birth on the full moon day in Kārttika (October-November). (Lord) Hari has laid down her worship long ago.

35. One that worships the Viśvapāvanī then with devotion, would become free from all sins and reach the world of Viṣṇu.

36. One that offers the holy basil to (Lord) Viṣṇu in Kārttika, would certainly get the benefit of offering a gift of ten thousand cows.

37-38. A childless one would get a child, one without a wife would get a wife, people bereft of relatives would get kinsmen by mere remembrance of this hymn. A sick person would become free from disease. The fetters of a bonded one would go. A person having fear will get rid of his fear. A sinner will get rid of his sins.

39. I have described you thus the hymn (on Tulasī). Listen to me now for the mode of meditation and worship. You alone know the *veda* pertaining to the Kaṇva recension.

40. One should worship her with devotion without invoking her, offering the sixteen services and meditation that destroys sins.

41. Tulasī, the essence of flowers, chaste, adorable and charming, resembles the flame of the glowing fire for burning the fuel of entire sins.

42. O Sage ! There was no flower equal to her, nor among the goddesses. Tulasī has been declared as the holiest among all.

43. She should be held on the head by all. The covetable one, the sanctifier of the universe, liberated while alive, conferrer of liberation and the conferrer of devotion to (Lord) Hari on the worshippers should be adored.

44. After contemplating, worshipping and eulogising her thus, the wise man should bow to her. I have described you the episode of Tulasī. What else you desire to hear from me?

CHAPTER TWENTY-THREE

The Legend of Sāvitrī

Nārada said:

1. O Lord ! I have heard the nectar like legend of Tulasī. You may describe me the legend of Sāvitrī.

2. I have already heard about her origin from the scriptures. By whom was she at first worshipped and then by others ?

Nārāyaṇa said:

3. O Sage ! That one, from whom scriptures originated, was at first worshipped by (Lord) Brahmā, secondly by the hosts of gods and then by the hosts of learned men.

4. Then Aśvapati worshipped her first in Bhārata. Then (the people belonging to) the four castes worshipped her.

Nārada said:

5. O Brahman ! Who was that Aśvapati and why did he adore her ? You are fit to explain me why Sāvitrī is adored by all.

Nārāyaṇa said:

6. O Sage ! Aśvapati was a great king in the country of Madra. He was the shatterer of the strength of the enemies and dispeller of the miseries of friends.

7. He had the pious Mālatī as his great queen just like Lakṣmī for Viṣṇu (the wielder of the mace).

8. O Nārada ! On the advice of (the sage) Vasiṣṭha that most pious queen adored Sāvitrī with devotion.

9. The queen did not get any instruction from her (Sāvitrī) and did not behold her manifest. She returned home with broken heart oppressed by grief.

10. Finding her grief-stricken, the king consoled her and then repaired to Puṣkara in order to do penance on Sāvitrī with devotion.

11. With self-control he performed penance for hundred years there itself. He did not get a vision of Sāvitrī. But there was an instruction.

12. O Nārada ! The foremost king heard the incorporeal voice from the sky directing him to repeat the *gāyatrī* (*mantra*) ten lakhs times.

13. In the meanwhile (the sage) Parāśara arrived there. The king prostrated before him and the sage told the king.

Parāśara said:

14. The repetition of the *gāyatri* once would destroy the sin committed in a day. The repetition by men ten times (would remove) the sin incurred during the day and night.

15. The repetition for hundred times (would remove) thus the sin acquired in a month. Similarly the repetition for one thousand times (would remove) the sin accumulated in a year.

16. (Repetition) a lakh (times) (would remove) the sin acquired in one's life time, and ten lakh (times) that (acquired) in three births. The sins acquired in all births would be destroyed by (repetition) hundred lakh (times).

17a. The repetition for ten times more than that would make the brahmins get liberation (from birth and death).

17b-20a. With the hands raised above the head like the hood of a serpent, the head bent, remaining firm and facing the east, a twice-born has to mutter (the syllables). The procedure for the repetition is to begin from the middle of the ring finger and proceed left-wards upto the root of the first finger on the hand (to keep count). O King ! After making a garland from the seeds of white lotuses and purified crystals, one has to mutter (the *mantra*) in a sanctified place or temple of gods.

20b-21. After having placed the garland on seven leaves of holy fig tree with self-control, it should be anointed with *gorocana* (the pigment obtained from the cow) and bathed with (the repetition of) the *gāyatrī* by the wise (votary). It should be sanctified with the (repetition of) *gāyatrī* hundred times preceded by the procedure laid down.

22-23. Otherwise, the garland would be sanctified by being bathed in *pancagavya*.[1] It becomes sanctified well by being bathed with the water of the Ganges. O Saintly King ! You repeat thus ten lakh times. You will behold Sāvitrī after the sins of three births are destroyed.

24. You will perform it everyday during the three twilight (periods) at midday, in the evening and in the morning always (remaining) pure.

25. One that is bereft of the twilight worship daily becomes unfit for (performing) all religious rites. For such a person the rite performed during the day will not fetch him the (desired) fruit.

26. One that does not worship the east or the west (i.e. does not offer the twilight worship), should be expelled from all the rites of a twice-born like a *śūdra* (man of the fourth order).

27. A brahmin performing the three twilight worship during his life period is deemed always to be on par with the Sun in his lustre and penance.

28. The earth gets pure immediately by the dust from his lotus feet. The twice-born that is purified by the twilight (worship) becomes liberated while alive and lustrous.

29. The sacred places become sanctified by the mere touch of such a person. Then the sins would fied away like the serpents from the kite.

30. The gods do not accept the worship and the manes, the balls of rice, willingly from a twice-born bereft of the three twilight (worships).

31. A twice-born bereft of the sacred formula of (Lord) Viṣṇu, the three twilight (worships) and the (fasting on) eleventh day (of a lunar fortnight) would be like a serpent without the poison.

32. A brahmin that does not partake of the offerings made to (Lord) Hari, a washerman, a carrier of bull, one that eats the food from a *śūdra* is like a serpent without poison.

33. A brahmin that burns the corpse of a *śūdra*, one that is the husband of a *śūdra* woman, one that cooks food for the *śudras* are deemed to be like a serpent without poison.

34. A brahmin that accepts a gift from *śūdras,* one that officiates a rite performed by a *śūdra,* one that earns his livelihood by the sword or ink are considered like a serpent without poison.

35. A brahmin that partakes food from a coward (not valorous), or from a woman after her menses, or one that caters to satisfy the lust of a person, one that lives on usury are deemed as a serpent without poison.

36. O King ! A brahmin that sells the girl, the name of (Lord) Hari, and knowledge is like a serpent without poison.

37. A twice-born partaking food at Sunrise, a twice born eating fish, a person devoid of worship of images (of gods) is like a serpent bereft of poison.

38. That foremost sage after having described him all the modes of worship, explained him the most desired method of contemplation on Sāvitrī.

39. After having imparted everything to the king the sage went away to his abode. The king worshipped Sāvitrī, beheld her and obtained the boon.

Nārada said:

40. How is Sāvitrī contemplated ? What is the mode of her worship? After imparting which hymn and mystic formula, (sage) Parāśara went away ?

41. By what mode of worship the king adored the mother of the *vedas,* and describe me what favour the king Aśvapati obtained from her ?

Nārāyaṇa said:

42. After having controlled his senses on the thirteenth day of a dark fortnight in Jyeṣṭha (May-June) at an auspicious period, the votary should begin the austerity with devotion on the fourteenth day.

43-44a. The austerity (performed) for fourteen years with fourteen fruits, fourteen kinds of offerings, flowers, incense and other things, cloth, sacred thread and eatables as prescribed.

44b-45. After having set up firmly the auspicious pitcher endowed with fruits and vegetables, and after having, adored (Lords) Gaṇeśa, Sun, Fire, Viṣṇu, Śiva, Śivā (consort of Śiva), O Sage ! One should adore the favourite deity invoked in the pitcher.

46. Listen to me for the mode of contemplation on Sāvitrī laid down in the *mādhyandina* (text) as well as the hymn, mode of worship, and the mystic formula yielding all the desires.

47-50. I adore the mother of the *vedas*, resembling the hue of heated gold, glowing with the lustre of brahman, possessing the radiance of one thousand midday suns of the summer, having a gently smiling face, adorned with gem-studded ornaments, wearing the upper garment as pure as fire, eager to bless the devotees, conferrer of happiness, bestower of beatitude, tranquil, the pause of Brahmā, an embodiment of all fortunes, conferrer of all fortunes, presiding deity of the *vedas*, an embodiment of the science of scriptures and an embodiment of mystic seed of the scriptures.

51. After having contemplated thus and after having placed the flower on one's own head, the votary should contemplate the goddess and invoke her with devotion in the pitcher.

52. After having offered the sixteen services preceded by (the repetition of) the formula mentioned in the *vedas*, and after worship and extollation as laid down the votary should bow to the goddess.

53-55. One should offer the sixteen courtesies—seat, water for washing the feet, water for rinsing the mouth, water for bathing, unguent (for besmearing), incense, lamp, eatables, betel, cold water, dress, ornament, garland, perfume, water for sipping and a lovely bed-stead made of excellent wood or gold. I have offered daily a resting place for the deity conferring merits.

56. I have offered water from a sacred place for washing the feet that yields merits and gives great pleasure. I have offered with devotion that has been a pure accessory of the worship.

57. I have offered with devotion the holy water for rinsing containing the *dūrvā* (a kind of grass), flower and unbroken rice sprinkled with water from a conch and meritorious.

58. I have offered with devotion the fragrant myrabolan oil that is the cause of a beautiful body, for bathing. Kindly accept it.

59. I have offered you the fragrant (sandal), that has originated from the Malaya hill (Kerala) and which enhances the lustre of the body and brings happiness.

60. I have offered with devotion the incense that is originated from fragrant material, meritorious, delighting and yielding divine fragrance. Kindly accept.

61. That which is the cause of brightness and makes visible the objects ought to be seen and that which is the seed for destroying darkness, that I have offered you.

62. Kindly accept the sweet offering that pleases, nourishes, satisfies, destroys hunger and yields merit.

63. I have offered you the excellent betels that has been rendered charming and fragrant with camphor etc., that delights and nourishes.

64. Kindly accept the cool and fragrant water that destroys thirst and which constitutes the life of the world and livelihood.

65. Kindly accept the apparel made of cotton and made by insect that is of the form of the lustre of the body and that which enhances the grace of the assembly.

66. Kindly accept the ornament that is made of gold etc., endowed with fortune, yielding fortune always, conferring happiness and merit.

67. Kindly accept the garland made of different flowers and endowed with varied lustre that gives pleasure and merit.

68. Kindly accept the perfume, an embodiment of all auspiciousness, conferrer of all auspiciousness, outstanding, bestower of merit and much fragrant.

69. Kindly accept the delightful water for sipping offered by me. It is pure, yields purity and satisfies the pure ones.

70. Kindly accept the excellent bedstead, made of exquisite gems and endowed with flowers and sandal and that which bestows happiness and merit.

71. Kindly accept the fruits produced from various trees and having different shapes which are embodiments of the fruits and conferrer of benefits.

72. Kindly accept the vermilion that is outstanding, charming, enhancing the lustre of the forehead and an ornament for the ornaments.

73. Kindly accept the sacred thread endowed with pure knots and made of meritorious threads and sanctified with the mystic formula of the *vedas.*

74. A wiseman should offer these objects with the basic formula and repeat the hymn. Then after prostration, the votary should offer the fees to a brahmin.

75. (The word) Sāvitrī ending in its fourth case, ending with the spouse of Fire(*svāhā*) (oblation) preceded by the mystic seed letters of Lakṣmī, Māyā and Kāma, is known to the eight-syllabled basic formula.

76. *Śrīm, hrīm, klīm,* oblations to Sāvitrī. I will impart you the hymn described in the *mādhyandina* text that confers all the desired fruits and which is an embodiment of the life of a brahmin.

77. O Nārada ! Sāvitrī was gifted to Brahmā by Kṛṣṇa in the past at Goloka. She did not go with him to the world of Brahmā.

78. As directed by Kṛṣṇa, Brahmā worshipped the mother of the *vedas* with devotion. Becoming extremely pleased, that chaste one liked Brahmā.

Brahmā said:

79. O Beautiful one ! An embodiment of Nārāyaṇa ! Nārāyaṇi ! The Eternal one ! Originated from Nārāyaṇa ! Be gracious.

80. O Beautiful one ! An embodiment of lustre! The Supreme one ! An embodiment of supreme bliss ! One of the form of the *jāti* of the twice-born ! Be gracious.

81. O Beautiful one ! Eternal one ! Fond of permanence! O Goddess an embodiment of eternal bliss ! You be gracious in the form of all auspicious things.

82. O Fair one ! An embodiment of all the brahmins ! The essence of the mystic formula ! The Foremost one ! Conferrer of happiness ! Bestower of beatitude ! O Goddess! Be gracious.

83. O Fair one ! O Goddess ! Conferrer of the lustre of brahman ! One resembling the flame of the glowing fire for consuming the fuel, the sins of the brahmins ! Be gracious.

84. Whatever sin a twice-born does physically, mentally or verbally, that would become an ash by your mere remembrance.

85. After having extolled thus, the creator of the world stood there in the assembly. Sāvitrī went away to Brahmaloka along with Brahmā.

86. After having glorified (the goddess) with this excellent hymn, King Aśvapati beheld (goddess) Sāvitrī and gained the desired boon.

87. One that reads this excellent hymn in the three twilight periods would certainly reap the fruits of repeating the four *vedas.*

CHAPTER TWENTY-FOUR

The Birth of Sāvitrī and the Story of Satyavān

Nārāyaṇa said:

1. After having extolled and worshipped her as laid down, (King) Aśvapati beheld there the goddess, luminous like thousand suns.

2. Like a mother to her son she spoke to the king with a gracious smile lighting the quarters with her radiance.

Sāvitrī said:

3. O Great King ! I know what you have in your mind. I will definitely confer on you what you and your wife desire.

4. Your pious spouse desires to have a daughter and you want to have a son. It will duly take place.

5. After having uttered thus that great goddess went away to Brahmaloka. The king went back to his abode. He had a daughter at first.

6. On account of the worship of the king, Kamalā, a digit of Sāvitrī was born. King Aśvapati named her as Sāvitrī.

7. She grew up everyday and in course of time was endowed with beautiful form and maidenhood like the digits of the waxing moon.

8. Sāvitrī chose (to marry) Satyavān, the son of Dyumatsena, endowed with all (good) qualities.

9. The King gave her away to him adorning her with gems and ornaments. He also repaired to his abode with delight along with her.

10. After the lapse of one year, Satyavān, the truthful and valorous one, went away to the forest with delight at the behest of his father for the sake of (collecting) fruits and wood.

11. On account of destiny Sāvitrī accompanied him. On account of fate Satyavān fell down from the tree and died.

12. O Sage ! Yama tied up his sentient soul of the size of a thumb and started moving. The chaste lady followed him.

13. Beholding the beautiful (lady) following him, Yama, the Lord of Saṁyaminī, the foremost among the virtuous, spoke sweet words to that pious lady.

Yama said:

14. O Sāvitrī ! Where do you go with your mortal frame ? If you desire to accompany your husband, then you (should) discard your body.

15. A mortal is not capable of going to Yamaloka (world of Yama) with the body composed of the five elements. The perishable one is always perishable.

16. O Chaste one ! The life period of your husband has ended in Bhārata. In order to reap the fruits of his action, Satyavān is proceeding to my place.

17. A being is born on account of one's action and has the end on account of action. Happiness, misery, fear and grief are the resultants of action.

18. It is only by his own action, Indra would become Jīva, the son of Brahmā. It is only by his own action, he would become the attendant on Hari and devoid of birth and death.

19. He would attain all perfections and firm position as immortal on account of his own action. He would attain the states of *sālokya* (remaining in the same place) etc., of Viṣṇu on account of his own action.

20. A man would become a brahmin, a liberated one, a celestial, a mortal or a king on account of action.

21. The position as a foremost sage, an ascetic, a *kṣatriya* and a *vaiśya* are resultants of one's own action.

22. One attains the states of a *śūdra* and the last order by means of one's own action.

23. There is no doubt that one attains the state of barbarian by one's own action. One gets the states of being immobile or mobile on account of one's own action.

24. One (gains) the states of a mountain, tree, animal and bird on account of one's action.

25. One becomes a small creature or an insect, or a serpent or a *gandharva* as a resultant of his own action.

26. One attains the states of a *rākṣasa, kinnara, yakṣa* and a pumpkin (false appearance) on account of one's own action.

27. One gains the states of *preta* (corpse), *vetāla, bhūta, piśāca* and *ḍakinī* (different kinds of spirits) by means of one's own deeds.

28. The states of a *daitya, dānava* and *asura* (different evil forces) (are resultants) of one's action. One is virtuous or sinful on account of his own action.

29. One becomes, beautiful and robust or extremely sick due to one's own action. One becomes blind, one eyed and censured on account of one's deeds.

30. The beings go to hell or heaven because of their own deeds. (The beings) go to the Śakraloka (world of Indra) or the world of Sun on account of their own actions.

31. (The beings) go to the worlds of Moon, or Fire, or Vāyu, or Varuṇa as a result of their own actions.

32. In the same manner a man goes to the worlds of Kubera or Dhruva or Śiva on account of his own deeds.

33. One attains the worlds of asterism or *satya, jana, tapa* and *mahas* [1] on account of one's action.

34. One goes to the nether world or the world of Brahmā by means of his own action. One is born in the sacred Bhārata, that confers all the desired favours on account of one's own action.

35. One goes to the Vaikuṇṭha or Goloka, a region free from disease, as a resultant of one's action. One becomes long-lived or short lived because of one's own deeds.

36. One lives for crore *kalpa* periods or short lived on account of one's own actions. One dies soon after birth or dies in the womb on account of one's own deeds.

37. O Fair One ! I have thus described you the entire principle. Your husband has died on account of his own deed. Hence you go back home as it is congenial to you.

CHAPTER TWENTY-FIVE

The Dialogue between Sāvitrī and Yama

Śrī Nārāyaṇa said:

1. After listening to the words of Yama, the chaste and self-controlled Sāvitrī extolled him with great devotion and spoke.

Sāvitrī said:

2. O Lord of piety ! What are the auspicious and inauspicious acts of men ? By what means the pious men destroy their deeds ?

3. Who is the seed of actions and who is the bestower of the fruits of actions ? What is action and what is its genesis ?

4. Who enjoys the fruits of action and who does not get stained by it ? Who is corporeal ? What is the body ? Who is the agent of the action ?

5. What is knowledge, mind and intellect ? What is life of man? What are the organs and their characteristics? Who are the presiding deities ?

6. Who is the enjoyer (of the fruits of actions)? Who causes one to enjoy? What is it that being enjoyed ? What is the redemption from-it? Who is the soul ? Who is the Supreme Soul? You are fit to explain these.

Yama said:

7. The acts laid down in the scriptures are extremely auspicious. The acts opposed to the scriptures are inauspicious.

8. Service rendered to (Lord) Viṣṇu without any motive and resolve is the means of getting rid of action for pious men. It is the only means of gaining devotion to (Lord) Hari.

9. It is known from the scriptures that one who is a devotee of Hari is liberated. (He becomes) free from birth, death, decrepitude, sickness and fear.

10. O Pious one ! It has been told in the scriptures that liberation is of two kinds. It has been agreed by all. It confers on men liberation and devotion to (Lord) Hari.

11. The *vaiṣṇavas* (devotees of Lord Viṣṇu) desire for liberation of the nature of devotion to (Lord) Hari. The other pious men desire to get redemption of the form of liberation (from cycles of birth).

12. Lord Śrī Kṛṣṇa is of the form of action and of the form of the seeds of action yielding always the appropriate fruits. He is above primordial nature.

13. He is also of the form of its cause. O Chaste one ! The acts are due to him. Sentient beings ripe the fruit of their actions. The soul does not get stained by it.

14. The individual soul that animates the body is the reflection of the Supreme soul. The body composed of the five elements is indeed perishable.

15. The earth, wind, ether, water and lustre are the elements which are the primary creations in the process of creation by (Lord) Hari.

16. The animate being is the doer and enjoyer and the Supreme Being is always that makes one to act. Enjoyment is another form of one's fortune. Liberation is a cessation of that.

17. Knowledge that is the basis for the distinction of good and bad is of various kinds. It has been declared as the basis for the distinction of objects and their classifications.

18. (It has been stated) in the scriptures that intellect is of the form of discrimination that ignites knowledge. The vital breaths are modifications of wind and are of the forms of strength for animate beings.

19-20. Mind is the foremost among the organs and is a collective force of the organ.[1] It cannot be determined. It is invisible and is known to be a form of knowledge. The eyes, ears, nose, skin and tongue are the organs.

21. It constitutes the limbs of the animate being and it directs one to do things. It is of the form of a foe or friend. It yields always pleasure and pain.

22. Sun, wind, earth and Vāṇī (Sarasvatī) and others are known to be gods. The animate being is stated to be sustaining the life, breath and the body.

23. The Supreme soul is the Supreme Brahman. He is without attributes. He is above the primordial nature. Lord Śrī Kṛṣṇa himself is the cause of causes.

24. Thus as requested by you I have described you everything as told in the scriptural texts. It is of the form of knowledge for learned men. O Child ! You go back comfortably.

Sāvitrī said:

25. Where shall I go leaving my husband ? Or (where shall I go leaving) you, the wise one, the ocean of wisdom ? You are fit to explain me whatever I ask.

26. O Yama ! What acts lead one to different kinds of births ? O Father ! What acts lead one to heaven and what is hell ?

27. By what actions one gets liberation and by what actions one gets devotion to (Lord) Hari ? By what actions one gets disease and by what actions one becomes free from disease ?

28. How is one long-lived or short-lived ? How does one exprerience grief and how does one get happy?

29. How does one become disabled, one-eyed, deaf, blind, miserly and infatuated ?

30. How does one become mad, extremely greedy, or a murderer ? How does one attain perfection and the four (states) such as *sālokya* (same world as god)?

31. How does one get the state of a brahmin or an ascetic? By what acts one attains heaven, pleasure etc. or Vaikuṇṭha (the world of Viṣṇu)?

32. O Brahman how does one get the Goloka, the most outstanding one, free from disease ? How many are the hells and what are their names ?

33. Who reaches which hell and how long he remains there ? What disease is the result of which acts of the sinners?

34. You deserve to explain me what all I have asked.

CHAPTER TWENTY-SIX

The Fruits of the Actions

Nārāyaṇa said:

1. Hearing the words of Sāvitrī, Yama was surprised. He smiled and began describing the fruits of former actions of the beings.

Yama said:

2. O Child ! You are now a child aged twelve years. But you possess more wisdom than those of learned ascetics and old wise men.

3. O Auspicious one ! You have been gained by the king in the past by means of penance as a part of Sāvitrī by the favour of Sāvitrī.

4-9. I confer on you the boon to be the dear one of Satyavān, endowed with fortune, like Śrī on the lap of the consort of Śrī (Viṣṇu), Bhavānī on the lap of Bhava, Rādhā on the lap of Śrīkṛṣṇa, Sāvitrī on the chest of Brahmā, Mūrti on the lap of Dharma, Śatarūpā in respect of Manu, Devahūti in respect of Kardama, Arundhati for Vasiṣṭha, Aditi for Kaśyapa, Ahalyā for Gautama, Śacī for Mahendra, Rohiṇī for Candra (Moon), Rati for Kāmadeva (God of love), Svāhā for Fire-god, Svadhā for the manes, Samjñā for the Sun, Varuṇānī for Varuṇa, Dakṣiṇā (fee) for Sacrifice, the Earth for the Boar (form assumed by Viṣṇu) and Devasenā for Kārttika. O Most fortunate one ! You seek any other favour. I shall certainly grant you everything.

Sāvitrī said:

10. O Blessed one ! I desire this favour from you that I may have hundred sons through Satyavān.

11. (May) my father beget hundred sons and my father-in-law (regain) his eyesight and kingdom. This is the favour desired by me.

12. O Lord of the world ! After the lapse of lakh years, may I go to the abode of Hari along with Satyavān.

13. I am eager to listen to the fruits of the former actions of beings which are the seeds for the expansion of the universe. You are fit to explain me.

Yama said:

14. Most pious one ! All your desires will be fulfilled. Listen to me. I shall describe you the fruits of former actions of beings.

15. In the entire sacred land of Bhārata, one is born according to the good and bad acts. People do not enjoy elsewhere.

16. The celestials, progeny of Diti, progeny of *danu*, *gandharvas*, *rākṣasa*, men and others are all subjects to acts. But all do not have the same pattern of life.

17. Beings of distinct birth gain their birth through wombs. Especially men attain their birth through all wombs.

18. One enjoys the fruits of good or bad actions done in the previous (life). People attain heaven etc., by doing good deeds.

19-20. People wander in hell etc., by performing bad acts. When the (fruits of) acts get exhausted, one gets liberation. It is of two types—Emancipation and service to (Lord) Kṛṣṇa the Supreme soul. One gets diseases on account of evil deeds and free from diseases on account of good deeds.

21. It is certain that one is long lived or short-lived, happy or unhappy (on account of one's deeds). One becomes blind or disabled etc., owing to his evil deed.

22-23. One gains perfection etc., because of his outstanding acts. O Beautiful girl ! I have described you in general. Listen to me for particular things very difficult to find in the *purāṇas* or even in the scriptures and difficult to be enjoyed.

24-27. It is very difficult to be born as a man among all species of beings in Bhārata. A brahmin is outstanding among all species. He is commended in all acts. Then a devotee of (Lord) Viṣṇu and a twice born are more superior in Bhārata. A *vaiṣṇava* (devotee of Viṣṇu) is of two types— desireless and with desire. One with desire is the principal one and the desireless is a devotee. One with desire enjoys the fruits of the deeds and the desireless one is free from trouble. After discarding the body he attains the place of Viṣṇu, free from sickness. The desireless persons are not reborn.

28. Those devotees who worship Lord Kṛṣṇa, the Supreme soul, the suzerain one having two arms, attains Goloka assuming divine form.

29. Those devotees who worship Lord Nārāyaṇa, the four-armed one, reach Vaikuṇṭha assuming divine form.

30. The devotees of Viṣṇu possessing desire attain Vaikuṇṭha and return to Bhārata and are born as twice-borns.

31. In course of time they certainly become desireless. (The Lord) confers on them devotion and stainless intellect.

32. Among all those born, those other than a brahmin and a *vaiṣṇava*, are with desire. Those who are devoid of devotion to (Lord) Viṣṇu, do not have stainless intellect.

33. The twice-borns who visit the sacred places and are bent on doing penance attain the world of Brahmā and are reborn in Bhārata.

34. The brahmins practising their own duties and are devoted to Sun in Bhārata attain the world of Sun and are reborn in Bhārata.

35. The brahmin practising their own duties and are devoted to Lord Śiva, Śakti (goddess), and Gaṇapati attain the world of Śiva and are reborn in Bhārata.

36. The brahmins devoted to other gods and are pursuing their duties attain the world of Indra and are reborn in Bhārata.

37. The twice-borns devoted to (Lord) Hari, practising their own duties without desire, they also attain the world of Hari in due course on account of the strength of (their) devotion.

38. The brahmins not practising their own duties and are always serving the other gods, having fallen from good conduct and ignorant certainly go to hell.

39. Thus the four castes practising their own duties would be enjoying the fruits of their good deeds.

40. Those who do not practise their own duties would certainly go to hell. They would be born in Bhārata and would enjoy the fruits of their deeds.

41. Those brahmins who practise their own duties would give their daughter to a brahmin practising his duty. They would attain the world of Moon.

42. O Pious lady ! They remain their during the periods of fourteen Indras. It is stated that there would be two-fold merits by making a gift of an adorned (girl).

43. The devotees of Viṣṇu possessing desire attain that world, but not those not having desire. They attain the world of Viṣṇu devoid of the fruits.

44-45. Those who bestow on brahmins cow, silver, wife, clothes, food and water, they would attain that world. They remain in that world for a period of a *manvantara.* Those men stay there for a long period.

46-47. Those who give a pure brahmin gold, cow and copper etc., would attain the wide world of Sun and live there ten thousand years free from disease.

48-49. One who makes a gift of land and large quantity of grain to brahmins, would attain the world of Viṣṇu and the charming *śvetadvīpa.* He would stay there so long as the Moon and Sun (last). Being a meritorious person he would stay in that extensive (region) for a long (period).

50-52. Those who give with devotion a house to a brahmin, they would go to the celestial region and stay there for a long time. If the gift has been made on an auspicious day, they would remain there as many years as the particles of dust in the house. O Chaste lady! Such men would live in that extensive region for a long period. A person who consecrates an abode for any god would attain that world (and stay) as many years as the particles of dust (in the abode).

53. (Lord) Brahmā has stated that one would get four-fold merits by making a gift of a big mansion, hundred-fold fruits by making a pious act and eight-fold benefits by a distinguished act.

54. O Chaste one ! One who consecrates a tank for all the beings in Bhārata, would reach the Jñaloka and stay there for ten thousand years.

55-56. A man would get hundred-fold merit by (dedicating) a tank. Similarly a gift of a bridge yields certainly the same benefit as that of a tank as the measure of length of four thousand bows. It is lesser or the same (benefit) in (giving a gift of) a table land or a well.

57. (Giving a gift) of a girl is equal to that of (giving) ten wells if it is made to a worthy person. It yields two-fold benefits if (the girl) is adorned.

58. The same fruits (would accrue) by removal of mud from the tank. Removal of mud from a well confers the same benefit as that of (giving) a well.

59. One who grows a holy fig-tree and dedicates, it would go to the Tapoloka and live there for ten thousand years.

60. O Sāvitri ! One who dedicates a flower garden for the sake of all, would certainly stay in the world of Dhruva for ten thousand years.

61. O Chaste lady ! One who dedicates a vehicle for (Lord) Viṣṇu in Bhārata would stay in the world of Viṣṇu for the period of Manu.

62. If it is large and endowed with painting, fruits will be four-fold. Making a gift of a palanquin would fetch half the benefit of that of a chariot.

63. Whoever dedicates with devotion, a chamber of swing would attain the world of Viṣṇu and stay there for a period of Manu.

64. O Chaste lady ! One who gifts a royal path endowed with mansions would enjoy the stay in the world of Indra for ten thousand years.

65. Gift made to brahmins and gods would confer the same benefit. That which is given by one comes back to him. That which is not given does not return.

66. After having enjoyed the pleasures such as the heaven etc., one returns to Bhārata. One is born in the family of a brahmin and in order in the noble family etc.

67. A brahmin in Bhārata after having enjoyed the supreme heaven etc., is again born as a brahmin and not as a *kṣatriya* etc.

68. It is known from the scriptures that a *kṣatriya* or a *vaiśya* does not attain the state of a brahmin even after hundreds of crores of *kalpas* and by (doing) penance.

69. Brahmins devoid of their own duties attain different births and are again born as brahmins after having enjoyed the fruits of their deeds.

70. Deeds do not get destroyed even after hundreds of crores of *kalpas* without being enjoyed. They are certainly to be enjoyed even after hundred crores of *kalpas.*

71. Good or bad deed done has certainly to be enjoyed. One becomes pure at a sacred place after several births.

72. I have described you all matters. What else would you like to listen ?

CHAPTER TWENTY-SEVEN

Fruits of Good Actions

Sāvitrī said:

1. You are fit to explain me by what deeds men attain heaven and become meritorious.

Yama said:

2. Whoever gives food to a brahmin in Bhārata would enjoy stay in the world of Indra as many years as the quantity of food.

3. Neither there was, nor there will be a greater gift than good. Neither there is any test for a deserving person, nor any kind of regulation of time.

4. If one offers a seat to the gods or the brahmins, he would certainly enjoy stay in the world of Fire for ten thousand years.

5. Whoever gives an excellent milch-cow to a brahmin, would enjoy stay in Vaikuṇṭha as many years as the hair (on its body).

6. (If the gift is made) on an auspicious day, (it would have) four-fold benefits, and (if done) at an ass three times, and as a jackal three times and would surely become pure thereafter a sacred place, (it would confer) hundred-fold benefits. A gift made at a sacred spot dedicated to (Lord) Nārāyaṇa would confer crore times benefits.

7. Whoever gives a cow with devotion to a brahmin in Bhārata, would enjoy stay in the world of Moon for ten thousand years.

8. Whoever gives as a gift a cow and a calf to a brahmin, would enjoy stay in Vaikuṇṭha as many years as the hair (on its body).

9. Whoever gives a *śāligrāma*[1] together with the clothes, would enjoy stay in Vaikuṇṭha till the Moon and Sun last.

10. Whoever gives a charming umbrella to a brahmin, would rejoice in the world of Varuṇa for ten thousand years.

11. O Chaste lady ! Whoever gives a pair of sandals to a brahmin in Bhārata, would enjoy stay in the world of Vāyu for ten thousand years.

12. Whoever gives a divine charming bed to a brahmin, would enjoy stay in the world of moon till the moon and sun last.

13. Whoever offers a lamp to the god or a brahmin, would enjoy stay in the world of Brahmā for a period of Manu.

14. He would certainly be born as a man possessing good eyes. O Beautiful one ! On account of the merit he would not go to the world of Yama.

15. Whoever makes a gift of an elephant to a brahmin in Bhārata, would live in the world of Indra and other gods.

16. Whoever makes a gift of a horse to a brahmin in Bhārata, would rejoice in the world of Varuṇa for a period of 14 Indras.

17. O Chaste lady ! Whoever gives an excellent palanquin to a brahmin, would enjoy stay in the world of Viṣṇu for a period of Manu.

18. Whoever gives a country fan and white chowrie to a brahmin, would certainly stay in the world of Vāyu for ten thousand years.

19-20. Whoever makes a gift of a mountain of grains to a brahmin in Bhārata, would enjoy stay in the world of Viṣṇu as many years as the number of grains. Then he is born in the same womb and enjoys an eternal happy life. Both the donor and the recipient would certainly go to Vaikuṇṭha (world of Viṣṇu).

21. Whoever mutters always the name of Śrīhari in Bhārata, would be eternal and death would flee away (from him).

22-23. Whoever arranges for the swing of Hari (Viṣṇu) at the end of the night in full moon in Bhārata would be liberated while living. He would go to the abode of Viṣṇu after having enjoyed happiness in this world. He would cerainly remain there till the end of hundred Manu periods.

24. The benefits would be two-fold than that if done in the (asterism) *uttaraphālguni*. (Lord) Brahmā has stated that such a person would live till the end of a *kalpa*.

25-26. Whoever makes a gift of sesamum to a brahmin in Bhārata, would rejoice in the abode of Viṣṇu as many years as the quantity of sesamum. Then he would be born again in the same position and would enjoy a happy eternal life. One would get a two-fold benefit, if the gift is made in a copper vessel.

27-30. Whoever gives away a worthy, chaste, beautiful girl, adorned with ornaments and dress to a brahmin in Bhārata would enjoy stay in the world of Moon for a period of fourteen Indras. There he rejoices day and night in the company of a nymph. Then he would spend ten thousand years in the world of the *gandharvas* and rejoice happily the company of Urvaśī (a nymph) day and night. Then he would get a beautiful, chaste and graceful wife speaking pleasant words and endowed with all prosperity for thousand births.

31-32. Whoever makes a gift of a tree together with the fruits to a brahmin, would enjoy in the world of Indra as many years as the quantity of fruits. He would be born in the own position and get an excellent son. (Making a gift) of thousand trees together with fruits is commended.

33. Whoever gives fruit alone to a brahmin, would stay in the heaven for a long time and return to Bhārata.

34-35. Whoever makes a gift of a big house endowed with all materials and grains to a brahmin in Bhārata, would dwell in the world of Kubera (god of wealth) till the *manvantara* (period of Manu). Then he would be born in his original position and be very rich.

36-38. O Chaste one ! Whoever makes a gift of good land together with crops with devotion to a brahmin or at a sacred place, would certainly enjoy stay in the Vaikuṇṭha (abode of Viṣṇu) for hundred Manu periods. He would be reborn in his original position and would possess extensive land. The land will never desert him in hundred births. He would be endowed with prosperity, wealth and progeny.

39-40. Whoever makes a gift of a village together with the residents to a brahmin, would enjoy stay in Vaikuṇṭha for a lakh *manvantaras*. He would be reborn in his own position and gain certainly a lakh villages. The earth will not desert him even after a lakh births.

41-44. Whoever makes a gift of an excellent town together with the residents, five kinds of crops and endowed with many tanks, trees, fruits and objects of pleasure to a brahmin in Bhārata, would enjoy stay in Vaikuṇṭha for ten lakh times the period of Indra. He would be reborn in his own position and be a monarch in Bhārata. There is no doubt that he would get million cities. Certainly the earth would not desert him for million years. He would be endowed with all prosperity on the earth.

45-48. Whoever makes a gift of hundred cities or a country with excellent residents, wells, tanks and different kinds of trees to a brahmin, would enjoy stay in Vaikuṇṭha for a crore Manu periods. He would be reborn in his own position and become the ruler of *jambūdvīpa*[2] endowed with all prosperity. He would be like Indra on the earth. The earth would not desert him for crore births. He would live till the end of the *kalpa* and would be a mighty king of kings.

49. Whoever gives away his entire authority to a twice-born, there is no doubt that he would enjoy four-fold fruits as a consequence.

50. O Chaste one ! Whoever makes a gift of *jambūdvīpa* to a brahmin, would enjoy fruits hundred-fold without any doubt.

51-52. A donor of the earth with the seven continents, a person that visits all the sacred places, a doer of all kinds of penances, a practitioner of all austerities, a donor of all kinds of gifts, and a person that has accomplished everything there is rebirth certainly. But indeed it is not so far a devotee of Hari.

53. O Chaste one ! The devotees of Viṣṇu residing in Goloka or Vaikuṇṭha or at the place of Hari witness the fall of countless Brahmās.

54-55. A votary of the formula of Viṣṇu would discard his mortal body and attain a divine form that removes birth, death and decrepitude. He would obtain the same form as Viṣṇu and do service to him. Remaining in Goloka he would behold countless primary dissolutions.

56. Gods, accomplished persons, and the entire universe would perish. But the devotees of Kṛṣṇa devoid of birth, death and decrepitude would not perish.

57-58. Whoever offers Tulasī (leaf) (holy basil) to (Lord) Hari in (the month of) Kārttika (October-November), would rejoice in the abode of Hari as many *yugas* as the number of leaves. He would be reborn in the same position and would certainly gain devotion to Hari. He would be happy, long-lived in Bhārata on the earth.

59-60. Whoever offers a lamp with ghee to Hari in Kārttika, would rejoice in the abode of Hari as many years as the *pala*[3] (of glow). He would certainly be reborn in the same position and gain devotion to Viṣṇu. He would be endowed with much wealth, good eye-sight and radiance.

61-62. Whoever bathes in the Ganges at the time of Sunrise in Māgha (January-February), would rejoice in the abode of Hari for sixty thousand *yugas*. He would be reborn in his own position and certainly gain devotion to Viṣṇu. On the earth in Bhārata, he would be the foremost among the subduers of their senses.

63-65. Whoever bathes in the Ganges at Prayāga at the time of Sunrise in Māgha would rejoice in Vaikuṇṭha till the end of lakh Manu periods. Then he would be reborn in the same position and certainly get the formula of Viṣṇu. He would discard the mortal body and go back to Hari. He would never return to earth from Vaikuṇṭha. He would serve (Lord) Hari after having gained similar form.

66-68. Whoever bathes daily in the Ganges, would become pure on earth like the Sun. At every step there would certainly accrue to him the fruits of (performing) the horse sacrifice. The earth becomes purified at once by the dust of his feet. He would rejoice in Vaikuṇṭha till the Moon and Sun last. He would again get his previous position and be a foremost ascetic, devoted to his duties, pure, learned and controller of his senses.

69-70. Whoever gives fragrant water in Bhārata when the Sun is severely scorching between Pisces and Cancer,[4] would rejoice in Vaikuṇṭha till (the periods of) fourteen Indras. He would again be born in his previous position, be happy and devoid of conceit.

71. Whoever offers sandal to (Lord) Hari with devotion in Vaiśākha (April), would rejoice in the abode of Viṣṇu for sixty thousand *yugas*. He would again be born in his previous position with good physique and happiness.

72. Whoever makes a gift of flour of fried gram to a twice born in Vaiśākha, would rejoice in the abode of (Lord) Viṣṇu as many years as the particles in the flour.

73-74. Whoever practises the austerity of Kṛṣṇa Janmāṣṭamī (the birth day of Kṛṣṇa on the eighth day of a fortnight), would no doubt get free from sins committed in hundred births. He would rejoice in Vaikuṇṭha till (the periods) of fourteen Indras. He would be reborn in the same position and certainly gain devotion to (Lord) Kṛṣṇa.

75. Whoever practises the Śivarātri (the night auspicious for worship of Śiva in February) in Bhārata, would rejoice in the world of (Lord) Śiva till the end of seven Manu periods.

76-77. Whoever offers the leaf of bilva to (Lord) Śiva on the Śivarātri, would rejoice in the abode of (Lord) Śiva, as many *yugas* as the number of leaves. He would be reborn in the same position and certainly gain devotion to (Lord) Śiva, possessing knowledge, progeny, prosperity and land.

78-79. Whoever worships (Lord) Śaṅkara after practising austerity in the months of Caitra (April) or Māgha (February) and dances with devotion with a cane in his hand day and night for a month or half a month, or ten or seven days, would enjoy stay in the world of (Lord) Śiva as many *yugas* as the measure of days.

80-81. Whoever practises the Rāmanavamī (the ninth day celebrating the birth of Rāma) in Bhārata, would rejoice in the abode of (Lord) Viṣṇu for seven Manu periods. He would be reborn in the same position and gain certainly devotion to

Rāma. He would be foremost among controllers of senses and great righteous persons.

82-86a. Whoever worships primordial nature in autumn offering buffaloes, goats, rams, sugarcane and pumpkin and other foodstuffs, incense, lamp, dance, music, instrumental music and other auspicious merriment, would reside in the world of (lord) Śiva for seven Manu periods. He would again be born in the same position and possess spotless intellect, stable prosperity, furtherance of sons and grandsons, great glory and an elephant and horse. There is no doubt that he would be king of kings.

86b-88. Whoever worships Mahālakṣmī beginning on the eighth day in bright fortnight in Bhādra (October) with devotion for a fortnight in a sacred place, offering her sixteen excellent services,[5] would rejoice in Vaikuṇṭha as long as the Moon and Sun last. He would be reborn in the same position and be a king of kings.

89-93. Whoever sets up on the full moon in Kārttika (November), a dance-circle consisting of hundred cowherds and hundred cowherdesses and makes a stone idol of Śrīkṛṣṇa together with Rādhā and worships in Bhārata offering the sixteen services, would live in Goloka for a period equal to the life of Brahmā. Then he would return to Bhārata and have devotion to Hari certainly. After gradually gaining devotion and the formula of Hari, he would discard his body and return to Goloka. After having gained the same form as Kṛṣṇa there, he would become a member of his circle. He would not have a fall again. There would be great freedom from decrepitude and death.

94-95. Whoever practices (the austerity of) the eleventh day in the bright or dark fortnight.

96. Whoever worships Indra on the twelfth day in bright fortnight in Bhādra (September), would enjoy stay in the world of Indra for sixty thousand years.

97-98. Whoever worships the Sun on a Sunday, on the day of the transit of the Sun from a zodiacal sign to another or on the seventh day in the bright fortnight and prepares the boiled rice offering in Bhārata, would enjoy stay in the world of Sun till the Moon and Sun last. Afterwards he would return to Bhārata, be free from sickness and be endowed with prosperity.

99-100. Whoever worships (goddess) Sāvitrī on the fourteenth day in the bright fortnight in Jyeṣṭha (June), would enjoy stay in Brahmaloka till the end of seven Manu periods. He would return to earth, possess prosperity and unparalleled valour, eternal life, knowledge and wealth.

101-102. Whoever worships (goddess) Sarasvatī on the fifth day in the bright fortnight in Māgha (January) and offers with control (of the senses) and devotion the sixteen services, would enjoy stay in Vaikuṇṭha for a day and night of Brahmā. After being born again he would be a learned poet.

103-105. Whoever makes a gift of a cow, gold etc., to a brahmin, would be endowed with devotion everyday till the end of his life in Bhārata. He would rejoice in the abode of (Lord) Hari along with the latter with auspicious sport and amusements twice the number of years as that of hair on the body of the cow. Then he would return here and would certainly get devotion to (Lord)Viṣṇu. Then again he would come back and be a king of kings, possessing cows, progeny, learned, wise and happy in all respects.

106-107. Whoever offers sweets to Brahmins in India, would rejoice in the abode of Viṣṇu as many years as the hair on (the body of) the brahmin. Then he would return and be happy, rich, learned, long-lived, prosperous and have unparalleled valour.

108-109. Whoever utters or offers the names of Hari in Bhārata, he would enjoy stay in the world of Viṣṇu as many years as the name of *yugas*. He would then return here and certainly gain devotion to Viṣṇu. If that is done at a place sacred to (Lord)Nārāyaṇa, it would get crore times benefits.

110-111. Whoever mutters the names crore times at a place sacred for Nārāyaṇa, would become free from all sins and certainly be liberated while living. He would not have rebirth and would enjoy stay in Vaikuṇṭha. He would gain oneness of Viṣṇu's form and would not have a fall.

112-113. Whoever worships daily (Lord) Śiva making a liṅga out of earth and visits the temple of (Lord) Śiva throughout his life, would enjoy stay in the world of Śiva as many years as the particles in the earth. Then he would return and be a powerful king in Bhārata.

114-115. Whoever worships daily the (sacred) stone and partakes the water offered to the stone, would enjoy stay in Vaikuṇṭha as many years as (the period) of hundred Brahmās. Then he would be reborn and gain devotion to (Lord) Viṣṇu. Then he would enjoy stay in the world of Viṣṇu and would not have a fall.

116-117. Whoever performs all kinds of penances and practises all austerities, would stay in Vaikuṇṭha as long as (the periods of) fourteen Indras. Then he would be reborn and be a mighty king in Bhārata. Thereafter he would get liberated and then would never have rebirth.

118. Whoever bathes in all sacred waters on earth after doing circumambulation, would get liberated and would never have rebirth on earth.

119. Whoever performs the horse-sacrifice at a sacred place in Bhārata, would occupy half the seat of Indra as many years as the hair on the horse.

120-121. Man gets four-fold benefit in (the performance of) *rājasūya*[6] and half the benefit in sacrificing of a man or a cow. (One would get) half of the fruit in offering a son and would get a good son. The same benefit as the offering of a cow would accrue by the (performance of) plough-sacrifice.

122. The same benefit would accrue by the offer of a brahmin and by the *vṛddhiyāga* (rite at the time of the birth of a child). Half the fruit would accrue to a man in the lotus-sacrifice.

123. One would be free from grief in (performing) *viśoka* (sacrifice) and would enjoy half the fruit of the lotus sacrifice and heaven. The king would be victorious in performing (the rite) *vijaya* and would enjoy heaven similar to the lotus-sacrifice.

124. The kings would gain progeny and extension of territory by (the performance of) *prājāpatya* (giving away one's property before).

125. O Beautiful lady ! The sacrifice for Viṣṇu is the main one among all sacrifice. It was performed by Brahmā in the past, with lot of materials.

126-127. O Chaste one ! When there was a dispute between Dakṣa and Śaṅkara, the brahmins cursed Nandin the brahmins with wrath. Hence Candraśekhara destroyed the sacrifice of Dakṣa. The patriarch Dakṣa performed the Viṣṇu sacrifice in the past.

128-131. (Then) Dharma, Kaśyapa, Śeṣa, Kardama, Svāyambhuva Manu and his son Priyavrata, Śiva, Sanatkumāra, Kapila and Dhruva(performed this sacrifice). That rite could be accomplished with (the materials required for) thousand *rājasūya* rites. The fruits of that rite will be that of thousand *rājasūya* sacrifices. There is no other rite in the *vedas* that would yield more fruits than this *viṣṇu* rite. One would live till the end of many *kalpa* periods and would certainly be liberated while living (by this rite). He would become on par with *viṣṇu* in his wisdom and lustre.

132-137. O Child ! This *viṣṇu* rite is the foremost among the rites just as Viṣṇu among the gods, Śiva among the devotees of Viṣṇu, the *vedas* among the scriptural texts, the brahmins among the four stages, the Ganges among the sacred places, the devotees of Viṣṇu among the sanctified, the eleventh day among the austerities, the holy basil among the flowers, the moon among the asterisms, the Garuḍa among the birds, the *prakṛti* (Nature) among women, the earth among supports, the mind among the swiftest, organs and fickly-natured, Brahmā among the patriarchs, Prajāpati among the Lords of beings, the Vṛndāvana among the forests, Bhārata among the countries, (Goddess) Śrī among the fortunate, (Goddess) Sarasvatī among the learned, (Goddess) Durgā (Pārvatī) among the chaste and Rādhikā among the prosperous.

138. It is certain that one would attain the position of Indra by (the performance of) hundred horse sacrifices. (King) Pṛthu

also obtained the position of Viṣṇu by (the performance of) thousand (horse sacrifices).

139-140. Bathing in all sacred waters, initiation in all rites, practise of austerities and penances would doubtless be meritorious. But the seed of all fruits is the service rendered to (Lord) Kṛṣṇa conferring beatitude.

141. It has been established in the *purāṇas, vedas, itihāsas* (epics) and other texts that the worship of the feet of (Lord) Kṛṣṇa is the essence.

142-143. O Chaste one ! Describing him, meditating him, glorifying his name and virtues, eulogising him, remembering him, saluting him, muttering his name, partaking of the food offering and water offered at his feet daily is accepted and coveted by all.

144. O Child ! You worship (Lord) Kṛṣṇa, the Supreme Brahman, devoid of attributes and above Nature. You take your husband and go back to your abode.

145. I have thus described you the fruits of deeds of men, that is mostly desired, agreed upon and yielding the truth.

CHAPTER TWENTY-EIGHT

The Eulogy of Yama by Sāvitrī

Śrī Nārāyaṇa said:

1. After listening to the glory of (Lord) Hari from the mouth of Yama, Sāvitrī spoke again with tears in her eyes and horripilation.

Sāvitrī said:

2-4. I understand that glorifying Hari is the act of righteousness that is the cause of the redemption of one's ancestors and it gets rid of birth, death and decrepitude of the listeners and the reciters. Glorifying Hari is greater than the gifts, austerities, accomplishments, penances, yogic practices and scriptures. Liberation or immortality does not deserve one-sixteenth of the merits of serving (Lord) Śrī Kṛṣṇa.

5. O Venerable one ! Foremost among the knowers of scriptures ! Tell me, an ignorant one and orphan, the procedure for the worship of Śrī Kṛṣṇa, transcending *prakṛti* (Nature).

6. I have heard from you the interesting (details about) fruits of good deeds. You are fit to describe me the fruits of evil deeds.

7. O Brahman ! After having stated thus that chaste lady glorified with her head bent, the god of piety with a hymn told in the scriptures.

Sāvitrī said:

8. I bow to that lord of piety whom in days of yore the Sun-god obtained as a son, after penance and adoration of piety (*dharma*) at Puṣkara, as a part of piety.

9. I salute him witnessing and treating alike all beings and hence bearing the name Śamana (allaying).

10. I bow to that Kṛtāmta that puts an end to the lives of all beings befitting the time of their deeds.

11. I worship that Daṇḍadhara (the wielder of the staff) that holds the staff in order to punish the sinners for the sake of purifying them and that governs all deeds.

12. I bow to that unavoidable Time (*kāla*) who always controls all the lives in the world.

13. I adore that Yama—an ascetic, a devotee of Viṣṇu, pious, self-controlled subduer of the organs and conferrer of the results of the deeds of the beings.

14. He revels in his own self, omniscient, friend of doers of good deeds and giver of trouble to sinners. I worship that person having merit as the friend.

15. I bow to that family of Brahman born in the family of Brahmā with glowing brahman lustre and contemplating the Supreme Brahman.

16. O Sage ! After having spoken thus Sāvitrī saluted Yama. Yama described her the worship of Viṣṇu and the fruits of deeds.

17. Whoever reads this octad of Yama daily after getting up in the morning, would have no fear from Yama and would become free from all sins.

18. O Nārada ! If a great sinner reads this hymn daily with devotion, Yama would certainly render him pure from this bodily shackle.

CHAPTER TWENTY-NINE

Narration about Hells

Śrī Nārāyaṇa said:

1. After imparting her the formula of Viṣṇu preceded by the procedure, Yama described her the fruits of evil deeds.

Yama said:

2. O Chaste one ! You have heard (from me) the fruits of different good deeds. You listen to me now. I shall describe you the results of evil deeds.

3. The soul goes to different kinds of heaven on account of good deeds, and to various kinds of hells on account of evil deeds.

4. There are several kinds of pits of hells bearing different names on account of the difference in the various *purāṇas.*

5. O Child ! They are extensive, deep, causing grief for the beings, frightful, fierce and vile.

6. There are eighty-six pits in Yama's city. O Chaste one ! Listen to me for a description of their well-known names as in the *vedas.*

7-20. O Lady of good conduct ! (They are): pits of fire, molten hot lava, frightful alkali, odour, urine, the unbearable phlegm, poison, rheum, flesh, semen, blood, vile one, tears, bodily impurities, impurity of the ear, marrow, flesh, the impassable nail, hair on the body, hair on head bones, yielding grief, copper, heated iron causing great grief, sharp thorns, poison causing obstacles, perspiration, hot wine, well heated oil, the unbearable teeth, insects, pus, serpent causing fatal end, mosquito, stings, the frightful poison, powerful teeth, scorpions, arrows, spears, frightful swords, balls, alligators, crows, distressing one, quivering one, feather of arrow, the unfordable bonds, hot stones, sharp stones, saliva, sword, extremely painful powder pit, disc, thunderbolt, tortoise, thick flames, ashes, putrid, burning Sun, razor-edged leaves, razor like ones, needle faced ones, face of alligator, teeth of elephant, face of cow, *kumbhīpāka* (a baking pit), rope of time, water filled pit, inflicting wounds at the vital parts, abound with mass of dirt, encircled by noose, abound with spears, violently shaking one meteorlike one, blind well, piercing one, beating with stick, bound with nets, that which pounds the body, that which pierces, that which dries up one, one having the flame of serpent, deceitful one, blinding smoke, and girdle of serpents.

21-27. O Sāvitrī ! These are the pits causing misery for the sinners. They are always guarded by hosts of attendants instituted (for that purpose). (These attendants) are armed with frightful sticks, spears, noose, iron spears and clubs. They are mad with pride, cruel, endowed with the attribute *tamas*, devoid of compassion, unavoidable by any means, radiant and devoid of doubt. They possess eyes reddish brown like copper. They are endowed with asceticism. They are accomplished ascetics and capable of assuming different forms. They are beheld by the sinners belonging to all class of animate beings about to die. But they are never seen by devotees of (Lord) Śiva, (goddess) Śakti, Sun and Gaṇapati and always practising their duties, doing meritorious deeds and accomplished ascetics. Then devotees of Viṣṇu engaged in practising their duties, or ceased to practise, independent, strong and without any doubt perceive them in their dreams. O Pious one ! I have described you the details about the number of pits. Now you comprehend the details about the type of people destined to live in these pits.

CHAPTER THIRTY

The Description of the Sinners

Yama said:

1. O Chaste one ! An ardent devotee of Viṣṇu, a pure one, an ascetic, an accomplished one, one practising austerities, one performing penance, a celibate and one that has controlled his senses would not go to hell.

2-3. Whoever wickedly and on account of his power scorches his kinsmen with harsh words would go to the pit of fire. After having stayed in the fire (pit) as many years as the hair on the body, he would gain his birth as an animal and would be scorched for three births in that terrible one.

4-5. Whoever does not feed a thirsty and hungry brahmin that has come to his house, that ignorant one would go to the pit of molten hot lava and stay there enjoying grief as a bird for seven births in the hot fire pit as many years as the hair.

6-7. Whoever applies alkali to the clothes on Sundays, the day of movement of Sun from one constellation to another, the new moon day and the day of ancestral rite, would go to the pit of alkali as many years as the thread. In Bhārata he would be born as a washerman for seven births.

8-9. Whoever takes away something given by himself or by others the means of living of a brahmin, would go to the pit of ordure for sixty thousand years, remains there partaking ordure for sixty thousand years and become insects in ordure for sixty thousand years on earth.

10-11. Whoever digs up a tank in another's tank and dedicates it, would go to the pit of urine on account of violating divine laws. He would dwell there as many years as the dust particles (of the tank) partaking (urine) and would then be born as an alligator for seven births in Bhārata.

12-13. Whoever partakes sweetmeat alone, would go to the pit of lizards and remain there hundred years consuming the same. He would then become a corpse for hundred years in Bhārata partaking phlegm, urine and poison and then would become pure.

14-15. Whoever does not support his parents, preceptor, wife, son, daughter and an orphan, would go to the pit of poison, remain partaking it for thousand years, become a goblin for hundred years and afterwards pure.

16-18. Whoever makes crooked eyes at a guest, the water (of libation) would not be accepted by the manes from him. He would incur all the sins such as the killing of brahmins and would finally go to the pit of rheum of the eyes. He would stay there for hundred years partaking the same. Then he would be born on the earth as a poor man seven times.

19-20. Whoever gives a material to a brahmin and then offers (the same) to another, would stay in the pit of marrow partaking the same for hundred years. Then he would become a *caṇḍāla* (low-born) for hundred years and then become pure. He would become a chameleon for seven births in Bhārata.

21-22. Whoever, a man or a woman causes a woman or man to partake[1] the semen, would go to the pit of semen and stay there consuming the same for hundred years. That person would become an insect in the private organ for hundred years on the earth and then pure, then become a corpse for hundred years in Bhārata partaking phlegm, urine and poison and then would become pure.

23-24. Whoever strikes a brahmin preceptor and causes bloodshed, would stay in the pit of blood consuming the same for hundred years. Then he would take birth as a hunter seven times in Bhārata and thus become pure.

25-26. Whoever laughs at a devotee (of Kṛṣṇa) shedding tears, singing and having choked throat after listening to music glorifying the virtues of Kṛṣṇa, would reside in the pit of tears partaking the same for hundred years. He would then be born as a *caṇḍāla* three times and then become pure.

27-28. Whoever is always wicked and has an impure heart, would go to the pit of bodily impurities for ten years. Then he would be born as an ass three times, and as a jackal three times and would surely become pure thereafter.

29-30. Whoever laughs at or censures a deaf man, would stay in the pit of ear wax consuming the same for hundred years. Then he would be born as deaf, poor and disabled seven times and then become pure certainly.

31-32. Whoever out of greed for his own maintenance, kills any being, would dwell in the pit of marrow partaking the same for lakh years. Then he would be born as a hare, fish and antelope etc., seven times and be pure thereafter.

33-37. Whoever protects his daughter and sells her on account of avarice, that extremely ignorant one, would go to the pit of flesh and remain there as many years as the hair of the girl consuming the flesh. The attendants of Yama would beat him in that pit. He would bear the load of flesh on his head and lick the flowing blood with hunger. He would be born as an insect in the ordure of girls in Bhārata, a hunter for sixty thousand years in seven births, a boar three times, a dog seven times, a frog seven times, leeches seven times and a crow seven times and would certainly become pure thereafter.

38-39. Whoever does not shave on the days of austerities or fast or the days of ancestral (funeral) rites, would be impure in all rites. O Beautiful girl ! He would stay in the pit of nails etc., consuming the same as many years as they are and being beaten by a stick.

40-41. Whoever worships an earthen *liṅga* (emblem of Śiva) along with hair (on it) in Bhārata, would remain in the pit of hair as many years as the particles of earth. Then he would be born as a Yavana[2] on account of the wrath of (Lord) Hara (Śiva). He would become pure after hundred years and would regain his original family.

42-43. Whoever does not offer cakes for the manes at the feet of Viṣṇu[3], would remain in the pit of bones as many years as the hair on his body. Then he would be born in his original position and be crippled and extremely poor seven times. He would then become pure after chastisement.

44. Whoever cohabits his pregnant wife would stay in the pit of hot copper for hundred years.

45-46. Whoever partakes food from a widow without sons or a menses woman, would stay in the pit of heated iron for hundred years. He would be born as a washerman and artisan seven times and then suffer severe sores and be poor. Then he would become pure.

47. Whoever touches the materials for god with hands drenched with perspiration, would stay in the pit of perspiration for a period of hundred years.

48-49. A twice born partaking food from a *śūdra* after being ordered by him, would remain in the pit of hot wine for hundred years. Then he would officiate the rite of a *śūdra* for seven births, eating food at the ancestral rite done by a *śūdra* and then become pure.

50-51. A shrew tormenting her husband always with foul and harsh words would remain in the pit of sharp thorns experiencing that pain. She would be beaten with stick by the messenger of Yama for four *yugas* and then be born as Uccaiśśravas (the divine horse) seven times and then become pure.

52-53. A rustic killing an animate being by means of poison without compassion would remain in a pit of poison for thousand years consuming that. Then he would become a killer of men and afflicted with wounds in seven births and leper in seven births and then would surely get pure.

54-55. If a person driving a bullock beats the bull with a stick by himself or through his servant in a sacred place in Bhārata, he would stay in the pit of hot oil for four *yuga* periods and then would be a bullock as many years as the hair on the bullock.

56-57. O Chaste one ! Whoever kills an animate being with the tooth, iron or hook, would dwell in the pit of teeth for a million years. Then he would be born in his same position suffering stomach disease and after suffering in one birth he would become pure.

58-59. A brahmin partaking flesh without any purpose or eating fish and has not consumed the offering made to Hari, would go to the pit of insects. He would stay there consuming the same as many years as his own hair. Then he would be born as a barbarian three times and (regain his form as) a twice-born.

60-62. A brahmin officiating at the rite of a *śūdra*, partaking food at the ancestral rite of a *śūdra* and lighting the funeral pyre of a *śūdra* would go to the pit of pus. O Lady of good conduct ! He would stay there being beaten by the messenger of Yama and partaking the pus as many years as the hair on (the body of) the sacrificer. Then he would be born as a *śūdra* in Bhārata for seven times experiencing excruciating pain and penury and would then be pure and again twice born.

63-65. Whoever kills a small, fierce or great serpent, would stay in the pit of serpent as many years as the hair on his body. He would be eaten by the serpent and beaten by the messenger of Yama. He would maintain himself by the excreta of the serpent. He would then become a serpent. Then he would be born as a short-lived man suffering ringworms. He would die with great pains. It is certain that he would be consumed by the serpent.

66-68. Whoever kills the beings and tiny creatures after promulgating the codes, would spend as many years as the days of his life in the pit of biting mosquitoes being bitten by them day and night without food and making sound. After his hands and legs are bound he would be beaten by the messenger of Yama. Then he would be born as a tiny creature and then as a disabled man and then pure.

69-70. An ignorant person collecting honey after killing the honey-bees, would remain in the pit of poison partaking the same as many years as the days of his life and being bitten and burnt by the poison and struck by the attendant of Yama. Then he would be born as a honey-bee and then become pure.

71-72. Whoever punishes a faultless one or a brahmin, would go to the pit of strong teeth and insects and stay there as many years as the hair (on the person), crying day and night being bitten by them. He would then be born as a *śūdra.*

73-74. On account of avarice if a king punishes his subject, he would certainly dwell in the pits of scorpions as many years as the hair on that person. Then he would be born as a scorpion seven times. Then he would become a crippled man with disease.

75-76. A brahmin wielding a weapon or serving as a washerman for others or bereft of the practice of twilight worship or ignorant or devoid of devotion to Viṣṇu, would remain in the pits of wine etc., being always pierced by arrows etc., as many years as his own hair and become pure.

77-79. Whoever confines the subjects in a dark prison for petty offences with pride, would go to the pit of balls. That pit of balls would be dark, flooded with boiling water, frightening and abound with insects possessing sharp teeth. He would stay there being pierced by the insects as many years as the hairs on (the body of) the people. Then he would become a vile servant and then pure on earth.

80-81. Whoever kills the alligator etc., coming out from the tank, would go to the pit of alligators as many years as the thorns of the crocodiles. Then he would surely be born as alligators etc., in rivers etc. Then he would become pure at once and be a man again only by punishment.

82-83. Whoever looks at the chest, loins, breasts and face of other women out of lust in the holy place of Bhārata, that lustful person would dwell in the pit of crows his body being pecked. He would be there as many years as his hair. Then he would be blind in three births and poor in seven births, very cruel and a sinner. He would then be a goldsmith and a gold merchant in Bhārata.

84-86. O beautiful one ! Whoever steals copper and iron in Bhārata, would go to the pit of *vajra* (an insect) as many years as his hair. He would stay there partaking the ordure of *vajra*, his eyes being pecked by *vajra* and being beaten by the messenger of Yama and then become pure as a man.

87-88. Whoever steals an idol or the material belonging to the god (temple) in Bhārata, would stay in the difficult pit of *vajra* as many years as his own hair. His body being burnt by the thunderbolt, remaining without food and making sound, and beaten by the messenger of Yama, that man would become pure then.

89-91. Whoever steals silver items, cows or dress[4] from the gods (temples) and brahmins, would certainly dwell in the pit of heated stone as many years as his hair. He would be born as a crane three times, as a white swan three times, once as a kite and other white birds. Then he would be born suffering from deranged blood.

92-93. Whoever steals silver[5] and bronze vessels of gods and brahmins would dwell in the pit of sharp stones as many years as his hair. Then he would be born as a horse seven times in Bhārata. Then he would be born as having extra limbs and with afflicted foot and then pure.

94-95. Whoever partakes food from a wanton woman or subsists on her earning, would dwell in the pit of saliva as many years as his hair. Being beaten by the messenger of Yama, he would remain there partaking the same. Then he would suffer eyesore and become pure thereafter in due course.

96-98. Whoever serves a barbarian and subsists on dyes, that brahmin in Bhārata would dwell in the pit of hot dye as many years as his hair. Then being beaten by the messenger of Yama, he would dwell there partaking the same. O Chaste one! He would then become a black coloured animal in three births, a goat in three births, a black serpent in three births, and then a palm tree and then become pure.

99-101. Whoever steals the foodgrains, betel, seat and conch belonging to the gods and brahmins, would go to the pit of powder, dwell there hundred years, being beaten by the messenger of Yama. Then he would be born as a ram and cock three times and then as a man suffering from disease of the lungs, without progeny, poor and short-lived and then pure.

102-103. Whoever steals the material belonging to a brahmin and makes a disc, would dwell in the pit of disc for hundred years, being beaten by a stick. Then he would become an oilman in three births, suffering from disease, without progeny and then pure.

104-105. O Chaste one! Whoever is deceitful to his kinsmen and brahmins, would go to the pit of *vajra* (an insect) and dwell there a period of a *yuga*. Then he becomes deformed and disabled for seven births and then poor, without progeny and wife and then pure.

106-107. A brahmin who eats the flesh of tortoise on *śayana* day (the eleventh day in the month of July), would dwell in the pit of tortoise for hundred years being bitten by a tortoise. He would be born as a tortoise and three times as a boar. He would be born three times as a cat and three times as a peacock.

108-109. Whoever steals ghee, oil etc., belonging to gods and brahmins, would go to the pit of flames and that sinner (would go) to the pit of ashes. He would stay for hundred years and then become a cockroach. He would be born as a fish seven times and then a mouse and then pure.

110-112. Whoever steals fragrant oil, emblic myrabolan or fragrant material from the gods or brahmins in the holy land of Bhārata, would dwell in the pit of foul smell getting always foul smell as many years as his hair and would then become a bad smelling substance in seven births, musk in three births, fragrance in seven births and then become a man.

113-117. O Chaste one ! Whoever takes away by force, by fraudulent ways or by causing trouble the paternal land of another person in Bhārata, would remain in the hot spike being scorched day and night just as a being turns round always in hot oil while being boiled. No doubt he would not be reduced to ashes as the body meant for experiencing (grief) would not perish. That sinner remains there for seven Manu periods experiencing heat. He would make sound, (remain) without food and be beaten by the messenger of Yama. Then he would be an insect in the ordure for sixty thousand years in

Bhārata. Then he would be without land, poor and then pure. Then he would regain his original position and become a doer of auspicious deeds again.

118-122. Whoever cruelly and without compassion cuts an animate being with a sword, and a killer of man on account of avarice in Bhārata, would stay in (pit of) sword-like leaves (as many years) as the periods of fourteen Indras. The killers of brahmins among them (would stay) for hundred Manu periods and that sinner would be having mutilated limbs being struck continuously by swords. He would then be born in Bhārata as a vile hundred times and then a boar, a dog hundred times, a jackal seven times, a tiger seven times, a wolf three times, a rhinoceros seven times, and a buffalo three times.

123-125. O Chaste one ! Whoever burns a village or a city, would also dwell on the edges of a sword with mutilated limbs for three yuga periods. Then he would become a corpse at once and wander the earth with fire as face. He would remain partaking ordures in seven births and the glow-worm in seven births. Then he would experience severe colic for seven births and a bleeding leper for seven births and then become pure.

126-128. Whoever slanders another by whispering in the ears of another person, and whoever finds great pleasure in the faults of others, whoever slanders the gods and brahmins, would dwell on the tip of a needle being pierced by the needle for three *yugas.* Then he would become a scorpion and a serpent in seven births, a *vajrakīṭa* (a small insect boring the stones) in seven births, then a mortal with a major disease and then pure.

129-131. Whoever breaks open the house of a householder and steals materials, would go to the wombs of cows, goats, sheep and alligators. Then he would be born as a cow seven times with disease, a sheep three times and a goat three times. Then he would become a man always sickly, poor, devoid of wife and kinsmen and tormented and then pure.

132. Whoever steals an ordinary item would reach the hell of an alligator for a *yuga* period. Then he would become a mortal with major disease and then pure.

133-134. Whoever kills cows, elephants, horses and men, that great sinner would go to (the pit of) elephant's tusk for three *yuga* periods. He would be beaten always by the messenger of Yama with the tusk of an elephant. He would become an elephant and a horse for three births. Then he would be born as a cow and a barbarian and then pure.

135-137. Whoever prevents a thirsty cow from drinking water or whoever does not tend a cow, would go to *gomukha*, hell of the shape of cow's face, containing insects and hot water. He stays there being tormented till the end of the Manu period. Then he would be a man without a cow, extremely sick, poor and a low caste man for seven births and then become pure.

138-145. Whoever commits cow-slaughter and slaughter of a brahmin or an induced one, cohabits the prohibited woman, does not perform twilight worship, whoever is not initiated (for religious rite), whoever accepts gifts at holy places, whoever officiates as a priest in a village, whoever subsists on the offering made to gods, whoever cooks for the *śūdras*, whoever is intoxicated, whoever is a husband of the low caste woman, whoever commits cow-slaughter or kills a brahmin or a woman and a great sinner who kills his friend or the embryo in Bhārata, would dwell in *kumbhīpāka* for a period of the fourteen Indras and being beaten by the messenger of Yama and always crushed. For a moment he would fall on the fire, for a while on the thorn, for a moment on heated oil and for another moment on heated water, for sometime on heated stone and then for a while on heated iron. He would then be born as a vulture crore thousand times, as a boar hundred times, as a crow seven times, as a serpent seven times and then as an insect in the ordure for sixty thousand years. Then he would be born as a *vṛṣala*[6] (vile), a bleeding leper and poor man seized by consumption, devoid of family and wife and then pure.

Sāvitrī said:

146-148. What is slaughter of a brahmin or cow-slaughter or an induced one? Who is prohibited for cohabiting ? Who is bereft of twilight worship? Who indeed is uninitiated ? Who is recipient of a gift in sacred places ? Which twice-born is a priest in a village ? Which brahmin subsists on the offering made to gods ? Who is the cook for *śūdras*? (Who is) intoxicated and a husband of the vile ? O Best among the learned in the *vedas* ! Describe me the characteristics of all these people.

Yama said:

149-150. O beautiful one ! Whoever holds a distinction between (Lord) Kṛṣṇa and the idol for his worship, an earthen image of nature, (Lord) Śiva and Śivaliṅga (the emblem of Śiva), Sun and the gem representing Sun, (Lord) Gaṇeśa and the idol for his worship, such a person would incur (the sin of) killing a brahmin.

151. Whoever entertains a distinction between his preceptor, his tutelary deity and his mother who had given birth to him, would incur (the sin of) killing a brahmin.

152. Whoever treats alike, the devotees of Viṣṇu, the devotees of other gods, brahmins and others, would incur (the sin of) killing a brahmin.

153. Whoever holds alike the offering made to (Lord) Viṣṇu and other gods, the water offered to the feet of (Lord) Viṣṇu and other gods, that ignorant person would incur (the sin of) killing a brahmin.

154-155. Whoever equates with other gods, (Lord) Kṛṣṇa, the lord of all gods, the cause of all causes, the first among all, a person to be served by all, an inner soul of all beings and the one without any attribute although assuming different forms on account of illusion, would incur (the sin of) killing a brahmin.

156. Whoever forbids the worship of the manes, the preceding one and the gods, the succeeding one, instituted in the *vedas*, would incur (the sin of) killing a brahmin.

157. Whoever censures (Lord) Hṛṣīkeśa[7] (a name of Viṣṇu) and the votaries of his formula, most holy among the holy would incur (the sin of) killing a brahmin.

158-159. Whoever do not worship and censure (Lord) Śiva and the form of Śiva endearing to Lord Kṛṣṇa more than his life, most holy among the holy, bliss of knowledge, eternal, foremost among the devotees of Viṣṇu, adorable by (all) gods and master, would incur (the sin of) killing a brahmin.

160-161. Whoever slanders nature, the illusion of Viṣṇu, the chaste one yielding devotion to Viṣṇu, embodiment of all energies, the mother of all the beings, an embodiment of all goddesses, first among all, adored by all and an embodiment of all causes, would incur (the sin of) killing a brahmin.

162-163. Whoever does not practice the five auspicious periods such as the eighth day (associated with) the birth of Kṛṣṇa,[8] the most meritorious ninth day for Rāma, the night for Śiva, the eleventh day and the day for the Sun.[9]

164. O Child ! Whoever performs ablution in the waves of the water or that has been dug up in Bhārata, would incur (the sin of) killing a brahmin.

165. Whoever does not support the preceptor, mother, father, pious wife, son, daughter and destitutes, would incur (the sin of) killing a brahmin.

166. Whoever is unmarried, does not get a son and devoid of devotion to (Lord) Hari, would incur (the sin of) killing a brahmin.

167. Whoever partakes things not offered to Viṣṇu and whoever does not worship Viṣṇu daily or the meritorious earthen *liṅga* (symbol of Śiva), would incur (the sin of) killing a brahmin.

168. Whoever prevents a cow from eating or drinking and whoever goes in between a cow and a brahmin, would incur (the sin of) cow-slaughter.

169. Whichever ignorant brahmin driving a bull beats it with a stick, no doubt would incur (the sin of) cow-slaughter every day.

170. Whoever offers remnant of food to cows, engages a driver of a bull for officiating as a priest and feeds someone with the food from a driver of a bull, would certainly incur (the sin of) cow-slaughter.[10]

171. Whoever serves as a priest for a vile and whoever eats food from him, would also no doubt incur (the sin of) cow-slaughter hundred times.

172. Whoever places his foot on the fire or kicks a cow with his feet or enters the house and bathes without washing his feet, would incur (the sin of) cow-slaughter.

173. Whoever eats with wet feet and lies down with wet feet, whoever eats twice at sunrise, would certainly incur (the sin of) cow-slaughter.

174. Whoever partakes food from a childless widow, a twice-born living on gratifying lust, a person devoid of the three twilight worships, would certainly incur (the sin of) cow-slaughter.

175. Whoever does not serve the manes at the time of the *parvan* (days such as the New moon) and the gods on the (appropriate) days, would certainly incur (the sin of) cow-slaughter.

176. Whoever distinguishes between her husband and (Lord) Kṛṣṇa and threatens with abusive words, would certainly incur (the sin of) cow-slaughter.

177. Whoever sows grains after digging the pathway of cows or in the tank or on its banks, would certainly incur (the sin of) cow-slaughter.

178. Whoever violates the expiation for killing a cow on account of avarice or ignorance, would surely inherit (the sin of) cow-slaughter.

179. The ignorant cowherd who does not tend the cows with greater care on (the festive days of) the king or the god, and causes them hardship, would certainly incur (the sin of) cow-slaughter.

180. Whoever transgresses the animal engaged in the worship of gods, or water, or an offering, flowers and food, would certainly incur (the sin of) cow-slaughter.

181. Whoever always denies, or utters a lie or misleads or hates the gods or hates the preceptors, would certainly incur (the sin of) cow-slaughter.

182. Whoever does not hasten to bow on beholding an idol of the god, or the preceptor or a brahmin, would definitely incur (the sin of) cow-slaughter.

183. If a twice-born does not bless a saluting person on account of wrath, or (does not impart) knowledge to a student, he would surely incur (the sin of) cow-slaughter.

184. I have explained you cow-slaughter, slaughter of a brahmin and (the sin) due to inducement as I had heard from the mouth of the Sun. What else do you desire to hear?

Sāvitrī said:

185. You are fit to explain me the distinction between the actual and the induced one as related to sin and merit and their deficiency and excessiveness.

Yama said:

186. Sometimes the actual one is greater and the induced one is lower. Sometimes induced one is greater and the actual one is lower.

187. O Pious one! Sometimes they are equal on the authority of the Vedas. Whoever does not believe, would incur (the sin of) killing the preceptor.

188. Whoever imparts a potential formula to an already acquainted person is stated to be superior because of the super-imposition of the father on the preceptor.

189. The mother is hundred times (meritorious) than the father and the person imparting potential formula is hundred times (superior) to the mother and the *vedas* hence view that the preceptor is to be adored.

190. The wife of the preceptor is greater in respect than the preceptor. The consort of the god is to be adored well since she is the tutelary deity.

191. A brahmin equals (Lord)Śiva and is as valorous as (Lord)Viṣṇu. The king is superior to the induced one and an actual one lakh times.

192. All water equal the Ganges and all the twice-borns equal (sage) Vyāsa. The Sun and the Moon have equality in respect of the eclipse.

193. (Lord) Brahmā has stated as accepted by all the *vedas* that (the sin of killing) an actual one is four times that of killing an induced one.

194. O Chaste one ! The divisions of the killing of the induced one has been described. Listen to me. I shall describe you those not to be cohabited by men.

195. It has been established in the *vedas* that one's own wife may be cohabited. Those learned in the *vedas* declare that others are not to be cohabited.

196. O beautiful one ! I have told you in general. You now listen to me for particular kind. You listen to me I shall describe you those not at all to be cohabited.

197. O Chaste one ! It has been held in the world and in the *vedas* that a brahmin's wife of a *śūdra* and the *śūdra* wife of a brahmin are extremely condemned for cohabitation.

198. If a *śūdra* cohabits a brahmin woman, he would incur hundred times (the sin of) killing a brahmin. On par with it the brahmin woman also would certainly go to (the hell) *kumbhīpāka*.

199. If a brahmin cohabits a *śūdra* woman, he is only a husband of a *śūdra*. He would become an outcaste from the brahmin community and be considered as inferior to a *caṇḍāla*.

200. The ball of rice offered would be equal to ordure and water libation equal to urine. O chaste one ! The same is the case in the worship of his manes and gods.

201. There is no doubt that the merits earned by a twice-born in crore births by twilight worship and penance would get destroyed by cohabiting a *śūdra* woman.

202. A brahmin drinking wine, a person partaking ordure, a (brahmin) husband of a *śūdra* woman and a person partaking

food on the day of (Lord)Hari (i.e., eleventh day), would certainly go to (the hell) *kumbhīpāka*.

203-205. O Chaste one ! (Lord)Brahmā has stated that one should not cohabit with preceptor's wife, queen, step-mother, one's mother, daughter, daughter-in-law, mother-in-law, the sister of the mother-in-law, sister, brother's wife, wife of the maternal uncle, father's mother, mother's mother, mother's sister, one's sister, brother's daughter, girl student, student's wife, sister's son's wife and brother's son's wife.

206. Whoever does any one or more than one of the above is deemed in the *vedas* as having cohabited one's mother. That condemned one would incur (the sin of) killing a brahmin hundred times.

207-208. Whoever performs imperfect twilight worship or whoever does not perform twilight worship or whoever is bereft of all the three twilight worships, that twice-born is deemed to be devoid of twilight worship.

209. Whoever on account of pride does not receive the formula relating to Lords Viṣṇu or Śiva or Goddess or Gaṇapati or Sūrya, is known as not initiated.

210-214. (Lord) Nārāyaṇa is the master of four cubits in the excellent deep water of the Ganges having the current as the limit. Whoever wilfully accepts a gift therein or at the place of Nārāyaṇa, or at Kurukṣetra or at the feet of (Lord) Hari or at Vārāṇasī or at Badarī or at the confluence of the Ganges and the ocean or at Puṣkara or at the sacred place of the Sun, or at Prabhāsa or at the dance circle or at Haridvāra or at Kedāra or at Soma (Somanatha ?) or at the holy Badara or on the banks of the river Sarasvatī or at the sacred Vṛndāvana grove or on the Godāvarī[11] or on the Kauśikī or on the Triveṇī or on the Himālaya and other places is deemed to be receiving a gift at a sacred place and such a person would go to *kumbhīpāka*.

215. One officiating the sacrifice of those other than the *śūdra* is said to be officiating for the village (*grāmayājī*). Then a person subsisting on offerings made to god is stated to be Devala.

216. A person making a living by cooking for a *śūdra* is deemed to be a Supakāra. A person bereft of the twilight worship is intoxicated. He is deemed to be fallen.

217. I have described in the previous context the characteristics of a Vṛṣalīpati (the husband of a *śudra* woman), These great sinners would go to *kumbhīpāka*.

218. You listen to me. I shall describe you the other pits to which others go.

CHAPTER THIRTY-ONE

Description of the Other Hells

Yama said:

1. O pious one ! One may not destroy one's deeds without service to (Lord) Hari. Good deeds are the seeds for heaven and hell is the resultant of bad deeds.

2-3. O chaste one ! Whoever partakes food from a *puṁścalī*[1] or *veśyā*[2] and the twice-born cohabiting her would go to (the hell) *kālasūtra* (thread of time). After having stayed hundred years in *kālasūtra*, he would certainly become a *śūdra*. Then the twice-born would be suffering disease and then pure.

4-5. A chaste one is known as having a single husband. One is a *kulaṭā* having two. *Dharṣiṇī* is known to have a third one. One is known to be *puṁścalī* having four. When it is five, she is *veśyā*. One is stated to be *yugmī* having six.

Above that is *mahāveśyā*. She is untouchable by any one of the castes.

6. A twice-born cohabiting a *kulaṭā* or *dharṣiṇī* or *puṁścalī* or *veśyā* or *yugmī* or *mahāveśyā*, would go to (the hell) *avaṭa*.

7-8. Whoever cohabits a *kulaṭā*, would dwell (in *avsṭa*) hundred years. One cohabiting *dhṛṣṭā* (*dharṣiṇī*) (would stay for) four times (the previous). One cohabiting *puṁścalī* (would) six times that, one cohabiting *veśyā* (would) eight times that and one cohabiting *yugmī* would stay ten times that without any doubt. The paramour cohabiting a *mahāveśyā* would stay for hundred times that.

9. (Lord) Brahmā has stated that it is as follows if he cohabits all the above. He would experience the sufferings there itself being beaten by the messenger of Yama.

10-11. A person cohabiting a *kulaṭā* would become the *tittiri* (bird), a *dhṛṣṭā* (would become) a cow, a *puṁścalī* (would become) a cuckoo, a *veśyā* (would become) a wolf, a *yugmī* (would become) a boar seven times in Bhārata. The paramour of *mahāveśyā* (would become) a silk-cotton tree in the cremation ground.

12-13. Whoever eats foolishly at the time of the eclipse of the moon and sun, would go to (the hell) *aruntuda* as many years as the moon. Then he would be born as a man suffering from stomach disease and dropsy, one-eyed and devoid of teeth and then pure.

14. Whoever offers a girl to another after promising one, would dwell in the hell of *pāṁśubhoga* consuming the same (dust) for hundred years.

15. O pious one ! Whoever takes away the gift (would go to) *pāśaveṣṭa* (bound by noose) for hundred years. He would remain on the bed of arrows being beaten by the messenger of Yama.

16-17. Whoever does not worship with devotion the earthen emblem of (Lord Śiva) would go to the extremely painful (hell) *śulapota* (bound with the spear) on account of the wrath of (Lord) Śiva. He would remain there for hundred years and be born as a beast seven times. Then he becomes a *devala*[3] in seven births and then pure.

18. Whoever chastises a brahmin with a stick and makes him tremble on account of fear, that person would dwell in (the hell) *prakampana* (shaking) as many years as the hair on (the body of) the brahmin.

19-21. Whoever looks angrily at her husband and utters harsh words, would go to (the hell) *ulkāmukha* (fiery-mouthed). The attendant of Yama would always put fire-brand in her mouth and would strike her on the head with a stick as many years as the hair (on the person). Then she would be a mortal and a widow in seven births. After having experienced pain, widowhood and disease, she (would become) pure thereafter.

22-26. A brahmin woman cohabited by a *śūdra* would go to (the hell) *andhakūpa* (dark well). She would dwell there in hot impure water in darkness without food day and night. She would experience much pain being beaten by the messenger of Yama. She would remain immersed in that water for a period of the fourteen Indras. Then she would be a female crow in thousand births, a female boar in hundred births, a hen in hundred births, a female jackal in seven births, a female pigeon in seven births and a female monkey in seven births. Then she would become a *caṇḍāla* woman cohabited by all in Bhārata. Then she would become a washerwoman seized by consumption and a *puṁścalī*.[4] Then she would be having leprosy and become an oil-monger woman. Then she would become pure.

27-29. A *veśyā*[5] would dwell in (the hell) *vedhana* (perforation), a *yugmī* in *daṇḍatāḍana* (chastised by rod), a *mahāveśyā* in *jālabandha* (mesh), a *kulaṭā* in *dehacūrṇaka* (pounding the body to dust), and a wanton woman in *dalana* (breaking one) and *dhṛṣṭā* in *śoṣaṇa* (dehydration) experiencing pain and being beaten by the messenger of Yama. O chaste one! Such a person would consume ordure and urine for the period of Manu. Then she would become an insect in the ordure for lakh years and then pure.

30-32. (Lord) Brahmā has stated that if a brahmin cohabits a brahmin woman (other than his wife), a *kṣatriya* a *kṣatriya* woman, a *vaiśya* a *vaiśya* woman and a *śūdra* a *śūdra* woman, would go to bitter water with the woman and dwell there for ten years consuming bitter water. Then the brahmin would become pure. Similarly *kṣatriya* and others would be. The women also would become pure.

33-35. If a *kṣatriya* or *vaiśya* cohabits a brahmin woman he would be deemed to be cohabiting his mother. He would go to the hell *sūrpa* (winnowing basket). He would be bitten by insects of the shape of the winnowing baskets along with the brahmin woman. Then he would be drinking hot urine and beaten by the messenger of Yama. He experiences suffering there itself for a period of fourteen Indras. He would then become a boar and a goat for seven times and then pure.

36. Whoever holds the Tulasī (holy basil) in the hand and does not maintain his resolve or makes a false swearing, would go to *jvālāmukha* (fiery mouth).

37. Whoever holds the water of the Ganges in the hand (or touches) the holy stone idol and does not maintain his resolve, would go to (the hell) *jvālāmukha.*

38. Whoever extends his right hand or stays in the abode of god and does not maintain his resolve, would go to *jvālāmukha.*

39. O chaste one ! Whoever touches a brahmin, cow or fire equal to (Lord) Viṣṇu, and does not maintain his resolve, would go to *jvālāmukha.*

40. Whoever betrays his friend, is ungrateful or has belied one's faith, such a person would go to *jvālāmukha.*

41. These people dwell there itself for a period of fourteen Indras being burnt by embers and chastised by the messengers of Yama.

42-46. Whoever touches the holy basil (and does not maintain his resolve) would become a *caṇḍāla* for seven times and then become pure. Whoever touches the water of the Ganges similarly, would be a barbarian in five births and then pure. O beautiful one ! Whoever touches a stone idol similarly, would be an insect in the ordure in seven births. Whoever touches an idol that is worshipped, would similarly become an insect in the wound for seven births and then pure. Whoever extends the right hand, would similarly be a serpent for seven births. Then he would be born as a man bereft of the hand and then pure. Whoever utters a lie in the abode of the god, would similarly become a *devala* for seven births. Whoever touches a brahmin etc., would similarly become a degraded brahmin certainly. They would then become dumb and deaf three times, bereft of wife, without progeny and without intellect and then pure.

47. Whoever betrays his friend (would be) a mongoose, an ungrateful one (would be) a rhinoceros, a traitor (would be) a tiger for seven births in Bhārata.

48. Whoever gives false evidence, (would become) a bear in seven births. They pull down the ancestors and descendants of them for seven generations.

49-51. A dull twice-born bereft of the daily duties, not having faith in the statements of the *vedas*, mocking at them, devoid of austerities and fasts, scoffing at the words of the pious, and conceitful towards the conceited would dwell in icy water for hundred years. He would become a water-creature duly for hundred births. Then he would be born in the different species of fish and then pure.

52-56. Whoever steals the wealth of the gods or brahmins, would cause the downfall of the ancestors and descendants for ten generations. He would go to (the hell) *dhūmāndha* (dark with smoke) having darkness due to smoke. He would dwell for four *yuga* periods tormented by smoke and consuming smoke. Then he would become a mouse in Bhārata for hundred births. Then he would be born in different species of birds and insects, then as different species of trees and then as a man. (He would then be) bereft of a wife and progeny. (He would be) a hunter with disease. Then he becomes a goldsmith and a gold merchant. Then he would be an attendant on an infidel and a brahmin astrologer.

57-59. A brahmin taking the profession as an astrologer, or as a physician, or as an iron merchant, a trader in arrack etc., and a seller of alchemy materials would go to Nāgaveṣṭa (encircled by serpents), be encircled by serpents and dwell there as many years as his hair and being bitten by serpents. Then he would become an astrologer and a physician for seven births, and then a blacksmith, cowherd and maker of conches and then pure.

60. O Chaste lady ! I have described you the well-known pits. There are other minor pits not well-known.

61. There are sinners in them enjoying the fruits of their deeds. They also wander in mundane existence. Would you like to hear more ?

CHAPTER THIRTY-TWO

Deeds Conveying One to Heaven

Sāvitrī said:

1-7. O Master of piety ! Blessed one ! Proficient in the *vedas* and accessory texts ! Expounder of the different *purāṇas, itihāsas* and *pāñcarātra* texts ! O Virtuous one ! You tell me that which is the essence of everything, liked mostly by all, agreeable to all, the seed of destruction of one's deeds, commendable, conferring happiness on men, bestowing fame, yielding piety, auspicious among all those auspicious and on account of which people do not go to hell and experience misery in worldly life, do not perceive the pits and do not fall into them, and there will not be birth. O Brahman ! You are fit to tell me about the shapes and size of the pits and the forms assumed by the sinners dwelling there. How do men go to other worlds when their bodies had been reduced to ashes ? With which body one enjoys the fruits of good and bad actions ? How the body does not perish after enjoying miseries for a long time? What kind of body is that ?

Nārāyaṇa said:

8. O Nārada ! After having listened to the words of Sāvitrī, Dharmarāja remembered Hari and began narrating the legend after bowing to the preceptor.

Yama said:

9-10. O Child ! In all the *vedas, dharmasaṁhitās, purāṇas, itihāsas, pāñcarātra* texts, in all other *śāstra* texts and *vedāṅgas,* O Pious one ! The essence and auspicious thing is the service to (Lord) Kṛṣṇa.

11-13. O Auspicious one ! It makes one cross the grief and torment of birth, death, decrepitude and disease. It is the embodiment of all auspiciousness. It is the cause of supreme bliss. It is the cause of all perfections. It makes one ford the ocean of hells. It enables the tree of devotion to sprout. It cuts the tree of deeds. It is the steps leading to Goloka. It confers an indestructible position. It confers the states such as oneness of position, oneness of rank, oneness of form and proximity.

14. O Chaste one ! The servants of (Lord) Kṛṣṇa do not behold the pits, the messenger of Yama, Yama and the servants of Yama even in their dreams.

15-16. Whoever practices the austerities of Hari enjoying the fruits of their deeds, whoever bathes in the sacred water of Hari, whoever do not eat on the day of Hari (eleventh day), salute Hari daily and worship the idol of Hari, they do not go to my aweful city Samyamanī.

17. Those brahmins purified by the three twilight worships, endowed with good conduct always bent on their own duties and tranquil do not go to the abode of Yama.

18. They always enjoy heaven. But the other worshippers of other gods go to the mortal world and come back to heaven and do not have liberation. Men do not get liberation without service to (Lord) Kṛṣṇa.

19-20a. Whether people are bent on their duties or they cease to do their duties, when they go to the mortal world, the servants of Yama do not approach them being afraid of the devotees of Kṛṣṇa like the serpents from Vainateya (Garuḍa) (Eagle).

20b-22. I tell my messenger proceeding to the mortal world with noose in hand to go anywhere except the hermitage of the devotee of Hari. Citragupta (the chief among the attendants of Yama) himself removes as if afraid with folded palms the names of the votaries of the formula of Kṛṣṇa. (Lord) Brahmā renders them (the services) such as *madhuparka.*[1]

23-24. The ordeals of the pious crossing the Brahmaloka and proceeding to the Goloka would perish the moment they touch the pious. Just like the fuel and grass in the glowing fire, delusion gets deluded on beholding them as if much frightened.

25-26a. Lust goes to a licentious person. O Chaste one ! Avarice, anger, death, disease, decrepitude, grief, fear, time, good and bad deeds, pleasure and enjoyment run away.

26b. O Chaste one ! I have described you the type of persons who do not go to the place of Yama.

27. Listen to me. I shall describe you the corporeal frame as in the sacred texts. The earth, wind, sky, heat and water are explicit.

28-29a. These are the primary basis of the creation of beings by the creator. The body that has been made up of the five elements such as the earth etc., is artificial and perishable. It gets almost reduced to dust.

29b-33. The individual soul of the size of the thumb having the shape of the person supports the subtle body and its form for the sake of enjoyment. That body does not get reduced to ashes in glowing fire in my place. The body does not get lost in water or if it is beaten long, or by weapons and missiles, sharp thorns, hot liquid, hot iron, hot stone or by embracing a heated image or by falling[2] from above. It is neither burnt nor broken and it enjoys only torments. O Noble lady ! I have described you the details about the cause as in the religious texts. Listen to me. I shall describe you the characteristics of the pits.

CHAPTER THIRTY-THREE

Description of the Pits in Yamaloka

Yama said:

1. O chaste one ! All the pits (in the hell) are circular like the orb of the moon. They are very deep and set up with different varieties of stones.

2. They are indestructible and outside the pale of deluge established by the will of god. That abode is of varied forms giving grief to the sinners.

3-4. The pit of fire is stated to be of the form of glowing embers, the flames extending to hundred cubits (high) and extending to a *krośa*[1] around. It is abound with sinners screaming loud and guarded by my messengers who always beat (the sinners).

5-6. The pit of hot water extending to half a *krośa* is filled with wild creatures, intensively and terribly dark filled with hosts of sinners making screams on being beaten by my messengers guarding it.

7-8. The frightening pit of hot saline water extending to a *krośa*, is abound with alligators and sinners crying aloud requesting for rescue when they are beaten by my messengers and are having parched throat and palates due to wandering without food.

9-10. The pit filled with ordure and urine extending to a *krośa* is condemned with extremely foul smell and filled with sinners being beaten by my messengers and experiencing miseries like not having food and crying for protection and bitten by the worms therein.

11-12. The pit full with hot urine abound with worms in the urine is filled with great sinners being always bitten by those worms. It extends to a *gavyūti*,[2] and shrouded in darkness. It is filled with the perennial screams (of sinners) being thrashed by my terrible messengers and having parched throat and palates.

13. The pit of phlegm extending to a *krośa* is abound with sinners partaking the same and being bitten by the worms therein.

14-15. The pit of poison extending to half a *krośa* is abound with sinners being bitten by the poisonous worms, consuming poison and thrashed by my messengers. The sinners scream and shake on account of the cruel worms resembling snakes having powerful teeth.

16. The pit filled with the rheum of the eye extending to half a *krośa* has worms and is abound with floating sinners being bitten by the worms.

17. The pit filled with the marrow extending to one fourth *krośa* is unbearable and abound with sinners partaking the same end being thrashed by (my messengers).

18. The pit filled with semen extending to one fourth *krośa* is abound with sinners wailing and being bitten by the worms in the semen and agitated on account of fear.

19. The pit filled with foul smelling blood is deep resembling a well. It is abound with sinners consuming that and being bitten by the worms.

20. The pit filled with the tears of men extending to half a well is abound with sinners consuming the same and being thrashed by my messengers and bitten by the worms.

21. The pit filled with the bodily impurities of man has bewildered sinners consuming the same and being beaten by my messengers and bitten by the worms.

22. (The pit) filled with the ear-wax extends to a quarter of a well and abounds with sinners consuming the same and wailing on account of being bitten by the worms.

23-25. (The pit) filled with the marrow of men having much bad smell containing great sinners, is of the extent of a quarter of a well. (The pit) filled with sticky flesh and abound with sinners beaten by my messengers is of the measure of a well and frightening. It is filled with those selling the girls and who are eating the same and being bitten by the worms and crying for protection and being threatened. It is frightening.

26. The four (pits) of nails etc., are of the measure of one fourth of a well abound with sinners always beaten by my messengers.

27-28. The pit of heated copper with fire brands of copper is always surrounded by a lakh hot copper images. Each one of the image is embraced by crying sinners. Its extent is two miles. (The sinners) are beaten by my messengers.

29-31. The pit of iron has heated iron pieces containing burning embers and always surrounded by lakh heated iron images. Each one is embraced by great sinners always running about with fear, crying for protection and being beaten by the messengers. It is of the measure of four miles. It is frightening and dark.

32. The pit of heat and pit of hot wine is half the well. It is abound with the sinners partaking the same and beaten by my messengers.

33-36. The pit of sharp thorns is at the bottom of silk-cotton tree. It is of the measure of lakh *puruṣa* (height of a man) (in length)and two miles in breadth. It is painful. It is encircled by sharp thorns measuring (the length of) four cubits. Each one of the great sinners is being pierced by the thorns. They are falling down from the top of trees and beaten by my messengers. (The sinners) with their palates parched would cry for water. They would be agitated with great fear, their hands smashed by the clubs and tossed about in hot oil.

37. (The pit) flooded with poison of (serpents such as) Takṣaka etc., measures two miles. The sinners therein partaking the same would be beaten by my messengers.

38-39. (The pit) filled with hot oil contains worms etc. The great sinners partaking (oil) would be besmeared with oil. They will be moving here and there crying while being beaten by the messengers. It measures four miles.

40-42. The pit of weapons is dark measuring two miles and frightening. It is encircled by sharp-edged iron weapons of the shape of a spear. It is of the form of a bed of weapons extending to two miles. It is abound with sinners pierced by the spears. (The sinners) are beaten by my messengers and have their throats and palates parched. They are being tormented by frightful worms creeping therein.

43. (The pit) extending to two miles is filled with sharp teeth hideous in their form and dark. It is filled with frightened great sinners being bitten by worms and crying while being beaten by my messengers.

44. The pit filled with pus has much foul smell and extends to half a mile. It is abound with sinners partaking the same and being beaten by my messengers.

45-46. (The pit) filled with ice water extending to four miles and encircled by crore serpents of the size of the palm tree is abound with sinners with their bodies encircled by serpents and bitten by them. They raise sounds while being beaten by my messengers.

47-48. The three pits of mosquitoes etc., are full with mosquitoes. All are measuring one mile. They are abound with great sinners with their hand and feet bound. They are besmeared with blood being beaten by the guards with iron. They move around wailing aloud hā ! hā !

49. The pit of *vajra* (an insect) and scorpion is abound with these two. It extends to half a well. It contains sinners being bitten by *vajra* and scorpion.

50. The three pits of arrows etc., are filled with the same. They abound with sinners being pierced by them and besmeared with blood. They extend to half a well.

51. The pit containing heated mud and water is dark and circular in shape. It contains sinners tormented and bitten by worms.

52-53. The pit abound with crore water creatures like alligators, wild and hideous, abounds with sinners bitten by them. It extends to half a well. The pit abounds with hundred crore sinners partaking ordure, urine and phlegm. (The pit) extending to four cubits and abound with hideous ravens contains a lakh sinners.

54. The pit of Sañcala and Vāji (variety of birds) is abound with them. It contains sinners being bitten by them and always crying.

55. The pit containing *vajra* extends to 400 cubits and abounds with sinners always making sound and being scorched by the *vajra*, (the pit) is always dark.

56. (The pit) measuring twice that of a well and set up with hot couch like burning embers is abound with moving sinners.

57. (The pit) set up with stones sharp like the edges of the swords contains great sinners shedding blood being struck by iron.

58. (The pit) full of foul smelling saliva contains sinners partaking the same. It extends to two miles and deep. (The sinners) are beaten by my messengers.

59. (The pit) filled with hot water like the collyrium extends to four hundred cubits. It contains moving sinners being beaten by my messengers.

60. (The pit) filled with powder like thing extending to two miles abounds with sinners consuming them and scorched by them and beaten by my messengers.

61. The pit resembling a potter's wheel, revolving always has sixteen sharp spokes and contains sinners who are revolved.

62-64. (The pit) extremely crooked and deep extending to four miles set up in the shape of a cave is endowed with hot water. It is dark and frightening. It contains great sinners being bitten by water creatures and moving around raising sounds. They are bitten by crore hideous looking turtles in the water.

65. (The pit) set up with glowing band extends to two miles. It is abound with sinners crying and moving around always.

66. The pit containing hot dust extending to two miles is deep. It is abound with moving sinners partaking the dust.

67-68. The *dagdha-kuṇḍa* (hot pit) is stated to be filled with collections of hot stones. It is dark and deep. It is abound with sinners with burnt bodies, dried up palates and beaten by my frightful messengers. It extends to two miles.

69-71. The dreadful pit of husk is abound with husk, water and hot alkali. It contains various water creatures hideous in their forms. It extends to four miles, deep and dark. It contains sinners consuming the same and bitten by the water creatures. They move about wailing without beholding each other.

72-74. The pit of sword-edged leaf is like a forest of sword-edged leans, tall under the palm tree, extending to one mile and containing falling leaves. It is filled with the blood of unholy sinners falling from the top of the tree, making sound seeking protection. (The pit) is deep, dark, dreadful and endowed with blood worms.

75. The pit of the shape of a dagger are abound with weapons measures 400 cubits. It is filled with the blood of sinners, like the edges of the dagger and is dreadful.

76. The needle-faced pit is endowed with needle-tipped weapons and filled with a flood of blood of the sinners. It extends to 200 cubits and is painful.

77-78. (The pit) resembling the face of the species of creature such as alligators is of the form of a deep well extending to 80 cubits. That is filled with great sinners having hung faces always and are bitten by worms therein.

79. The pit of the shape of the face of men measures 64 cubits. It is deep in the form of a well and always filled with sinners.

80-81. The pit known as the tusk of elephant is pervaded by hosts of elephants and the place is like a pit. It is filled with the blood of sinners killed by the tusk of the elephants. (The sinners) are bitten by the worms therein. They always make feeble sounds. (The pit) measures 400 cubits.

82. The pit of cow's face is declared as measuring one hundred and twenty cubits in the shape of cow's face painful to the sinners.

83-90. The pit of the shape of a pot always made to revolve by the wheel of time is dreadful. It is dark and it measures four miles. Its depth equals lakh times the height of man. It is very extensive. Inside the pit in some corner it contains hot oil. Somewhere inside it has the pit of hot iron etc. Somewhere inside it has the pit of hot stone. It contains the prime sinners and great sinners. They always raise sounds but do not behold one another. They are then beaten by my messengers with rods and clubs. Being revolved they fall down unconscious repeatedly being pushed down by my messengers and fallen down from high above. O Beautiful one ! In the unfordable *kumbhīpāka*, there are four times the sinners in all the other pits. *Kumbhīpāka* is declared as the main among all pits (where the sinners fallen for a long time and devoid of all pleasures dwell).

91-93. The pit of thread of time is declared as that wherein the sinners are bound by the thread set up by time. It is endowed with hot water. They (sinners) are lifted by my messengers and immersed for a moment. They are bound by the exhaling breath for some time in between the pits. They experience much torment. The bodies of enjoyment are not perishable. They are beaten by my messengers with rods and clubs.

94-95. (The pit) is said to be *avaṭoda* (pit with water), it is a type of well where the water takes its shape. It is full of hot water extending to eighty cubits. It is always pervaded by great sinners with scorched bodies and always beaten by my messengers.

96-97. (The pit) *Aruntuda* is known to be that where all the diseases would come to the sinners the moment they touch the water here by falling into the pit extending to four hundred cubits. All the sinners held up there feel agony and raise hā, hā sound.

98. The *pāṁsubhoja* is filled with hot dust and glowing wherein the sinners are scorched and are partaking the dust.

99-100a. Where the sinner feel shaking, the moment they fall in it, is (the pit) *prakampana, pāśaveṣṭana* is that where the sinner gets encircled by the noose. This pit measures two miles.

100b-101a. The *śūlaprota* measures eighty cubits. The sinner would be strung to the spear soon after he falls into it.

101b-102a. Where the falling sinners tremble, that is *prakampana* filled with ice water extending to one mile.

102b-103a. Where my messengers place burning torches into the mouth of sinners, (that pit) extending to eighty cubits and filled with burning torches (is called *ulkāmukha*).

103b-105. *Andhakūpa* is declared as measuring lakh times the height of man, deep and circular. It is abound with different kinds of insects. It is dreadful. The pit is circular in the shape of a well and pervaded by darkness. It is abound with sinners partaking that and not perceiving each other. They are burnt by hot water. They move about being bitten by worms. There is darkness and (the sinners) are blind.

106. (The pit) *vedhana* is declared as that extending to eighty cubits in which the sinners are pierced with different kinds of weapons.

107. The pit is known to *daṇḍatāḍana* extending to sixty-four cubits in which the sinners are beaten by my messengers with rods.

108. Just as the fish (are caught) in big nets, the sinners are caught. It is known as *jālavat* extending to one hundred and twenty cubits.

109-110. The pit in which the falling sinners are pounded by iron altar set up inside, is crore times the height of man in depth dark and eighty cubits wide. It is declared as the *dehacūrṇa* of the unconscious ignorant ones.

111. The pit extending to sixty four cubits wherein the sinners are crushed by my messengers with clubs is known as *dalana.*

112-113. (The pit) is declared as *śoṣaṇa* hundred times the height of a man in its depth and extending to one hundred and twenty cubits, in which the sinner feels parched throat and palate soon after the fall into hot gravels. It is dark and devoid of water and food.

114. The pit full with bitter water of various hide extending to four hundred cubits having foul smell is abound with sinners partaking the same.

115-117. The pit in the shape of a winnowing basket extending to forty eight cubits is full with hot iron fire-brands gravels and sinners. O beautiful one ! That pit inside which is always pervaded by the flames of glowing fire extending to eighty cubits filled with sinners scorched by the flames causing great pain, is known as *jvālāmukha.*

118. The pit is known as *jihma* extending to half a well between hot bricks in which the sinner becomes unconscious and distressed.

119. (The pit) is declared as *dūmāndha* pervaded by darkness on account of smoke and abound with sinners blinded by smoke. It extends to four hundred cubits

120. The pit is (known as) *nāgaveṣṭana* extending to four hundred cubits and filled with serpents, in which the sinner soon after his fall is encircled by the serpents.

121. I have described you the characteristics of eighty-six pits. What else you would like to hear ?

CHAPTER THIRTY-FOUR

The Description of Lord Kṛṣṇa and the Revival of Satyavān

Sāvitrī said:

1. O Lord ! Bless me with devotion to Lord Hari, that is the essence and difficult to get. I have heard everything from you. There is nothing left out now.

2. Describe me a little about the glory of the attributes of (Lord) Kṛṣṇa, that is the seed of redemption of lakh men and that which makes one ford the ocean of hell.

3. It is the cause of all deeds relating to liberation. It wards off all inauspicious things. It cuts the trees of deed. It destroys the floods of committed sins.

4. How many are the types of liberation and what are their characteristics ? What is the nature of devotion to (Lord) Hari and the enjoyment of one's deeds ?

5. (Lord) Brahmā had made women bereft of knowledge about the reality. O Foremost among the knowers of the *vedas,* describe me that knowledge that is the essence.

6. All types of gifts, fasting, bathing in sacred places, austerity and penance do not deserve one-sixteenth (merit) of imparting knowledge to an ignorant one.

7. Mother excels the father hundred times in her merits. O Lord ! The preceptor imparting knowledge is adorable hundred times than the mother.

Yama said:

8. I have already conferred on you all that you desired in your mind. O Child ! Now let you have devotion to (Lord) Hari on account of my favour.

9-16. O Auspicious one ! You desire to hear the glory of the virtues of (Lord) Kṛṣṇa that elevates the family of the expounders, interrogators and listeners. (Lord) Śeṣa (the serpent vehicle of Viṣṇu) is not capable (of describing) with his thousand mouths. Lord Mṛtyuñjaya (Śiva) is not capable of describing with his five faces. Neither (Lord) Brahmā, the support of the four *vedas* and the creator of the universe with his four faces, nor Viṣṇu, the omniscient, are capable. Certainly Lord Kārttikeya cannot describe with his six faces. Lord Gaṇeśa, the preceptor of preceptors of the foremost ascetics is not proficient. The four *vedas* which are the essence of all the *śāstras* (treatises) and the wisemen do not know even a digit of the virtues. (Goddess) Sarasvatī is not capable in her effort to describe the virtues. Sanatkumāra, Dharma, Sanaka, Sanātana, Sananda, Kapila, Sūrya and other sons of Brahmā, the accomplished ones are not capable of describing (the virtues). What about others with dull intellect? The accomplished ones, great ascetics, yogins and others are not capable of describing. Who else and we would be capable of describing the virtues of the Lord ?

17. Whose lotus feet (Lords) Brahmā, Viṣṇu, Śiva and others meditate, only by his devotees it is extremely possible. It is extremely difficult for others.

18. Some know the glory of his virtues to a certain extent. Brahmā and the sons of Brahmā and others know something more.

19. Gaṇeśa, the preceptor of the wise knows something more than that. The omniscient Śambhu (Śiva) alone knows them above all.

20. Lord Kṛṣṇa, the supreme soul, had imparted him wisdom in days of yore at the dance-circle at Goloka at a charming extremely secluded place.

21. There itself some more virtues were glorified again. Śiva himself narrated it to Dharma at Śivaloka.

22. Dharma narrated it to Bhāskara (Sun) at Puṣkara. O Chaste one ! My father then propitiated him and obtained me.[1]

23. O Pious one ! In the past I had a detachment towards my personal work and I had desired to do penance.

24. Then my father narrated me the glory of his virtues. Listen to me. I shall describe you the incomprehensible thing as in the *āgama*[2] texts.

25. O Fair one ! Just as the sky does not know its own limits, he himself does not know his own virtues. How can others know that ?

26. The Lord is the soul of all beings. He is the cause of all causes. He is Lord of all beings. He is the first being. He is omniscient. He takes all the forms.

27. He has an external form, eternal body, eternal bliss. He is formless. He is without trouble and free from fear. He is void of all virtues. He is without support.

28. He is unstained. He is the witness of all and support of all. He is the most supreme. The Nature is his modification. All the objects of Nature are his modifications.

29. He himself is the Absolute Being, the Nature and above Nature. He takes different forms, yet he is formless for the sake of blessing the devotee.

30. The childhood form as a cowherd, dark like the fresh cloud, is very much attractive, beautiful and charming.

31. (That form) is the beautiful sporting ground for the beauty of crore gods of love. His eyes surpass the grace of the lotuses of the midday of the autumn.

32. His face is adorned with the beauty of crore full moons of the autumn. He is adorned with gemmed ornaments studded with invaluable gems.

33. He has a graceful smile. He is always beautified with invaluable yellow garment. He is the supreme form of Brahman. He is radiant with the lustre of Brahman.

34. He is easily perceivable, tranquil, the consort of Rādhā and endless. He is beheld by the smiling cowherdesses around him.

35. He is at the centre of the sphere of dance. He is seated on a gemmed throne. He is playing on his flute. He has two arms. He is adorned by the garland of wild flowers.

36. His radiant chest is beautiful with the excellent gem *kaustubha*[3]. His body is besmeared with saffron, *agallochum*, musk and sandal.

37. He is adorned by the graceful flowers like *campaka*, lotus and jasmine. His diadem is radiant with the graceful beauty of *campaka*.

38. His devotees meditate him as described above overwhelmed with devotion. The creator of the world performs his creation being afraid of him.

39. He writes down the fruits of all the beings according to their deeds. He (Brahmā) confers the fruits of penance and deeds at his command.

40. Viṣṇu is the protector of all beings and protects always being afraid of him. Kālāgnirudra (Rudra at the time of deluge) is the destroyer being afraid of him.

41-42. Śiva, the conqueror of death, preceptor of the preceptors of wise, is an accomplished one, an ascetic and omniscient on account of wisdom conferred by him. He is endowed with supreme bliss, devotion and detachment. The wind, foremost among the swift moving, blows by his grace.

43. O Chaste one ! The Sun is always shining being afraid of him. By his command Indra rains and Mṛtyu (God of death) moves among beings.

44. By his order the fire burns and the water is cold. The guardians of the directions guard by his order being much afraid.

45. The zodiac and the planets revolve being afraid of him. The trees bear fruits and flowers on account of fear.

46-47a. Being afraid of him the fruits become ripe and the trees are fruitless. Fearing him the beings on the land do not survive in water. Similarly by his command the beings in the water do not live on land.

47b-48. Fearing him I practise and uphold the law of righteousness and unrighteousness. By his order *kāla* takes everything and rotates them. Death takes away (the life) untimely afraid of him.

49-51a. *Kāla* takes away (the life) of those falling into glowing fire, or into deep ocean, or from the top of a tree, or at a sharp sword or into the mouths of serpents etc., as well as those pierced by various kinds of weapons and missiles in fierce battles, and those lying on flower beds being guarded by the kinsmen by means of *tantra* (incantations etc.) and *mantra* (formula).

51b-52. Wind supports the column of water, column of water the tortoise, the tortoise the serpent Ananta, and Ananta the earth, the ocean and the seven mountains by his order. He bears the various forms in the form of the earth.

53a-57a. All beings are from him and all beings get merged in him in the end. The life of Indra is seventy-one divine *yugas*. A day and night of Brahmā consists of 28 revolutions. Experts in reckoning time have known that 25560[4] *yugas* of the mortals equal the life of Indra. In the same way thirty days make up a month and two such months a season. Six seasons constitute a year and one hundred such years constitute the age of Brahmā. The period of Brahmā is covered by the opening of the eyes of (Lord) Hari. When he is shutting his eyes, people know that it is the dissolution of nature.

57b-73a. In that deluge all the nature, gods, etc., both animate and inanimate beings repose in Brahmā and Brahmā in the navel lotus of Śrī Kṛṣṇa. (Lord) Viṣṇu, the four-armed, reclining in the milky ocean at Vaikuṇṭha, repose on the left side of the Supreme soul, Kṛṣṇa. Rudra and others, Bhairava and others and all other attendants of (Lord) Śiva get dissolved in Lord Śiva, their support, the eternal bliss of wisdom, when the presiding one of wisdom gets dissolved in Kṛṣṇa, the soul of Lord Mahādeva. All the energies get dissolved in Durgā, the illusion of Viṣṇu. She (gets dissolved) in the intellect of (Lord) Kṛṣṇa as presiding deity of the intellect. (Lord) Skanda, a part-manifestation of (Lord) Nārāyaṇa, gets dissolved in his chest. Gaṇeśvara (the master of the *gaṇas*), the Lord of the gods, a part-manifestation of Śrī Kṛṣṇa (rests) on his arms. O Pious one ! (Women) forming part of Padmā (Lakṣmī) (disslove) in Padmā and she herself in Rādhā. The cowherdesses as well as all the consorts of the gods (dissolve) in her. She is the presiding deity of the life-breath of Kṛṣṇa. She rests in his life-breath. Sāvitrī as well as all the *vedas* and *śāstras* dissolve in Sarasvatī. Vāṇī (Sarasvatī) remains in the tongue of that Supreme soul. The cowherds in the Goloka get dissolved in his hair. The life-breaths of all beings and wind dossolve in his life-breath. Fire dissolves into his digestive fire in the stomach and water in the tip of his tongue. The devotees of Viṣṇu (get dissolved) in his lotus feet with supreme happiness, drinking the excellent essence of honey of devotion. The minor Virāṭ dissolves in Mahat[5] and the great Virāṭ in Kṛṣṇa. The entire universe (dissolves) in the pores of his skin. By the winking of his eye great deluge takes place. When that Supreme soul opens his eyes creation takes place. Whatever creation remains at the time of shutting of his eyes, so much gets destroyed at the time of opening (of his eyes). After hundred years of Brahmā's life, the creation gets dissolved again. O Pious one ! There is no count for the creation and dissolution made by Brahmā. You understand that the number is similar to the dust of earth. Dissolution takes place by the closing of the eyes by that soul of all beings. By the will of god, creation takes place again by the opening of the eyes.

73b-74a.Who indeed in the whole universe is capable of describing his virtues ? I have described you as I have heard from my father as in the *āgama* texts.

74b-76. Four kinds of liberation have been explained in the four *vedas.* The chief among is devotion to Hari and it is greater than liberation. One of them is oneness of place with Hari. The next one is oneness of form. (The third one) is proximity. (The fourth one) is absolute emancipation according to the codes. The devotees do not desire these bereft of service to him etc.

77-78. The worshippers can easily become an accomplished one, immortal (god) and Brahmā, cutting the birth and death, decrepitude, disease, fear, grief etc. The retention of the divine form is said to yield absolute liberation. Liberation is void of service and devotion furthers service.

79-82a. This is the difference between devotion and service. Listen to me for a description of the characteristic of enjoyment. The wise men knew '*niṣeka*' as enjoyment (of the fruits) of one's action. The service to Śrī Kṛṣṇa destroys that and confers supreme good. O Pious one ! This is the quintessence knowledge of the metaphysics and *vedas.* This has been declared as remover of obstacles and conferrer of good. O Child ! You go back as you wish. After having spoken thus, the son of Sun revived her husband, conferred on her good wishes and was about to leave.

82b-84. Beholding Yama about to leave, Sāvitrī saluted, held his feet and wept, since separation from good people causes grief. O Nārada ! Yama, the mine of compassion, beheld her weeping, became pleased, wept and spoke to her thus:

Yama said:

85-86. After having enjoyed happiness for lakh years in the sacred land of Bhārata, you will go to Goloka the abode of Śrī Kṛṣṇa, in the end. O Good one! You go home and practise the austerity of Sāvitrī. It would confer liberation for women (if practised) for fourteen years.

87-88. The austerity of Sāvitrī is good if practised on the fourteenth day of the bright fortnight in (the month of) Jyeṣṭha (May-June). The austerity of Mahālakṣmī is good if practised on the eighth day of the bright fortnight in (the month of) Bhādrapada (August-September). Whoever practises this austerity every year for sixteen years till the end of that fortnight with great devotion, would go to the place of Hari.

89-93. Whoever worships with devotion for the sake of progeny and wealth, the goddess Maṅgalacaṇḍikā on every Tuesday, or (the goddess) Ṣaṣṭhī, conferring auspiciousness, on the sixth day of the bright fortnight every month or (the goddess) Manasā, accomplishing all things, on the *āṣāḍha-saṅkrānti*[6], or Rādhā, the most endearing one of Kṛṣṇa more than his life, in the sphere of dance in Kārttika (November) or Goddess Durgā, the dispeller of all impediments, the illusion of Viṣṇu and conferrer of boons , on the eighth day of the bright fortnight every month after fasting, or Nature, the mother of the Universe, or a chaste woman having the husband and children, may be invoked on chaste and pure women or plates or images, would enjoy happiness in this world and reach the place of Śrī Hari in the end.

94. After having stated thus Dharmarāja returned to his abode. Sāvitrī also escorted her husband to her abode.

95. O Nārada ! Sāvitrī narrated to Satyavān and other relatives, the whole episode as it had happened.

96. On account of the boon, the father of Sāvitrī got sons in due course, her father-in-law regained his sight and kingdom and she (got) sons.

97. That chaste woman enjoyed happiness for lakh years in the holy land of Bhārata, and went to Goloka along with her husband.

98. Sāvitrī, the presiding deity of Savitā as well as the formulae and *vedas*, is hence declared as Sāvitrī.

99. O Child ! I have described you the excellent story of Sāvitrī. Would you like to hear again about the fruits of deeds of a being ?

NOTES

CHAPTER ONE

69.1. The present and the last among the periods believed to be lasting for 432000 human years.

89.2. Consisting of offering a seat, reception, water for cleansing the feet, water for cleansing the mouth and respectful offering of water.

92.3. For details see Mār. P. chs. 89-90.

117.4. *Satyayuga* otherwise known as *kṛtayuga* is equal to 17,28,000 years. Each succeeding *yuga* is less by a quarter than the preceding *yuga.*

CHAPTER TWO

45.1. These are vital breath, wind going down the body, wind in the cavity of the navel essential for digestion, wind going upwards from the throat extending upto the head and that which is diffused through the whole body.

47.2. A *manvantara* is equal to 4,320,000 years.

80.3. The word Padmanābha in this verse means 'One having the lotus in his navel' referring to Viṣṇu. It has been left out in the translation as it does not fit in with the context.

CHAPTER THREE

10.1. A measure of distance equal to eight or nine miles.

27.2. *Om kṛṣṇāya svāhā.*

CHAPTER FOUR

25.1. A day of Brahmā equal to 1000 *yugas.*

25.2. Offering seat, invocation, water for washing the feet, respectful water, water for sipping, fire sweet things, dress, ornaments and other materials for worship.

CHAPTER FIVE

14.1. A symbol used in writing, representing a hard aspirated sound and marked as ':'.

CHAPTER SIX

6.1. Denotes the third day in the bright half of Vaiśākha.

6.2. A portent foreboding in a great calamity.

CHAPTER EIGHT

7.1. Powerful demons said to have sprung from the ears of Viṣṇu while he was asleep. As they threatened to devour Brahmā, they were killed by Viṣṇu.

27.2. Hiraṇyakṣa was a demon. He rolled the earth and kept it hidden in the nether world. Lord Viṣṇu assumed the form of a boar, killed the demon and rescued the earth.

CHAPTER TEN

35.1. Denotes the *akṣayatṛtiya* falling on the third day of the bright half of Vaiśākha (May-June).

71.2. About 8 or 9 miles.

118.3. A *yojana* is about to 8 or 9 miles.

164.4. The reading yen iṇ the text should be corrected as ye-n to make sense.

CHAPTER TWELVE

11.1. One of the eight forms of marriage in which it is done with mutual consent of the two.

CHAPTER FIFTEEN

7.1. One of the five constituent units of a day based on the asterism ruling over a day and the day associated with it.

13.2. The reading should be nyagrodhaparimaṇḍalam having hard breasts, broad hips and slender waist.

18.3. Agreeing with the preceding and succeeding expressions it seems to be thirty thousand.

CHAPTER SIXTEEN

1. A Rākṣasa who kills secretly.

CHAPTER SEVENTEEN

32.1. Son of Lord Śiva.

32.2. This and the rest are different minor divinities.

46.3. These and the rest are supernatural beings.

84.4. Lord Śiva and Pārvatī in their hermaphrodite form.

CHAPTER EIGHTEEN

13.1. An *akṣauhiṇī* is a large army consisting of 21870 chariots, and equal number of elephants, 65610 horses and 109350 infantry.

CHAPTER NINETEEN

37.1. For its explanation see 18.13.1 above.

43.2. The word *balāhaka* seems to have been used in the sense of commander, although it means also a mountain and the devastating clouds at the time of a deluge.

CHAPTER TWENTY-THREE

22.1. The five products got from a cow-urine, cowdung, milk, curd and clarified butter.

CHAPTER TWENTY-FOUR

33.1. These are worlds one above the other in the celestial region.

CHAPTER TWENTY-FIVE

19.1. *Indriyaṇaṁ* has been taken as a better reading instead of *īśvaraṇaṁ.*

CHAPTER TWENTY-SEVEN

9.1. Sacred emblem of Lord Viṣṇu. For details see 21.58 ff.–

47.2. Traditionally the world is divided into seven continents, Jambūdvīpa extends from north of Himālayas to the whole of the sub-continent.

59.3. Equal to 24 seconds.

69.4. Imaginary zodiacal houses (corresponding to the period between March and July).

87.5. These are offering water for rinsing the mouth, water for sipping, water for washing the feet etc.

120.6. A sacrifice performed by an universal monarch.

CHAPTER THIRTY

21.1. Suggested reading *payayati* is better than *patayati.*

41.2. Barbarian.

42.3. One of the sanctified place at Gayā, where one has to offer cakes for the sake of the manes.

89.4. The printed text wrongly reads *śaivyagandhaṁ śukanaṁ* as two words. They should be read together.

92.5 The printed text wrongly reads Raitya, to be corrected as Raupya.

145.6. The reading *vṛṣala* is more appropriate than *vṛṣaṇa.*

157.7. The Master of sense-organs.

162.8. These days occur respectively in the months of August, April and February.

162.9. Occurring in January.

170.10. *Yo jayet* in the printed text should be read together to make it sensible.

213.11. These are rivers flowing in India.

CHAPTER THIRTY-ONE

2.1. See Verse 4.

2.2. See Verse 5.

17.3. See 30.215.

26.4. See verse 4 above.

27.5. For this and other terms here see verse 5 above.

CHAPTER THIRTY-TWO

22.1. Offering of a mixture of curd, clarified butter, water, honey and sandal paste.

32.2. The letters *patane* have not come off well in the printed text.

CHAPTER THIRTY-THREE

4.1. Equals 1/4th of a *yojana* (eight or nine miles).
12.2. Equals two miles.

CHAPTER THIRTY-FOUR

22.1. *Gaṁ* in printed text to be corrected as *maṁ*.
24.2. Texts laying down procedures.
36.3. The curl of hair on the chest described as a *gem*.
54.4. An alternate reading gives it as 25508.
68.5. The great principle.
90.6. The day of the entry of the Sun into the constellation Cancer (in July).